COMPUTER PROGRAMMING

The Most Complete Crash Course for Learning The Perfect Skills To Coding Your Project Even If You Are an Absolute Beginner. Learn and Master The Best Programming Languages!

Michail Kölling

CODING
HOOD

Table of Contents

PYTHON PROGRAMMING FOR BEGINNERS

After work guide to start learning Python on your own. Ideal for beginners to study coding with hands on exercises and projects for a new possible job career.

Michail Kölling

Introduction

The Python coding language is a great way to start your journey by learning more about computers, learning how to code, and even making some of your games and apps. This is one of the best languages to get started because it is simple, based on the English language, and many of those who decide to get started with a coding language will naturally fall with this one. This guidebook is going to take some time to discuss the Python language and help you to learn some of the basics that come with it to help you to get started.

While the Python language is a simple and basic language that is perfect for the beginner, it also has a lot of power that you are going to enjoy when creating your codes. Inside this guidebook, you are going to learn everything that you need to get started with the Python language and to make it work well for your needs!

This book is primarily for people who are relatively new to programming and, more specifically, those who want to discover the world of Python. This book will take you through the fundamentals of programming and Python.

Computer programming sounds scary, but it really isn't. The hardest part is choosing which language you want to learn because there are so many to choose from. Python is one of the easiest of all of computer programming languages; indeed, pretty much everything you need is right there, at your disposal. All you need to do is learn how to use what the program gives you to write programs.

Go ahead and read through the entire book, get the knowledge, and be informed about the key things that you need to know about this particular topic.

If you are as excited as I am to learn everything Python and how to program with it, let us get started.

Chapter 1

Datatype in python

The Python Data Types

The next thing that we need to take a look at is the Python data types. Each value in Python has a type of data.

Python numbers

The first option that we can work on Python data includes the Python numbers. These are going to include things like complex numbers, floating-point numbers, and even integers. They are going to be defined as complex, float, and int classes in Python. For example, we can work with the type() function to identify which category a value or a variable affiliated with to, and then the isinstance() function to audit if an object exists to a distinct class.

When we work with integers can be of any length, it is going only to find limitations in how much memory you have available on your computer. Then there is the floating-point number.

This is going to be accurate up to 15 decimal places, though you can go with a smaller amount as well.

The floating points are going to be separated by a decimal point. 1 is going to be an integer, and 10 will be a floating-point number.

And finally, we have complex numbers. These are going to be the numbers that we will want to write out as x + y, where x is going to be the real point, and then they are going to be the imaginary part.

We need to have these two put together to make up the complexity that we need with this kind of number.

Python lists

The Python list is going to be a regulated series of items. It is going to be one of the data types that are used the most in Python, and it is exceedingly responsive.

All of the items that will show up on the list can be similar, but this is not a requirement. You can work with a lot of different items on your list, without them being the same type, to make it easier to work with.

Being able to declare a list is going to be a straightforward option that we can work with. The items are going to be separated by commas, and then we just need to include them inside some brackets like this: [ ] we can also employ the slicing operator to help us obtain out a piece or a selection of items out of that list.

The index starts at 0 in Python.

And we have to remember while working on these that lists are going to be mutable.

It means that the value of the elements that are on your list can be altered or updated.

The lists in Python are going to be the most basic data structure because they are going to fall in a sequence.

The elements that are inside of the list are all going to have a number that is assigned to them. In other words, they all have a place that is assigned to them.

Not only are they simple, but lists are going to be versatile.

When creating a list, the objects are going to be separated by a comma, and all of these objects are going to fall inside a set of square brackets.

Items in a list are not going to have to be of the same data type.

Example

First list = [' science', 'history,' , 2002, 2030] ;

Second list = [2, 4, 6 ,8 ,10];

Third list = [" b", "d", "e", "g"]

The index for a list is going to start at zero, and you are going to have the ability to cut it so that you can create sub lists **Getting values inside of your list.**

When you want to get a value inside of the list so that you can slice it at a specific index.

Example

#! usr bin/ python

First list = [' science', 'history,' , 2002, 2030] ;

Second list = [2, 4, 6 ,8 ,10];

Print "first list [2] : " , fist list [2]

Print "second list [2:4] : " , second list [2 : 4]

Output

First list [2]: history

Second list [2:4] : [4, 6,]

Python Strings

Python strings are a series of characters enclosed within quotes. Use any type of quotes to enclose Python strings, that is, either single, double, or triple quotes. To access string elements, we use the slice operator. String characters begin at index 0, meaning that the first character string is at index 0. This is good when you need to access string characters. To concatenate strings in Python, we use + operator, the asterisk 9*) is used for repetition.

Example:

#!usrbin/python3

thanks = 'Thank You'

print (thanks) # to print the complete string

print (thanks[0]) # to print the first character of string

print (thanks[2:7]) # to print the 3rd to the 7th character of string

print (thanks[4:]) # to print from the 5th character of string

print (thanks * 2) # to print the string two times

print (thanks + "\tAgain!") # to print a concatenated string

The program prints the following once executed:

```
Thank You
T
ank Y
k You
Thank YouThank You
Thank You        Again!
```

Notice that we have text beginning with # symbol. The symbol denotes the beginning of a comment. The Python print will not act on the text from the symbol to the end of the line. Comments are meant to enhance the readability of code by explaining. We defined a string named thanks with the value Thank You. The print (thanks[0]) statement helps us access the first character of the string. Hence it prints T. You also notice that the space between the two words is counted as a character.

We can work with either a single quote or a double quote to show off our strings, but we need to make sure that the type of quote that we use at the beginning is the one that we finish it off with, or we will cause some confusion with the compiler.

We can even work with multi-line strings with the help of a triple quite.

Like what we are going to see when we use the tuple or the list that we talked about above, the slicing operator is something that we can use with our string as well. And just like with what we see in the tuples, we will find that the string is going to be immutable.

Python Set
Next on the list is going to be the Python set. The set is going to be an option from Python that will include an unordered collection of unique items. The set is going to be defined by values that we can separate with a comma in braces. The elements in the batch are not going to be ordered, so we can use them in any manner that we would like.

We have the option to perform this set of operations at the same time as a union or have an intersection on two sets.

The sets that we work with are going to be unique values, and they will make sure that we eliminate the duplicates since the set is going to be an unordered compilation. Cataloged has no aim.
Therefore the slicing operator is not going to work for this kind of option.

Python Lists
Lists consist of items enclosed within square brackets ([]), and the items are separated using commas (,). They are similar to the C arrays. Although all array elements must belong to a similar type, lists support the storage of items belonging to different types in a single list.

We use the slice operator ([ ] and [:]) for accessing the elements of a list. The indices start at 0 and end at -1. Also, the plus symbol (+) represents the concatenation operator, while the asterisk (*) represents the repetition operator.

Example:

#!usrbin/python3

listA = ['john', 3356 , 8.90, 'sister', 34.21]

listB = [120, 'sister']

print listA # will print the complete list

print listA[0] # will print the first element of the list

print listA[1:3] # will print the elements starting from the 2nd till 3rd

print listA[2:] # will print the elements starting from the 3rd element

print listB * 2 # will print the list two times

print listA + listB # will print a concatenated lists

There is no much difference in what is happening in the above code compared to the previous one for strings. When executed, the program outputs:

```
['john', 3356, 8.9, 'sister', 34.21]
john
[3356, 8.9]
[8.9, 'sister', 34.21]
[120, 'sister', 120, 'sister']
['john', 3356, 8.9, 'sister', 34.21, 120, 'sister']
```

In the statement "print listA", we print the contents of listA. Note that each element is treated to be at its index as a whole, for example, element 'john' is treated as a single element of a list at index 0.

Python Tuples

Tuples are going to be like lists in the fact that they are going to be a sequence of objects, but they are going to be immutable.

You can use a set of parentheses or not make a tuple, all you need to ensure is that you are using commas between the different objects that you want in your tuple.

Example:

Tup1 = ('science' , 'history', 2002, 2030)

Tup2 = (5, 9, 7, 4, 2)

Tup3 = "f", "b", "e", "t"

To write a tuple that is going to be returned as empty, it is going to use the tuple function and a set of empty parentheses.

We can also work with something that is known as a Python Tuple. The Tuple is going to be an ordered series of components that is the duplicate as a list, and it is sometimes hard to see how these are going to be similar and how they are going to be different.

The gigantic diversity that we are going to see with a Tuple and a list is that the tuples are going to be immutable.

Tuples, once you create them, are not modifiable.

Tuples are applied to write-protect data, and we are generally quicker than a list, as they cannot shift actively. It is going to be determined with parentheses (), where the items are also going to be separated by a comma as we see with the lists.

We can then use the slicing operator to help us wring some of the components that we want to use, but we still are not able to change the value while we are working with the code or the program.

Python tuples are similar to lists with the difference being after creating a tuple; you cannot add, delete, or change the tuple elements. Tuple elements should be enclosed within parenthesis ().

Example:

#!lusrbin/python3
t1 = () # creating an empty tuple, that is, no data

t2 = (22,34,55)

t3 = tuple([10,23,78,110,89]) # creating a tuple from an array

t4 = tuple("xyz") # creating tuple from a string

print t1

print t2

print t3

print t4

The values of the 4 tuples will be printed:

```
()
(22, 34, 55)
(10, 23, 78, 110, 89)
('x', 'y', 'z')
```

There are a number of functions that can be applied on tuples.

Example:

```
#!usrbin/python3

t1 = (23, 11, 35, 19, 98)

print("The minimum element in the tuple is", min(t1))

print("The sum of tuple elements is", sum(t1))

print("The maximum element in the tuple is", max(t1))

print("The tuple has a length of", len(t1))
```

When executed, it gives this result:

```
The minimum element in the tuple is 11
The sum of tuple elements is 186
The maximum element in the tuple is 98
The tuple has a length of 5
```

First, we called the min() function, which returns the smallest element in the tuple. We then called the sum() function, which returned the total sum of tuple elements. The max() function returned the maximum element in the tuple. The len() function counted all elements in the tuple and returned their number.

You can use the slice operator to access some of the tuple elements, not all. Example:

```
#!usrbin/python3

t = (23, 26, 46, 59, 64)

print(t[0:2])
```

When executed, it prints:

```
(23, 26)
```

We have used the slice operator to access elements from index 0 to index 2 in the tuple. Note that tuple elements begin at index 0.

Python Dictionaries

Python dictionaries are used for the storage of key-value pairs. With dictionaries, you can use a key to retrieve, remove, add, or modify values. Dictionaries are also mutable, meaning you can't their values once declared.

To create dictionaries, we use curly braces. Every dictionary item has a key, then followed by a colon, then a value. The items are separated using a comma (,). Example:

```
#!usrbin/python3

classmates = {

'john' : '234-221-323',

'alice' : '364-32-141'

}
```

We have created a dictionary named classmates with two items. Note that the key must be of a hashable type, but you may use any value. Each dictionary key must be unique. I first element, john, is the key, followed by the value. In the second element, alice is the element. To access dictionary elements, use the dictionary name and the key. Example:

```
#!usrbin/python3
classmates = {

'john' : '234-221-323',

'alice' : '364-32-141'

}

print("The number for john is", classmates['john'])

print("The number for alice is", classmates['alice'])
```

The last two statements help us access the dictionary values. It prints:

```
The number for john is 234-221-323
The number for alice is 364-32-141
```

.

To know the dictionary length, run the len() function as follows:

```
len(classmates)
```
The above will return 2 as the dictionary has only two elements.

When working with Python, a dictionary is going to be decided inside braces, with every component being a combination in the form of key: value. The key and the value can be any type that you would like based on the kind of code that you would like to write. We can also use the key to help us retrieve the respective value that we need. But we are not able to turn this around and work it in that manner at all.

Working with the different types of data is going to be so important for all of the work that you can do in a Python coding, and can help you out when it is time to work with data science.

Take a look at the different types of data that are available with the Python language, and see how great this can be to any of the codes and algorithms that you want to write into your data science project overall.

Datatype Conversion

Python allows you to convert data from one type to another. The process of converting from one data type to another is known as typecasting.

If you need to convert your int datatype into a float, you call the float() function.

Example:

```
#!usrbin/python3

height=20

print("The value of height in int is", height)

print("The value of height in float is", float(height))
```

In the above example, height has been initialized to 20. We have called the float() function and passed height to it as the parameter. The integer value, that is, 20 has been converted into a float value, that is, 20.0. The program prints the following:

```
The value of height in int is 20
The value of height in float is 20.0
```

.

To convert a float into an int, you call the **int()** function. Example:

```
#!usrbin/python3

height=20.0

print("The value of height in float is", height)

print("The value of height in int is", int(height))
```

The program prints the following:

```
The value of height in float is 20.0
The value of height in int is 20
```

We have called the int() function and passed the parameter height to it. It has converted 20.0 to 20, which is a float to integer conversion.

If you need to convert a number to a string, you call the str() function. The number will then be converted into a string.

Example:

#!usrbin/python3

num=20

print("The value of num in int is", num)
print("The value of num in string is", str(num))

The program outputs:

```
The value of num in int is 20
The value of num in string is 20
```

Although the value is the same, it is treated differently by a Python interpreter. The conversion of a float to a string can also be done similarly.

Chapter 2

Variables Operator the types and their use

Python Operators

Operators are symbols that indicate the implementation of a specific process. They are used to manipulate data within a program. Python uses different types of operators.

Arithmetic Operators

Addition (+)

The addition operator adds the operands on both sides of the operator:

>>>12 + 8

20
Subtraction (-)

The subtraction operator subtracts the value of the right operand from that of the left operand.

>>>40 – 3

37

Multiplication (*)

The multiplication operator multiples the values on the left and right side of the operator:

>>>20 * 3

60

Division (/)

The division operator divides the left operand with the value of the right operand:

>>>20 / 5

4.0

Exponent (**)

The exponent operator raises the first operand to the power indicated by the second operand.

>>> 4**4

256

Modulos (%)

The modulos operator returns the remainder after performing a division of the left operand by the right operand.

>>> 38%5

.

3

Floor Division (//)

The floor division operator performs a division of the left operand by the right operand and returns the quotient as a whole number while dropping the decimal numbers.

>>> 35//3

11

Comparison Operators

Operator Meaning

==   is equal to

!=   is not equal to

<   is less than

>   is greater than

<=   is less than or equal to

>=   is greater than or equal to

Logical Operators

Python supports 3 logical operators:

or

and

not

x or y If x is false, then it evaluates y. Else, it returns the evaluation of x.

x and y If x is false, then it returns the evaluation of x. Else, if x is true, it evaluates y.

not x If x is false, it returns True. Else, if x is true, it returns False.

6

INPUT AND OUTPUT

Input
Many programs require the user's input to function. Input can come from sources such as keyboard, mouse clicks, database, external storage, or the internet. The keyboard is the most common channel to gather user input. For this reason, Python features a built-in input() function to recognize keyboard entry.

The input() Function
Python's input() function collects keyboard input interactively through an optional parameter called a prompt string.

The program displays the prompt string whenever the input function is called. Program execution is suspended until the user enters a response to the prompt.

To illustrate this function, here's a simple program that collects name and age information from a user:

name = input("Please type your name: ")

print("Welcome, " + name + "!")

age = input("How old are you, " + name + "? ")

print("Thank you. You are " + name + " and you're " + age + " years old.")

When you run the program and input Marky for name and 24 for age, here's what the screen would display on a per-line basis: Please encode your name: Marky

Welcome, Marky!
How old are you, Marky? 24

Thank you. You are Marky, and you're 24 years old.

Output

Python's built-in print() function is used to output data to the screen, which is the standard output device.

The syntax for the print command is: print(value)

Here are examples of its usage:

>>> print("I am a programming student.")

I am a programming student.

>>> print(25)

25

>>> print(4**3)

64

>>> xyz = 50

>>> print('The value of xyz is' , xyz)

The value of xyz is 50

>>> animal = "rhinoceros "

>>>print(animal)

rhinoceros

Python allows printing of several values or variables which must be separated by a comma inside the parentheses.

For example, the following is a series of assignment statements:

a = "unemployed "

b = "16 years old "

c = "resident "

Assuming you want to print the above values as requirements, you can make a print statement like:

>>>print("Job requirements: ", a, b, c)

The output would be:

Job requirements: unemployed 16 years old resident

Output or String Formatting

Formatting options allow users to create a more readable output. Python provides the str.format() method to format string.

Using Curly Braces as Placeholders

Curly braces {} are used as placeholders for the formatted value specified in the str. format() statement.

If the position of the arguments given in str.format() statement coincides with your desired output order, you can use empty braces in your print statement: >>> x = 50; y = 100

>>> print('The value of x is {} and y is {}.'.format(x,y))

The value of x is 50 and y is 100.

If, however, you want the given arguments to appear in an order that is different from their position in the str.format() statement, you will need to specify their index inside the curly braces. The first argument has index 0, the second argument index 1, and so on.

Using the above example, assuming you want the value of variable b to appear before the value of variable a: >>> x = 50; y = 100

>>> print('The value of y is {1} and x is {0}.'.format(x,y))

The value of y is 100 and x is 50.

Here are other examples. This time, the values themselves are given and not stored in variables:

```
>>> print('I buy {}, {}, and {} coins.'.format('gold', 'silver', 'numismatic'))
```

I buy gold, silver, and numismatic coins.
```
>>> print('I collect {2}, {0}, and {1} coins.'.format('gold', 'silver', 'numismatic'))
```

I collect numismatic, gold, and silver coins.

String Formatting with sprint() style

Python 3 still supports string formatting using the sprint() style associated with the C language.

Here's an example:

```
>>> print('Catalog No.: %6d, Price per unit: %7.2f'% (6450, 159.8745))
```

Catalog No.: 6450, Price per unit: 159.87

Take note that the first argument, 6450, was formatted to print up to 6 digits (%6d). Since only 4 digits were used, 2 leading spaces were added to the output. The second argument was formatted to print a floating-point number with 7 digits, including 2 decimal numbers (%7.2f). Since only two decimal places were provided, the float was rounded off to two decimal places.

The above print statement uses the string modulo operator to format the string. You can translate this statement to the string format method by using curly braces and positional arguments. Here's how it would be written: >>> print('Catalog No.: {0:6d}, Price per piece: {1:7.2f}'.format(6450, 159.8745))

Catalog No.: 6450, Price per piece: 159.87
Python operators help us manipulate the value of operands in operations. Example:

10 * 34 = 340

In the above example, the values 10 and 34 are known as operands, while * is known as the operator. Python supports different types of operators.

Arithmetic Operators
These are the operators used for performing the basic mathematical operations. They include multiplication (*), addition(+), subtraction (-), division (/), modulus (%) and others. Example:

```
#!usrbin/python3

n1 = 6
```

```
n2 = 5

n3 = 0

n3 = n1 + n2

print("The value of sum is: ", n3)

n3 = n1 - n2

print("The result of subtraction is: ", n3)

n3 = n1 * n2
print("The result of multiplication is:", n3)

n3 = n1 / n2

print ("The result of division is: ", n3)

n3 = n1 % n2

print ("The remainder after division is: ", n3)

n1 = 2

n2 = 3

n3 = n1**n2

print ("The exponential value is: ", n3)

n1 = 20

n2 = 4

n3 = n1//n2

print ("The result of floor division is: ", n3)
```

The code prints the following when executed:

```
The value of sum is:    11
The result of subtraction is:    1
The result of multiplication is:  30
The result of division is:    1.2
The remainder after division is:    1
The exponential value is:    8
The result of floor division is:    5
```

That is how the arithmetic operations work in Python. The modulus operator (%) returns the remainder after a division has been done. In our case, we are dividing 6 by 5, and the remainder is 1.

Comparison Operators

These operators are used for comparing the values of operands and identify the relationship between them. They include the equal to (==), not equal to (!=), less than (<), greater than (>), greater than or equal to (>=) and less than or equal to (<=).

Example:

#!usrbin/python3

n1 = 6

n2 = 5

if (n1 == n2):

print ("The two numbers have equal values")

else:

print ("The two numbers are not equal in value")

if (n1 != n2):

print ("The two numbers are not equal in value")

else:

print ("The two numbers are equal in value")

if (n1 < n2):

print ("n1 is less than n2")

else:

print ("n1 is not less than n2")

if (n1 > n2):

 print ("n1 is greater than n2")

else:

 print ("n1 is not greater than n2")

n1,n2=n2,n1 #the values of n1 and n2 will be swapped. n1=5, n2=6

if (n1 <= n2):

The code will print the following:

```
The two numbers are not equal in value
The two numbers are not equal in value
n1 is not less than n2
n1 is greater than n2
n1 is either less than or equal to   n2
n2 is either greater than or equal to n1
```

The value of n1 is 6, while that of n2 is 5. The use of the equal to (==) operator on the two operands will return a false as the two operands are not equal. This will lead to the execution of the "else" part. The operator not equal to (!=) will return a true as the values of the two operands are not equal. The only logic which might seem complex in this case is the swapping of the values. The value of n1, which is 6 becomes 5, while that of n2 becomes 6. The statements which are below this swapping statement will then operate with these two new values.

Assignment Operators

These operators, the combination of the assignment operator (=) with the other operators. A good example of an assignment operator is "+=". The expression p+=q means "p=p + q". The expression "p/=q" means that "p=p / q". The assignment operators involve combining the assignment operator with the rest of the other operators.

 Example:

#!usrbin/python3

n1 = 6

n2 = 5

n3 = 0

n3 = n1 + n2

print ("The value of n3 is: ", n3)

n3 += n1

print ("The value of n3 is: ", n3)

n3 *= n1

print ("The value of n3 is: ", n3)

n3 /= n1

print ("The value of n3 ", n3)

n3 = 2

n3 %= n1

print ("The value of n3 is: ", n3)

n3 **= n1

print ("The value of n3 is: ", n3)

n3 //= n1

print ("The value of n3 is: ", n3)

The code will print the following when executed:

```
The value of n3 is:   11
The value of n3 is:   17
The value of n3 is:   102
The value of n3   17.0
The value of n3 is:   2
The value of n3 is:   64
The value of n3 is:   10
```

The statement "n3 = n1 + n2" is very straight forward as we are just adding the value of n1 to that of n2. In the expression "n3 += n1", we are adding the value of n3 to that of n1 and then assign the result to n3. However, note that in the previous statement, the value of n3 changed to "11" after adding n1 to n2. So we have 11+6, which gives 17. After that, the new value of the variable n3 will be 17. The expression "n3 = n1" means "n3= n3 n1". This will be 17 * 6, and the result will be 102. That is how these operators work in Python!

Membership Operators

These are the operators that are used for testing membership in a certain sequence of elements. The sequence of elements can be a string, a list, or a tuple. The two membership operators include "in" and "not in".

The "in" operator returns true if the value you specify is found in the sequence. The operator "not in" will evaluate to a true if the specified element is not found in the sequence.

Example:

```
#!usrbin/python3

n1 = 7

n2 = 21

ls = [10, 20, 30, 40, 50 ]

if ( n1 in ls ):

 print ("n1 was found in the list")

else:

 print ("n1 was not found in the list")

if ( n2 not in ls ):

 print ("n2 was not found in the list")

else:

 print ("n2 was found in the list")

n3=n2/n1

if ( n3 in ls ):

 print ("n1 was found in the list")

else:

 print ("n1 was not found in the list")
```

The code will print the following once executed:

```
n1 was not found in the list
n2 was not found in the list
n1 was not found in the list
```

.

The value of num1 is 7. This is not part of the list; it is why the use of the "in" operator returns a false. This causes the "else" part to be executed. The value of n2 is 21. This is not in the list. This expression returns a true, and the first part below the expression is executed. 21 divide by 7 is 3. This value is not in the list. The use of the last "in" operator evaluates to a false, and that is why the "else" part below it is executed.

Identity Operators

These operators are used to compare the values of two memory locations. Python has a method named "id()" that returns the unique identifier of the object. Python has two identity operators:

is- this operator evaluates to a true in case the variables used on either side of the operator are pointing to a similar object. It evaluates to false otherwise.

is not- this operator evaluates to a false if the variables on either side of the operator are pointing to a similar object, and true otherwise.

Example:

```
#!usrbin/python3

n1 = 45
n2 = 45

print ('The initial values are','n1=',n1,':',id(n1), 'n2=',n2,':',id(n2))

if ( n1 is n2 ):

 print ("1. n1 and n2 share an identity")

else:

 print ("2. n1 and n2 do not share identity")

if ( id(n1) == id(n2) ):

 print ("3. n1 and n2 share an identity")

else:

 print ("4. n1 and n2 do not share identity")

n2 = 100

print ('The variable values are','n1=',n1,':',id(n1), 'n2=',n2,':',id(n2))
```

if (n1 is not n2):

print ("5. n1 and n2 do not share identity")

else:

print ("6. n1 and n2 share identity")

The code will print the following once executed:

```
The initial values are n1= 45 : 1730008176 n2= 45 : 1730008176
1. n1 and n2 share an identity
3. n1 and n2 share an identity
The variable values are n1= 45 : 1730008176 n2= 100 : 1730009936
5. n1 and n2 do not share identity
```

Note that I have numbered some of the print statements so that it may be easy to differentiate them. In the first instance, the values of variables n1 and n2 are equal. The first statement of the output shows the respective values for the variables together with their unique identifier. Note that the identifier has been obtained by use if the id() Python method, and the name of the variable has been passed inside the function as the argument. The expression "if (n1 is n2):" will evaluate to a true since the values of the two variables are equal, or they are pointing to a similar object. This is why the print statement labeled 1 was executed!

You must also have noticed that the unique identifiers of the two variables are equal. In the expression "if (id(n1) == id(n2)):", we are testing whether the values of the identifiers for the two variables are the same. This evaluates to a true; hence the print statement labeled 3 has been executed!

The expression "n2 = 100" changes the value of variable n2 from 45 to 100. At this point, the values of the two variables will not be equal. This is because n1 has a value of 45, while n2 has a value of 100. This is clearly in the next print statement, which shows the values of the variables together with their corresponding ids. You must also have noticed that the ids of the two variables are not equal at this point.

The expression "if (n1 is not n2):" evaluates to a true; hence the print statement labeled 5 was executed. If we test to check whether the values of the ids for the two variables are equal, you will notice that they are not equal.

Chapter 3

Loops and function – variable function in python

Loops
The ability to make decisions is a critical component of most computer programs. Another is the ability to repeat or loop the program through a specific set of tasks.

All programs, other than those that perform a specific task and exit, contain at least one loop. Typically, this is the main loop, where the program continually loops, waiting for user or object input for it to act upon.

Additionally, loops can be used to apply repetitive processes on objects using a compact set of instructions.

Python offers two types of loops.

The for loop and the while loop.

They both allow for the repetitive looping through a specific operation but differ in how they test if the loop should continue to be processed.

For Loop
In the for loop, the loop will execute over a given range of items.

For example:

```
>>> for x in range(0,3):

print(x)
0
1
2
```

There are several things to note in this example.
First off, the syntax is similar to the if statements we covered earlier.

The for loop is ended with a colon.

With a single instruction in the for loop, we can leave that instruction on the same line immediately after the colon. A return after that will indent to the next instruction outside the for a loop.

If the for command contains multiple instructions, start those instructions on the next line. They will be indented to show they are contained within the loop.
A blank line entered at the end will close out the loop and drop the indent down from the loop for the next instructions outside the loop.

Range Command
Next, we have the range() command.

The range command is a built-in python method used to generate a range of numbers and is not explicitly part of the for loop syntax.

It is just there to make the numbers to iterate through. Like other ranges in python, the numbers provided do not represent a range from 0 – 3. They represent outputting three numbers starting at 0, which gives us 0, 1, and 2.

3 is not output in the range.

This is slightly different than the for loops you might be accustomed to in other languages. In those, a given range generally included the last number defined – for x=1 to 10, for example, would output 1 – 10, not one through 9.

While we use the range() function to generate the numbers to iterate over in the for loop, it is by no means the only option.

We can pull numerical values from any iterable source to iterate over that source.

For example, we can use the length of lists, tuples, or strings to process through that item.

```
>>> x=['apples', 'oranges', 'bananas', 'peaches', 'plums']

>>> for y in x:

print(y)

apples
oranges
bananas
peaches
```

plums

It is important to note, in this case, that we are iterating sequentially through the list values and setting y equal to those.

We are not setting y to the position values of 0 through 4.

If we had used print(x[y]) - or print the string at the position y in the list - we would get an exception stating that y cannot be str.

To iterate through a list using the position number, we would have to set y to a numeric range and iterate through it that way.

>>> for y in range(0, len(x)):

 print(x[y])

apples
oranges
bananas
peaches
plums

Going this route makes it easier to get every x value within the list.

The range method includes a step value attribute that allows us to step through the list in spaces other than 1.

For example, to get every other item in our list we would use:

>>> for y in range(0, len(x), 2):

 print(x[y])

apples
bananas
plums

Or, get the list backwards:

>>> for y in range(len(x)-1, -1, -1):

 print(x[y])

plums
peaches

bananas
oranges
apples

While Loop

The while loop continues while a specified condition is true.
For example:

```
>>> y=1
>>> while y<=10:
print(y)
y+=1
```

```
1
2
3
4
5
6
7
8
9
10
```

In this case, the loop will continue as long as y is less than or equal to 10.

Unlike for loop, which is specified to execute over a prespecified range and then exit, the while loop will continue as long as the specified condition is true; therefore, while loops can become infinite loops or code that loops forever.

To prevent that, code must be included within the loop that will make the condition false at some point.

In this case, y+=1 increments y by one each time the loop executes. When y becomes 11, the conditional becomes false, and the loop ends.

If you make a mistake and your program gets stuck in an infinity loop, you can exit the program by pressing ctrl-c.

Break Command

There is one additional way of gracefully exiting a for or while loop.

The break command forces the loop to terminate prematurely.

When coupled with an if statement, **break** can be used to conditionally and exit a loop early.

In most cases, choosing which loop structure to use and properly designing the code within the loop will negate the need for the break statement, so it is generally considered better if you can avoid it.

There are some cases, however, where it can be necessary.

Functions, Classes, and Methods

We learned how to branch programs through conditional statements and how to repeat through a set of instructions with loops efficiently. The next level of sophistication to explore is the function.

A function is a block of code that performs a specific, repetitive task that can be compartmentalized and called by another piece of code.

Our first code example in this book looked at a small program that calculated the volume of a cylinder.

This is an excellent example of something that should be written as a function. It is a clearly defined task that will never change.

By placing the code in a function, we can write it once and call it as many times as we need without rewriting it within the program.

Additionally, we can pull that code from one program and use it in any program we want, provided we call it properly.

This write-once/use everywhere property is a key benefit to object-oriented programming tools like Python. It saves time not just in development, but in debugging and deployment as well because the code only has to be written and debugged once.

Our original program for calculating the volume of a cylinder looked like this:

```python
# import math

import math

# assign variables
r=5 # radius
h=10 # height
V=0 # volume

# calculate volume of a cylinder

V=(math.pi*math.pow(r,2))*h # volume=(π*r^2)*h
```

```
# output the result
print(V)
```

If we had a much bigger program in which we wanted to calculate the volume of various cylinders, we could copy and paste this where necessary within the program, and it would work fine.

The better way to handle that is to convert this to a function.

Ideally, well-written functions would be completely self-sufficient. By that, I mean they should rely only on local variables (no globals).

Any values they need to function should be passed from outside, and any results they produce should be returned to the calling source.

So, in this case, we will need to set up our function to accept the radius, height as parameters. From the provided parameters, we can calculate the volume and return that value to the calling code.

The structural syntax for a Python function makes this easy. The basic format is as follows:

```
Def functionName(arg1, arg2,..):
 code to run
 return return-value
```

The function name can be anything that is not a reserved word or reference already in use by the program.
arg1, arg2, ... are variables that can accept values from the calling code.

These parameters will be local variables to the function and follow the same rules as any variable in Python.

Functions do not require these parameters, but they will be used in most cases.

Code to run is any python code which is necessary for the function to perform its task.

The return command at the end will send the value of whatever variable you specify back to the calling code.

The return call is also not required but will be used in most cases.

So to convert our volume of a circle calculation to a function, it will look like this:

```
# import math

import math
```

```
# define function
def cylinderVol(r, h): # r=radius, h=height
V=(math.pi*math.pow(r,2))*h # volume=(π*r^2)*h

return V # return the volume

# output the result
print(cylinderVol(5, 10)) # print the volume of a cylinder r=5, h=10
```

So, what we did was take the repetitive code necessary for the actual calculation and put it in a function which we named 'cylinderVol'.

That function accepts two arguments – r for the radius and h for the height. Those two arguments are all that is needed to complete the calculation.

We then do that calculation and place the result in V, which is then returned to the caller.

Instead of simply calling the function from a **print()** statement, we could have assigned a variable to the call like this:

```
vol = cylinderVol(5,10)
```

vol would then be equal to 785.3981633974483 – or the returned value of the function.

Because this function relies only on the values it is passed by the caller, it is entirely portable and can be used in any program provided it is called in the same fashion. This fact allows us to build into the next level, which is the class.

A class is typically defined as a group of related functions.

We currently have the code established to calculate the volume of a circle. We could expand upon that to create a volume class that would include functions for calculating the volume of cylinders and cubes.

```
# import math

import math

# define class

class Volume(object):
def cylinderVol(self, r, h): # r=radius, h=height
self.V=(math.pi*math.pow(r,2))*h # volume=(π*r^2)*h
return self.V
```

```
def cubeVol(self, l, w, h):
self.V=(l*w*h)
return self.V
```

output the result

```
vI=Volume() #create an instance of the Volume class

V=vI.cylinderVol(5,10) #set V by calling cylinderVol in the volume class

print(V) #print the result

V=vI.cubeVol(5,10,10) #set V by calling cylinderVol in the volume class

print(V) #print the result
```

In this example, we create a class called Volume.

Within it, we define two methods - in a class, the functions are called methods – one for cylinderVol and one for cubeVol.

These take the same arguments we used for the corresponding freestanding functions with one exception. The first argument of self.

In object-oriented programming, the value of self is commonly used to refer to the instance of the object created by the class.

In our code above, we first create an instance of the class by assigning a variable to it (vI=Volume()).

The self term is used to access the class-specific values then assigned to the vI variable instance.

This allows different instances to have different values for the same variables, and it allows us to test those values.

A clearer example may be that if we were creating a racing game, we could have a car class. That class could have methods for assigning make, model, speed, color, or other variables to a 'car' object.

If we created two cars by calling carA=car() and carB=Car() then carA's self property will point to a different car object then the self-property of carB.

Those two objects can store different values for the variables defined in the class for make, model, speed, and color.

Once the object vI is created, we can call its' methods in the same fashion we called our function earlier.

The only difference is we call a method using dot syntax (V=vI.cylinderVol(5,10)). By doing so, we call the method specific to that object and therefore utilize any special properties that are unique to that instance.

To improve usability and portability, Python allows us to save files like this separately and import them into other files as a whole.

We can create a file called volumemath.py and include in it a whole series of classes and methods designed to handle whatever volume calculations we would like to address.

That file can be saved separately and imported into our python projects on an as-needed basis. The specific process for doing that will be discussed in the section covering library usage.

Python allows defining the main function.

The following code is used to define and execute that function.

```
def main():

 # main code

if __name__ == "__main__":
 main()
```

The whitespace between the def main(): and the start of the main code is required. Failure to include it will throw an exception.

The second statement is an if..then that ensures the code is only called from the main file.

If you always use that code and mistakenly include it in a module or library, then the main() will not be called because the __name__ property will be set to the module name, not main.

Since python executes the file starting at the beginning as soon as it loads, these should be called early in your main file.

While a main() function is not required, it offers several advantages over not using one.

First, as a function, all the variables used in main() will be local to main().
Without the main() function declaration, all the variables will be global. That is also the case for all variables declared outside any functions in the main file.

Finally, this allows the main function to be called safely from a loaded module. Loading the main function from a module will allow more options in debugging.

Infinite Loop

You should always be aware of the greatest problem with coding loops: infinity loops. Infinity loops are loops that never stop. And since they never stop, they can easily make your program unresponsive, crash, or hog all your computer's resources. Here is an example similar to the previous one but without the counter and the usage of a break.

```
>>> while (True):

 print("This will never end until you close the program")
```

This will never end until you close the program

This will never end until you close the program

This will never end until you close the program

Whenever possible, always include a counter and break statement in your loops. Doing this will prevent your program from having infinite loops.

Continue

The continue keyword is like a soft version of break. Instead of breaking out from the whole loop, "continue" just breaks away from one loop and directly goes back to the loop statement. For example: >>> password = "secret"

```
>>> userInput = ""

>>> while (userInput != password):

 userInput = input()

 continue

 print("This will not get printed.")
```

Wrongpassword

Test

secret

```
>>> _
```

When this example was used on the break keyword, the program only asks for user input once regardless of anything you enter, and it ends the loop if you enter anything. This version, on the other hand, will persist on asking input until you put the right password. However, it will always skip on the print statement and always go back directly to the while statement.

Here is a practical application to make it easier to know the purpose of the continue statement.

>>> carBrands = ["Toyota", "Volvo", "Mitsubishi", "Volkswagen"]

>>> for brands in carBrands:

if (brands == "Volvo"):

continue

print("I have a " + brands)
I have a Toyota

I have a Mitsubishi

I have a Volkswagen

>>> _

When you are parsing or looping a sequence, there are items that you do not want to process. You can skip the ones you do not want to process by using a continue statement. In the above example, the program did not print "I have a Volvo" because it hit continue when a Volvo was selected. This caused it to go back and process the next car brand in the list.

Syntax of a Function

The syntax of a function looks like this:

def function_name(parameters):

""""docstring""""

statement(s)

return [expression]

Here is a breakdown of what the syntax of a function:

def keyword: This marks the beginning of the function header.

function_name: This is a unique name that identifies the function. The rules of the function name are almost similar to those of a variable we learnt at the beginning of this book.

parameters or arguments: Values are passed to the function by enclosing them in parentheses (). Parameters are optional.

The colon marks the end of the function header.

"""docstring""": (Docstring) is an optional documentation string. It describes the purpose of the function.

statement(s): There must be one or more valid statements that make up the body of the function. Notice that the statements are indented (typically tab or four spaces).

There may be an optional return statement that returns a value or values from the function.

Creating and calling a function

To use a function you create in your script; you will need to call it from the Python prompt, program, or function.

Exercise55: Creating a function

def greeting(name):

"""This function greets the user when

the person's name is passed in as

a parameter"""

print ("Greetings,", name + "!")

You can call a function by simply typing its name along with the appropriate parameters.

Modify the previous Exercise55 code to see how you can call the function greeting.

Exercise56: Calling a function

def greeting(name):

"""This function greets the user when

the person's name is passed in as

a parameter"""

print ("Greetings,", name + "!")

username = str(input("Enter your name: "))

greeting(username)

The code in Exercise55 first defines a function called a greeting, which requires one argument, name. It will prompt the user to enter a string, which will be assigned the variable username and used as the argument when the function greeting is called.

Docstring

The first string of text immediately after the function header is called the documentation string, or in short, docstring. This section of the function is optional and briefly explains what the function does. It is a good practice to include a descriptive docstring whenever you create a new function because you, or another programmer going through your code at a later time, may need it to understand what the function does. Always document your code!

We have exhaustively explained what our greeting function does. As you can see, we used a triple quote string to make it possible for the description to extend to multiple lines. Within the attribute of the function, the docstring is available as __**doc**__.

For instance, the greeting function would appear in the Python shell print() function output as in Exercise57.

Printing the docstring

def greeting(name):

"""This function greets the user when

the person's name is passed in as

an argument."""

print ("Greetings,", name + "!")

print (greeting.__doc__)

The return statements

The optional return statement in a function is used as an exit to return execution back to where it was called. The syntax of the return statement as we have seen takes this form:

return [expression_list]

The return statement may contain expressions that get evaluated to return a value. If there is no expression in the statement or when the return statement is not included in the function, the defined function will return a None object when called. Our greeting function in Exercises 55 through 57 return a value of None because we have not included a return statement.

The return statement

```
def agegroup_checker(age):

    """This function returns the

    user's age group name based

    on the age entered."""

    if age >= 18:

        agegroup = "Adult"

    elif age >= 13:

        agegroup = "Teenager"

    elif age >=0:
        agegroup = "Child"

    else:

        agegroup = "Invalid"

    return (agegroup)

age = int(input("Enter your age to check age group:"))

print ("Your age group is:", agegroup_checker(age))
```

Function Arguments

In Python, you can call a function using any of these four types of formal arguments:

• Default arguments

• Required arguments

• Keyword arguments

• Variable-length arguments

Default arguments
A default argument assumes the default value if no value is specified within the function's call parameters.

Default arguments
def studentinfo(name, gender = "Male"):

"This function prints info passed in the function parameters.

print ("Name:", name)

print ("Gender:", gender)

return;

studentinfo (name = "John")

studentinfo (name = "Mary", gender = "Female")

In Exercise59, you can see how we have specified the default value for the parameter gender as "Male". When we do not define the gender within one of the values, the default value is used.

Required arguments
Required arguments must be passed to the function in the exact positional order to match the function definition. If the arguments are not passed in the right order, or if the arguments passed are more or less than the number defined in the function, a syntax error will be encountered.

Keyword arguments
Functions calls are related to keyword arguments. This means that when a keyword argument is used in a function call, the caller should identify the argument by the parameter name. With these arguments, you can place arguments out of order or even skip them entirely because the Python interpreter will be able to match the values provided with the keywords provided.
Keyword argument
def studentinfo(name, age):

"This function prints info passed in the function parameters."

print ("Name:", name, "Age:", age)

return;

studentinfo (age = 21, name = "John")

Note that with keyword arguments in Exercise60, the order of the parameters does not matter.

Variable-length arguments

In some cases, a function may need to process more arguments than the number you specified when you defined it. These variables are known as variable-length arguments. Unlike required and default arguments, variable-length arguments can be included in the definition of the function without being assigned a name.

The syntax for a function with non-keyword variable-length arguments takes this format:

def studentinfo(name, age):

"This function prints info passed in the function parameters."

print ("Name:", name, "Age:", age)

return;

studentinfo (age = 21, name = "John")

Notice that an asterisk is placed right before the tuple name that holds the values of non-keyword variable arguments. If no additional arguments are defined when the function is called, the tuple will remain empty.

Chapter 4

Working with files

File is a named memory location that can be used to store data. Saving your files allows them to be accessed in the future when needed. Python handles file management through the file object.

File Operations
Python supports 4 basic file-related operations, namely:

opening a file

reading a file

writing to a file

closing a file

File Opening Modes
A Python file may be opened using different modes. It's important to familiarize yourself with them to ensure file safety and integrity.

These modes are available for accessing files in binary format: rb+ opens a file for reading and writing wb+ opens a file for writing and reading: overwrites files of the same name or create a new one ab+ opens a file for appending and reading These are examples of file opening statements:

fileobj = open("myfile.txt") #opens a file in default mode fileobj = open(("myfile.txt", "w") #opens a file in write mode fileobj = open(("pict.bmp", "rb+") #opens a binary file in read and write mode.

Closing Files
Closing a file is an important step in Python file management and maintenance. Closing an open file frees up the resources used, prevents accidental modification or deletion of data, and instructs Python to write data to your file.

Here's the syntax for opening and closing a file:

fileobj = open("myfile.txt") # open myfile.txt fileobj.close() # close open file.

Writing to a File
This section will illustrate how you can write data to a Python file.

First, to build a file, open a new file with the 'w' (write) mode and create a new file object to facilitate file access:
>>>fileobj = open("afile.txt","w") #opens a new file named 'afile.txt'.

Now, use the write() method to write strings to afile.txt:

>>> fileobj.write("A file is used to store important information.\n") 47

Notice that it returns the number of characters in the string. Likewise, the string is written with a new line \n character to tell Python to save it as a separate line.

>>> fileobj.write("You will use a file object to handle Python files.\n") 51

>>> fileobj.write("You can store program information on a file.\n") 45

Now that you're done writing to afile.txt, you must close the file: >>> fileobj.close()

Reading Files
There are different ways to read a text file in Python:

the readlines() method

'while' statement

with an iterator

'with statement'
The readlines() method

The readlines() method is one of the easiest ways to open a file in Python. It makes use of the file object to access and read the entire file. You will then create a variable to store the read file and use print to view the file.

To illustrate, open afile.txt with:

fileobj = open('afile.txt', "r")

Now, create a variable 'lines' that will store text from the readlines() method: >>> lines

= fileobj.readlines()

To access the content of the file, enter lines on the prompt:
>>>lines

['A file is used to store important information.\n', 'You will use a file object to handle Python files.\n', 'You can store program information on a file.\n']

Line by Line Reading with the 'while' loop

A simple while loop is a more efficient way to read files on a per line basis. Here is a simple 'while loop': # Open myfile.txt on read only mode:

fileobj = open('myfile.txt')

Read the first line

line = fileobj.readline()
# continue reading each line until file is empty

while line:

 print(line)

 line = fileobj.readline()

fileobj.close()

Here's the output when you run the while loop:

A file is used to store important information.

You will use a file object to handle Python files.

You can store program information on a file.

Line by Line Reading with an Iterator

Using an iterator is another way to read text files on a per-line basis. Here's a simple for loop that you can use to iterate through the myfile.txt: fo = open('myfile.txt')

for line in iter(fo):

 print(line)

fo.close()

Your output will be similar to per line reading using a while loop: A file is used to store

important information.
You will use a file object to handle Python files.

You can store program information on a file.

Using the 'with statement'

The 'with' structure facilitates a safe file opening and allows Python to close the file automatically without using the close() method. You can also use it to read through each line of a file.

Here's a 'with block' that can be used to read each line on myfile.txt: line_count = 0
with open('myfile.txt', 'r') as newfile:

 for line in newfile:

line_count += 1

 print('{:>3} {}'.format(line_count, line.rstrip()))

When you run the code, you'll get a per line output with line numbering:
1 A file is used to store important information.
2 You will use a file object to handle Python files.
3 You can store program information on a file.

Working with Files

Programs are made with input and output in mind. You input data to the program, the program processes the input, and it ultimately provides you with output.

For example, a calculator will take in numbers and operations you want. It will then process the operation you wanted. And then, it will display the result to you as its output.

There are multiple ways for a program to receive input and to produce output. One of those ways is to read and write data on files.

To start learning how to work with files, you need to learn the open() function.

The open() function has one **required** parameter and two **optional** parameters. The first and required parameter is the file name. The second parameter is the access mode. And the third parameter is buffering or buffer size.

The filename parameter requires string data. The access mode requires string data, but there is a set of string values that you can use and is defaulted to "r". The buffer size parameter requires an integer and is defaulted to 0.

To practice using the open() function, create a file with the name sampleFile.txt inside your Python directory.

Try this sample code:

```
>>> file1 = open("sampleFile.txt")
>>> _
```

Note that the file function returns a file object. The statement in the example assigns the file object to variable file1.

The file object has multiple attributes, and three of them are:
name: This contains the name of the file.
mode: This contains the access mode you used to access the file.
closed: This returns False if the file has been opened and True if the file is closed. When you use the open() function, the file is set to open.

Now, access those attributes.

```
>>> file1 = open("sampleFile.txt")

>>> file1.name

'sampleFile.txt'

>>> file1.mode

'r'

>>> file1.closed

False

>>> _
```

Whenever you are finished with a file, close them using the close() method.

```
>>> file1 = open("sampleFile.txt")

>>> file1.closed

False

>>> file1.close()

>>> file1.closed

True
```

>>> _

Remember that closing the file does not delete the variable or object. To reopen the file, just open and reassign the file object. For example:

>>> file1 = open("sampleFile.txt")

>>> file1.close()

>>> file1 = open(file1.name)

>>> file1.closed

False

>>> _

Reading from a File

Before proceeding, open the sampleFile.txt in your text editor. Type "Hello World" in it and save. Go back to Python.

To read the contents of the file, use the read() method. For example:
>>> file1 = open("sampleFile.txt")

>>> file1.read()

'Hello World'

>>> _

File Pointer

Whenever you access a file, Python sets the file pointer. The file pointer is like your word processor's cursor. Any operation on the file starts at where the file pointer is.

When you open a file and when it is set to the default access mode, which is "r" (read-only), the file pointer is set at the beginning of the file. To know the current position of the file pointer, you can use the tell() method. For example: >>> file1 = open("sampleFile. txt")

>>> file1.tell()

0

>>> _
Most of the actions you perform on the file move the file pointer. For example:

```
>>> file1 = open("sampleFile.txt")

>>> file1.tell()

0
>>> file1.read()

'Hello World'

>>> file1.tell()

11

>>> file1.read()

''

>>> _
```

To move the file pointer to a position you desire, you can use the seek() function. For example:

```
>>> file1 = open("sampleFile.txt")

>>> file1.tell()

0

>>> file1.read()

'Hello World'

>>> file1.tell()

11

>>> file1.seek(0)

0

>>> file1.read()

'Hello World'

>>> file1.seek(1)
```

1

>>> file1.read()

'ello World'

>>> _

The seek() method has two parameters. The first is offset, which sets the pointer's position depending on the second parameter. Also, argument for this parameter is required.

The second parameter is optional. It is for whence, which dictates where the "seek" will start. It is set to 0 by default.

If set to 0, Python will set the pointer's position to the offset argument.

If set to 1, Python will set the pointer's position relative or in addition to the current position of the pointer.

If set to 2, Python will set the pointer's position relative or in addition to the file's end.

Note that the last two options require the access mode to have binary access. If the access mode does not have binary access, the last two options will be useful to determine the current position of the pointer [seek(0, 1)] and the position at the end of the file [seek(0, 2)]. For example: >>> file1 = open("sampleFile.txt")

>>> file1.tell()

0

>>> file1.seek(1)

1

>>> file1.seek(0, 1)

0

>>> file1.seek(0, 2)

11

>>> _

File Access Modes

To write to a file, you will need to know more about file access modes in Python. There are three types of file operations: reading, writing and appending.

Reading allows you to access and copy any part of the file's content. Writing allows you to overwrite a file's contents and create a new one. Appending allows you to write on the file while keeping the other content intact.

There are two types of file access modes: string and binary. String access allows you to access a file's content as if you are opening a text file. Binary access allows you to access a file on its rawest form: binary.

In your sample file, accessing it using string access allows you to read the line "Hello World". Accessing the file using binary access will let you read "Hello World" in binary, which will be b'Hello World'. For example: >>> x = open("sampleFile.txt", "rb")

>>> x.read()

b'Hello World'

>>> _

String access is useful for editing text files. Binary access is useful for anything else, like pictures, compressed files, and executables. In this book, you will only be taught how to handle text files.

There are multiple values that you can enter in the file access mode parameter of the open() function. But you do not need to memorize the combination. You just need to know the letter combinations.

Each letter and symbol stands for an access mode and operation. For example:
r = read-only—file pointer placed at the beginning
r+ = read and write
a = append—file pointer placed at the end
a+ = read and append
w = overwrite/create—file pointer set to 0 since you create the file
w+ = read and overwrite/create
b = binary

By default, file access mode is set to string. You need to add b to allow binary access. For example: "rb".

Writing to a File

When writing to a file, you must always remember that Python overwrites and not insert file. For example:

>>> x = open("sampleFile.txt", "r+")

```
>>> x.read()

'Hello World'

>>> x.tell(0)

0

>>> x.write("text")

4

>>> x.tell()

4

>>> x.read()

'o World'

>>> x.seek(0)

0

>>> x.read()

'texto World'

>>> _
```

You might have expected that the resulting text will be "textHello World". The write method of the file object replaces each character one by one, starting from the current position of the pointer.

Practice Exercise

For practice, you need to perform the following tasks:

Create a new file named test.txt.
Write the complete practice exercise instructions on the file.
Close the file and reopen it.
Read the file and set the cursor back to 0.
Close the file and open it using append access mode.
Add a rewritten version of these instructions at the end of the file.
Create a new file and put similar content to it by copying the contents of the test.txt file.

Chapter 5

Object-oriented programming

Classes and Object-Oriented Programming

Python is an object-oriented programming language. It means that it focuses on working with data structures collectively known as objects. An object can be anything that could be named in Python, including strings, functions, integers, classes, floats, files, and methods. Objects can refer to the data and the methods that utilize these data. They can be used in many different ways. They can be passed as arguments and assigned to variables, lists, tuples, dictionaries, or sets. Practically everything is an object in Python.

A class is a data type like strings, lists, floats, integers, or dictionaries. The class belongs to a data type called 'type'. The data values that you store inside a class object are called attributes, while the functions that are associated with it are called methods. A class is simply a way to create, organize, and manage objects with similar attributes and methods. When you create objects out of a class, the object is called an instance of the class.

Defining a Class

A class definition statement starts with the keyword class, followed by a class identifier and a colon. By convention, the names of classes start in uppercase. A docstring that provides a short description of the class usually follows the class definition line.

Here is an example of a class definition:

class Furniture:

 #This is an example of a class definition.

 pass

The following defines a class that takes an object:

class Members(obj)

 #I have just defined a class that takes an object.

pass

When you use the keyword 'class' to create a new class, Python responds by creating a new class object with the same name as the class identifier. This new class object contains the definition of all attributes of the class. Hence, you can use it to access the attributes of the class and to instantiate new objects of the class.

To illustrate, create a new class and name it MyClass:
class MyClass:

"This is an independent class."

y = 100

def greet(self):

print ('Welcome, guest!')

To access the attributes of MyClass:

>>> MyClass.y

100

To access the function attribute of MyClass:

>>> MyClass.greet

<function MyClass.greet at 0x03025D20>

To access the docstring of MyClass:

>>> MyClass.__doc__

'This is an independent class.'

Creating Instances of the Class

The class object, which is created alongside the class, can be used to create instances of the class. Creating a new object is simple. You just have to assign that object to the class with a statement like>>>object_a = MyClass()
To access the attributes of an object, you will use the object name as prefix right before the dot and the attribute name after the dot. An object's attribute can be a method or data attribute. Methods refer to the functions of the class. To illustrate, you can use the class definition of MyClass above and create an object out of it: obj = MyClass()
MyClass.greet, an attribute of MyClass() is a method object because if defines a function for all objects that would be created from MyClass. Hence, obj.greet is a method object.

>>> obj.greet

<bound method MyClass.greet of <__main__.MyClass object at 0x0328DB90>>

In MyClass function definition, you might have noticed that the word self was used as an argument. Yet, in the above example, the method obj.greet was called without an argument. That's because when an object calls its method, the object itself becomes the first argument. By convention, the word 'self' is used to refer to the object. If there are other arguments, you can place them after 'self'.

The __init__() method

The __init__() method is a special class constructor method that is used to initialize the object it creates. Whenever you create a new instance of the class, Python calls this initialization method. The __init__ method() takes at least one argument, 'self', to identify each object.

Examples:

class Performers:

 def __init__(self) :

class Performers (object):

 def __init__(self, name, skills, salary) :

This class definition indicates that whenever an instance of the Performers class is created, each will have a copy of the variables initialized with the __init__ method.

To illustrate, you can instantiate members of the class Performers with these expressions:

mem_1 = Performers("Dolly", "singer", 5000.00)

mem_2 = Performers("Jayne", 'dancer', 5000.00)

mem_3 = Performers ("Lizah", 'pole dancer', 4750.00)

Use the print() function to see the connection between the initialized variables and the instance variables:

print(mem_1.name, mem_1.skills, mem_1.salary)

print(mem_2.name, mem_2.skills, mem_2.salary)

print(mem_3.name, mem_3.skills, mem_3.salary)

This is what you would see on your screen:

Dolly singer 5000.0

Jayne dancer 5000.0

Lizah pole dancer 4750.0

Chapter 6

Python list basics

What is a list?

A list is an ordered sequence of items enclosed in square brackets [] and separated by commas. A list is mutable, meaning that the values of its items and their index locations can be changed.

```
1 list = [item0, item1, item2, ... ,item-2, item-1]
```

Lists are one of the most important data structures in Python that every functional program must-have. It is a good thing that they are also one of the simplest to manipulate. Just like with the strings we looked at in the previous chapter, lists can be accessed with indexes that begin at 0 for the first item to -1 for the last item.

Creating a list

To create a list in Python, simply enclose one or more comma-separated values between square brackets and assign it a value.

Creating lists

```
1 Subjects = ["Math", "Physics", "Chemistry", "Biology",
"History"]
```

```
2 myLists = ["Pencil", "Scissor", 2020, ["Fruits", "Snacks"],
"Fare"]
```

```
3
```

```
4 print (Subjects) 5 print (myLists)
```

Did you notice that the second list in Exercise 12 has another list inside it? That type of list is known as a nested list, a list containing one or more lists in it.

Just like the string type we looked at in the previous chapter, a list type is a sequential data type in Python that we will learn to slice, concatenate, and iterate, and so on. First, though, let us look at how to access its values.

Accessing list values

We will use the square brackets to slice the items in a list then access them by referring to their indexed positions on the list.

Accessing values in a list

```
1 Subjects = ["Math", "Physics", "Chemistry", "Biology", "History",
"Art"]

2

3 print ("Print Subjects[0:2]:", Subjects[0:2]) 4 print ("Print
Subjects[2:]:", Subjects[2:]) 5 print ("Print Subjects[-3:-1]:",
Subjects[-3:-1])
```

You will discover that the slicing and indexing methods we learned when working with strings are used in the same way with lists. Perhaps you can practice creating a larger list then knock yourself out, trying out all the slicing and accessing operations we have learned so far.

Updating and deleting list values

We already mentioned that lists in Python are mutable, meaning that we can update the contents and the order of its sequential items. You can update a single or multiple elements of a list using an assignment operator (=) with the list name and index as the left operand and the new value as the right operand.

Adding list items

```
1 Subjects = ["Math", "Physics", "Chemistry", "Biology",
"History", "Art"]

2
```

3 print ("Current list items:", Subjects) 4 Subjects[3] = "Government"

5 Subjects[1] = "French"

6 del Subjects[-1]

7 print ("New list items:", Subjects)

When you run Exercise 14, you will notice that the list item "Government" is added at index 3 to replace "Biology" and the second item "Physics" at index [1] is replaced with "French". We also used the **del** statement to remove the last item in our list. An alternate approach in deleting an item from a list is the use of the **remove()** method, which we will cover briefly below.

Basic list operations with built-in functions and methods

There are a lot more operations we can carry out on a list, including concatenation (joining together using +) and iteration (using the asterisk *).

More operations on a list
This exercise will help reinforce what you already know about sequences by applying them to a list.

1 cont = ["Asia", "Africa", "America", "Europe", "Australia"]

2 oceans = ["Pacific", "Indian", "Atlantic"]

3

4 print ("Length of list 1:", len(cont)) 5 cont[2] = "North America"

6 cont.append("South America") 7 print ("New length of list 1:", len(cont)) 8 print ("List 1 + List 2:", cont + oceans) 9

10 oceans.remove("Indian") 11 print (oceans) 12 print ("List 2
* 3: ", oceans * 3) 13 print ("Are there 'ia' in either of the lists?",
'ia' in cont or Oceans)

Python includes a list of functions and methods that you can use to manipulate lists at an
advanced level.

Application of built-in functions and methods

Operation	Definition	Exercise example
Compare cmp	Compares the elements of two lists	cmp(cont, Oceans)
Length len	Returns the total length of the list	len(cont)
Maximum max	Returns the item with the most value in the list	max(cont)
Minimum min	Returns the item with the least value in the list	min(cont)
List list	Used to convert a string or tuple into a list.	list(Text)
Remove item list.remove(item)	Removes item from the list	cont.remove("Asia")
Item index list.index(item)	Returns the lowest index that item appears in the list	cont.index("Africa")
Extend list list.extend(list2)	Appends the contents of list2 to list	cont.extend("Antarctica")
Count items list.count(item)	Returns count of how many times item appears in list	cont.count("Europe")

Reverse list **list.reverse()**	**Reverses the order** **of items in the list**	**cont.reverse()**
Append item **list.append(item)**	**Appends object item** **to list**	**cont.** **append("Arctic")**
Sort items **list.sort([arg])**	**Sorts objects of list** **as per the argu-** **ment(s) if provided**	**cont.sort(0)**
Insert item list. **insert(index, item)**	**Inserts object item** **into the list at indi-** **cated index**	**cont.insert([6],** **"Madagas-car")**
Populate **list.** **pop(item=list[-1])**	**Removes and** **returns last object or** **item from list**	**cont.pop("India" =** **oceans[-1])**

Chapter 7

Python work list – tuples in python

Tuples

Tuples are similar to lists, and creating them is quite simple, one has to put commas to separate values, and these values can also be enclosed in parenthesis. For example *tup1 = ('chemistry', 'physics', 1998, 2000); tup2 = (7, 8, 9); tup3 = "x", "y", "z";* *Listed below are some of the basic features of a tuple: a)* For writing an empty tuple two parentheses is used – **tup1 = ();** **b)** Even of the tuple contains the single value one has to include comma—***tup1 = (50,);*** c) The indices in tuple start with at 0 and slicing can also be done.

d) Square brackets are used to access values in tuples e) One cannot change or update the values in tuples *f)* Removing tuple element is not possible; however, one can use del to remove entire tuple.

g) All general operators can be used. There are few built-in tuples like:

For comparing different elements - cmp(tuple1, tuple2)

To find the total length of tuple -len(tuple)

Converting list to tuple – tuple(seq)

Find maximum value—max(tuple)

Minimum value – min(tuple)

What is a tuple?

Tuples are used to group any number of items into a single sequential compound value.

Whereas lists are used when the length is not known or not fixed, tuples, because its sequential elements cannot be changed, are used in situations where the positions of each element is crucial to the use of the list.

Creating a tuple

The process of creating tuple objects in Python is the same as those of creating objects of any other type, such as numbers, strings, or lists we have already covered. Simply place values separated by commas and enclose them in parentheses or brackets.

The syntax takes this format:

```
Tuple_Identifier = (Item1, Item2, Item3, ... , Item-2, Item-1)
Tuple_Identifier = Item1, Item2, Item3, ... , Item-2, Item-1
```

The enclosing parentheses are not mandatory to create a tuple, as we will see in Exercise 17 below. In fact, any set of values in a sequence separated by commas and written with no identifying symbols such as square brackets to make them a list, default to a tuple. However, it is a good practice always to enclose the sequence items in parentheses.

Creating tuples

```
1 weekdays = ("Sun", "Mon", "Tue", "Wed", "Thu", "Fri", "Sat") 2
weekends = "Sun", "Mon"
3 years = (2017,) 4 decade = () 5
6 print(type(weekdays),type(weekends),type(years),type(decade))
```

Note that when you create a tuple with a single element, it must have a comma like the years tuple in exercise 17. You can create an empty tuple by identifying a pair of parentheses containing nothing as we created the decade tuple in the previous exercise.

Accessing tuple values

Like with strings and lists, the values of a tuple are sequentially arranged and can be accessed by indices starting at 0 for the first item to -1 for the last item. We use square brackets [ ] to slice and manipulate tuples in as many ways, same as in the case of lists.

In the next exercise, you will learn that we access and manipulate the elements of a tuple data type just as we did strings and lists.

Accessing the values of a tuple

```
1 weekdays = ("Sun", "Mon", "Tue", "Wed", "Thu", "Fri", "Sat") 2
3 print (weekdays) 4 print ("First day of the week is", weekdays[0])
5 print ("Print items [2:]:", weekdays[2:]) 6 print ("What is item
index [-1]?", weekdays [-1]) 7 print ("Print from first to second last
items:", weekdays[:-2])
```

You can see from Exercise 23 that the system of indexing we were introduced to with string object types is still used for the tuple types. Remember that the index location of the first item is 0 and not 1 and that accessing items [0:3] means the first (inclusive) through the fourth (exclusive). Our argument here, for instance, would access items 0, 1, and 2 of the tuple.

Updating tuple values

We have already learned that a tuple is an immutable data type, meaning that its values cannot be changed, updated, or deleted. However, should you need to make changes to the values of a tuple, you will have to take the portion of items you need from an existing tuple and create a new one. Let us try this in Exercise 24.

Creating a new tuple object from values of existing tuples

```
1 tuple1 = (2002, 2006, 2010, 2014) 2 tuple2 = ("Brazil", "Italy",
"Spain", "Germany") 3
4 #tuple1[0] = 2000 #This statement will generate an error.
5
6 tuple3 = tuple1 + tuple2
7 print (tuple3)
```

Exercise 24 above demonstrates how you can combine the values of two tuples to create a new tuple. Line 4 of the script is commented out. Still, if you uncomment and rerun the script, you will get a type error: TypeError: 'tuple' object does not support item assignment Practice creating new tuples from specific value indexes rather than whole tuples as we did in this exercise.

Basic tuple operations with built-in functions and methods

Python comes with a set of tuple functions and methods that you should discover and use during your practice to understand what each does. The table below summarizes what they are and how they are used.

You can concatenate tuples using the add (+) operand and iterate using the asterisk (*) just like you can strings and lists, except that the results of such manipulation is a new tuple and not a string. Here is a table with examples of the operations you can try to understand how the various basic tuple operations work.

Basic tuple operations

Operation	Description	Exercise example
Length (len)	Returns the length (number of items) of the tuple	len(weekdays)
Concatenate (+)	Combines two or more tuples to create a new one	tuple1 + tuple2

Repetition (*)	Repeats the tuple the defined number of times	tuple1 * 3
Membership (in)	Checks for the presence of a value in the tuple	"Fri" in weekdays
Comparison (cmp)	Compares the values of two tuples.	cmp(tuple1, tuple2)
Iteration for	Loops through the values of the tuple until a de-fined condition is met	for "Sun" in week-days: print "YES"
Sequence (seq)	Converts a list or string into a tuple	tuple(Continents)
Maximum (max)	Returns the item with the highest value in the tu-ple	max(tuple1)
Minimum (min)	Returns the item with the lowest value in the tu-ple	min(tuple1)

Chapter 8

Classes

Python Classes and Objects

Python is an object-oriented programming language. This means that a Python programmer can take advantage of the object-oriented programming features such as classes.

A class can be defined as a grouping of data and methods which operate on that data. This means that a class has date and methods, whereby the methods are used for manipulation of the data. The access to the methods of a class is done by use of the dot notation.

Class Definition

To define classes in Python, we use the class keyword. This should be followed by a colon. Example:

```
class testClass():
```

Once the class has been defined, you can create methods and functions inside it. These will help in data manipulation. Example:

```
#!usrbin/python3

class pythonMaths:

 def add(ax,bx):

 addition = ax + bx

 print(addition)

 def subtract(ax,bx):

 subt = ax - bx

 print(subt)
```

```
def multiply(ax,bx):

multiplication = ax * bx

print(multiplication)

def division(ax,bx):

div = ax / bx

 print(div)
```

We have defined a class named *pythonMaths*. The class can have some methods. To access any of these methods, you must use a class name, the dot (.), and the method name. Example:

To access the add method in above *pythonMaths* class, type the following on Python terminal:

```
pythonMaths.add(2,3)
```

Note that the class name comes first, followed by the method name then the parameters inside the parenthesis. The function expects two parameter values, that is, values for parameters ax and bx. If you pass values for more than two parameters or even one parameter, then an error will be returned.

Note that everything in the class has been indented. This should always be the case. If you don't, an error message will be generated.

The class methods may also be called from within the class itself. This calls for us to create an instance of the class which will be used for accessing the class methods. Example:

```
#!usrbin/python3

class class2():

 def firstMeth(self):

 print("The first method")

 def secondMeth(self,aString):
 print("Second method, string alongside:" + aString)
 def main():

  # instantiate class and call methods
```

c = class2 ()

c.firstMeth()

c.secondMeth(" We are now testing")

if __name__ == "__main__":

main()

The code prints the following when executed:

```
The first method
Second method, string alongside: We are now testing
```

The argument *self* is normally to refer to the object itself. That's why we use the word, and it's a keyword in Python. When used inside a method, *self* refers to a specific instance of the object being operated on. Whenever you see the keyword *self* in Python, know it refers to the first parameter of the instance methods. It is used for accessing member objects. However, you notice that when calling the two methods in our code, that is, *firstMeth()* and *secondMeth()*, we never specified the self-keyword as Python does this for us. After calling an instance method, Python knows how to automatically pass the *self*-argument whether it has been provided or not. This means you may choose to provide it or not. We created an instance of the class class2, and the instance was named c. This was done in the following line:

c = class2 ()

The c is an object of class class2. This means we can use the object to access all methods and properties of the class. You only have to care about the non-self-arguments. Notice how a string was appended to initial text in *secondMeth*.

Built-in Attributes
Some built-in attributes are kept by all classes, and to access them; we use the dot operator similar to the other attributes. These include the following:

___**dict**___ : This is a dictionary with the namespace for the class.

___**doc**___ : The class documentation string or none, in case it is not defined.

___**name**___ : The name of the class.

___**module**___ : The name of the module in which the class has been defined. In the interactive mode, the attribute becomes "__main__".

___**bases**___ : This is a tuple, possibly empty, having base classes, added in the order that they occur in your base class list.

Example:
```
#!usrbin/python3

class Worker:

'The base class. Its common to all instances'

workerCount = 0

def __init__(self, name, age):

self.name = name

self.age = age

Worker.workerCount += 1

def showCount(self):

print ("The total number of workers is %d" % Worker.workerCount)

def showWorker(self):

print ("Name : ", self.name, ", Age: ", self.age)

worker1 = Worker("Gishon", 26)

worker2 = Worker("Esther", 24)

print ("Worker.__doc__:", Worker.__doc__)

print ("Worker.__name__:", Worker.__name__)

print ("Worker.__module__:", Worker.__module__)
print ("Worker.__bases__:", Worker.__bases__)

print ("Worker.__dict__:", Worker.__dict__ )
```

The code prints the following when executed:

```
Worker.__doc__: The base class. Its common to all instances
Worker.__name__: Worker
Worker.__module__: __main__
Worker.__bases__: (,)
Worker.__dict__: {'__module__': '__main__', '__doc__': 'The base class. Its common to all instances', 'workerCount': 2, '__init__
```

Garbage Collection

Sometimes, the memory may be occupied by objects that are no longer needed. Python clears them from memory automatically, a process known as garbage collection. This way, Python can reclaim blocks of memory that are no longer in use. The garbage collector is launched when a program is executed, and it runs once a reference count to an object has reached a zero. The reference count to an object changes with change in the number of aliases pointing to it.

The reference count to an object increases when a new name is assigned or when it's added into a container such as tuple, list or dictionary. Once the del statement is used to delete the object, the value of count will decrease, or once its reference has gone out of scope or once the reference is reassigned.

Example:

ax = 5 # object created
bx = ax # Increase the ref. count for <5>

bz = [bx] # Increase the ref. count for <5>

del ax # Decrease the ref. count for <5>

bx = 70 # Decrease the ref. count for <5>

bz[0] = -1 # Decrease the ref. count for <5>

One is not capable of noticing once the garbage collector has destroyed an orphaned instance. However, in Python, a class can implement a destructor named "__del__()" which will be invoked when a particular object is almost destroyed. Any non-memory resources which are not being used by an instance can be cleaned by the use of this method. The __del__() destructor normally shows the class name for the instance that is almost being destroyed.

Example:

#!usrbin/python3

class Region:

def __init__(self, ax=0, bx=0):

```
self.ax = ax

self.bx = bx

def __del__(self):
class_name = self.__class__.__name__

    print (class_name, "already destroyed")

rg1 = Region()

rg2 = rg1

rg3 = rg1

print (id(rg1), id(rg2), id(rg3)); # to print object IDs.

del rg1

del rg2

del rg3
```

The code prints:

```
139921453750144 139921453750144 139921453750144
Region already destroyed
```

The best idea for you is to create your classes in some separate files. You can then use the "import" statement to import these classes into your main program. Suppose the code given above was created in the file "Region.py" and it has no executable code, then we can do this as follows:

```
#!usrbin/python3

import region

rg1=region.Region()
```

Inheritance

In Python, you don't have to create your class from scratch, but you can inherit from ma certain class, generally known as the "parent" class. The parent class should be placed in parenthesis after the definition of the new class.

Since the parent class has some attributes, the new class, which is the child class, will be allowed to use these attributes in such a manner that they have been defined in the child class. It is also possible for the child class to override the methods and the data members from the parent class.

Python inheritance takes the following syntax:

```
class DerivedClassName(BaseClassName):

derived_class_body
```

Example:

```
#!usrbin/python3

# Example file for working with classes

class parentClass():

def firstMeth(self):
print("The first method in parentClass")

def secondMeth(self,aString):

print("We are testing" + aString)

class childClass(parentClass):

#def firstMeth(self):

#parentClass.firstMeth(self);

#print "firstMeth for Child Class"

def secondMeth(self):

print("childClass secondMeth")

def main():

# exercising class methods

c = childClass()

c.firstMeth()

c.secondMeth()

if __name__ == "__main__":

main()
```

The code prints the following when executed:

```
The first method in parentClass
childClass secondMeth
```

In the *childClass*, we have not defined the *firstMethod*, but we have obtained it from the parent class. That is how inheritance works in Python. The child class has inherited a method from the parent class.

Another Example:

```
#!usrbin/python3

class Worker:

'A common class to all the workers'

workerCount = 0

def __init__(self, name, wage):

self.name = name

self.wage = wage

Worker.workerCount += 1

def showCount(self):

print ("Total Workers %d" % Workers.workerCount)

def showWorker(self):
print ("Name : ", self.name, ", Wage: ", self.wage)

#Creating first object of Worker class"

worker1 = Worker("Bosco", 2500)

#Creating second object of Worker class"

worker2 = Worker("June", 3000)

worker1.showWorker()

worker2.showWorker()
```

print ("Total Workers %d" % Worker.workerCount)

The above code clearly demonstrates how you can create an instance of a class and use it to access members or methods of the parent class. It gives the following result once executed:

```
Name :   Bosco , Wage:  2500
Name :   June , Wage:  3000
Total Workers 2
```

We have created two instances of the class Worker, that is, worker1 ad worker2. Each of these instances is a worker, the first one Bosco, and the second one June. We have used these instances to access the showWorker method defined in the class. This method returns the name and the wage for the worker.

Multiple Inheritance

In Python, one can inherit from more than one class at once. This is not the case with other languages like Java and C#. Python's multiple inheritance takes this syntax:

Class Childclass(ParentClass1, ParentClass2, …):
the initializer

 # the methods

Example of Python multiple inheritance:

#!usrbin/python3

class ParentClass1():

 def superMethod1(self):

 print("Calling superMethod1")

class ParentClass2():

 def superMethod2(self):

 print("Calling superMethod2")

class ChildClass(ParentClass1, ParentClass2):

def childMethod(self):

print("The child method")

```
ch = ChildClass()
ch.superMethod1()

ch.superMethod2()
```

The code will print:

```
Calling superMethod1
Calling superMethod2
```

We defined two methods, one in the first Super Class ad, the second one in the second Super Class. The child class has then inherited from these two classes. It has accessed the methods that have been defined in these two classes. That is how we can inherit from more than one classes in Python.

Python Constructors

A constructor refers to a class function for instantiating an object to some predefined values. It should begin with a double underscore (__). It is the ___ *init*___() method. Example:

```
#!usrbin/python3

class Worker:

workerName = ""

def __init__(self, workerName):
self.workerName = workerName

def sayHello(self):

print("Welcome to our company, " + self.workerName)

Worker1 = Worker("June")

Worker1.sayHello()
```

The code prints the following when executed:

```
Welcome to our company, June
```

What we have done is that we have used a constructor to get the name of the user.

Overriding Class Methods

When coding in Python, we are allowed to override methods that are defined in the parent class. You may need to have different functionality in the child class, and this is a good reason for overriding a parent method. To override the method, we only have to pass different arguments to it as demonstrated below:

```
#!usrbin/python3

class ParentClass: # define the parent class

 def firstMethod(self):

 print ('A call to parent method')
class ChildClass(ParentClass): # define the child class

 def firstMethod(self):

 print ('A call to child method')

c = ChildClass() # An instance of the child class

c.firstMethod() # The child calls the overridden method
```

The code will print the following once executed:

```
A call to child method
```

The method named firstMethod had been defined in the parent class. The function has been redefined in the child class, but this time, it prints a different text than what it was printing in the parent class. We have achieved method overriding.

Example 2:

```
#!usrbin/python3

class AB():

 def __init__(self):

 self.__ax = 2

 def method1(self):

 print("method1 from class AB")

class BC(AB):

 def __init__(self):
```

```
self.__bx = 2

def method1(self):

print("method1 from class BC")

bc = BC()

bc.method1()
```

The code prints the following once executed:

```
method1 from class BC
```

Creating an inheriting class

An inheriting class is a new class created that is based on a previous or proceeding class (otherwise known as a parent class or superclass). Don't worry if you are not following. This is an advanced use of Python and is presented as an example for educational purposes.

The output of the inheriting class program is similar to that of the normal class output. The differences are:

Another class is created (eg. "c2 =") in the function that was defined

The parent class will be returned, and then the information from the inheriting class will be returned

Follow the worked example below (done in Aptana Studio 3) and apply your mind to the process followed to understand the above statements.

Input Code:

```
class ClassOne():
    def method1(self):
        print ("ClassOne method1")
    def method2 (self, string):
        print ("ClassOne method2: " + string)

def function():
    c = ClassOne() # This is instantiating the class
    c.method1()    # Calling a method on the class by means of a class variable
    c.method2("string example") # Multiple methods can be called on a class'
function()         # Printing results for function1

class ClassTwo():
    def method1(self):
        print ("ClassTwo method1")

class InherrritingClass(ClassTwo):
    def method1(self):
        print ("InherrritingClass method1")

def function2():
    c = ClassTwo()
    c.method1()
    c2 = InherrritingClass()
    c2.method1() # Calling method 1 on class "c2"
function2()       # Printing results for function2
```

Output returned:

```
ClassOne method1
ClassOne method2: string example
ClassTwo method1
InherrritingClass method1
```

Creating a new class

```
class NewClass:
    """This is our first class. What it does
    is display a string text and a value of
    variable name"""
    name = str(input("Enter your name: "))
    def greeting (name):
        print ("Hello", name)
print (NewClass.name)
print (NewClass.greeting)
print (NewClass.__doc__)
```

What does your console display when you run the script in Exercise61?

Creating an Object

So far, we have learned that we can access the different attributes of a class using the class objects. We can use these objects also to instantiate new instances of that class using a procedure a lot similar to calling a function.

```
MyObject = NewClass()
```

In the example above, a new instance object called *MyObject* is created. This object can be used to access the attributes of the class NewClass using the class name as a prefix. The attributes, in this case, may include methods and variables. The methods of an object are the corresponding functions of a class, meaning that any class attribute function object defines the methods for objects in that class.

For instance, because *NewClass*.greeting is a function object and an attribute of *NewClass*, *MyObject.greeting* will be a method object.

Constructors

In python, the __init__() function is special because it is called when a new object of its class is instantiated. This object is also called a constructor because it is used to initialize all variables.

```
MyObject.greeting() # class ComplexNumbers:
 def __init__(self, x = 0, y = 0):
 self.real = x
 self.imagined = y
 def getNumbers(self):
  print ("Complex numbers are: {0}+{1}j".format(self.real, self.imagined))
Object1 = ComplexNumbers(2, 3) #Creates a new ComplexNumbers object
Object1.getNumbers() #Calls getNumbers() function
Object2     =     ComplexNumbers(10)     #Creates     another ComplexNumbers object
Object2.attr = 20 #Creates a new attribute 'attr'
print ((Object2.real, Object2.imagined, Object2.attr))
Object1.attr #Generates an error because c1 object doesn't have attribute 'attr'
```

In the above exercise, we have defined a new class that represents complex numbers. We have defined two functions, the __init__() function that initializes the variables and the *getNumbers()* function to properly display the numbers.

Note that the attributes of the objects in the exercise are created on the fly. For instance, the new attribute attr for *Object2* was created, but one for *Object1* was not (hence the error).

Deleting Attributes and Objects

You can delete the attributes of an object or even the object itself at any time using the statement del.

```
class ComplexNumbers:
 def __init__(self, x = 0, y = 0):
 self.real = x
 self.imagined = y
 def getNumbers(self):
  print ("Complex numbers are: {0}+{1}j".format(self.real, self.imagined))
Object1 = ComplexNumbers(2, 3) #Creates a new ComplexNumbers object
Object1.getNumbers() #Calls getNumbers() function
Object2 = ComplexNumbers(10) #Creates another ComplexNumbers object
Object2.attr = 20 #Creates a new attribute 'attr'
print ((Object2.real, Object2.imagined, Object2.attr))
del ComplexNumbers.getNumbers
Object1.getNumbers()
```

The error you get when you run the script in Exercise64 shows that the attribute getNumbers() has been deleted. Note, however, that since a new instance is created in memory when a new instance of the object is created, the object may continue to exist in memory even after it is deleted until the garbage collector automatically destroys unreferenced objects.

Chapter 9

Flow control

Flow Control

A loop is a program control structure which facilitates intricate execution paths and repetitive processing of a statement or a series of statements.

The For Loop

A for loop is used to iterate over items of sequential data types such as strings, lists, or tuples.

Syntax:

for val in sequence:

statement(s)
In a 'for loop', the variable holds the value of the item in the sequence with every iteration. The loop goes on until all items are processed.

Examples:
For Loop over a string:

for letter in 'Programming': #iterate over a string

print('<<*', letter, '*>>')

If you run the above code, this would be your output:
```
<<* P *>>
<<* r *>>
<<* o *>>
<<* g *>>
<<* r *>>
<<* a *>>
```

```
<<* m *>>
<<* m *>>
<<* i *>>
<<* n *>>
<<* g *>>
```

Take note that the printing ended when the 'for loop' reached the last letter in the string.

for Loop over a list:

```
#iterate over a list
```

```
dogs = ['Rottweiler', 'Pug', 'Bulldog', 'Beagle', 'Poodle']
```

```
for name in dogs:
```

```
print('happy dog :', name)
```

```
print("Lovely dogs!")
```

Here's the output when you run the program:

happy dog : Rottweiler

happy dog : Pug

happy dog : Bulldog

happy dog : Beagle

happy dog : Poodle

Lovely dogs!

Using the range() function in a for loop

The range() function is a built-in function that can be used with the 'for loop' to obtain the required numbers. For example, if you need a total of 1 and all numbers from 1 up to 10, you can create a 'for loop' with this program: x = 10

```
total = 0
```

```
for num in range(1, x+1):
```

```
total = total + num
```

print("Sum of 1 up to %d: %d" % (x, total))

Your output would be:

Sum of 1 up to 10: 55

The While Loop

The 'while loop' is used when you need to repeatedly execute a statement or group of the statements while the test expression is True. When it ceases to be true, control passes on to the line after the loop.

syntax:

while condition

statement(s)

Example:

#program adds number up to a number

#specified by the user

#total = 1+2+3+4...+number

num = int(input("Enter a number: "))

#initialize total and counter

total = 0

y = 1

while y <= num:

total = total + y

y = y+1 #update counter

#print the total

print("The total is: ", total)

Enter a number: 3

The total is: 6 #1+2+3

Enter a number: 7

The total is: 28 #1+2+3+4+5+6+7

Break Statement

A break statement terminates the loop and passes control to the first statement after the loop. It is commonly used when a quick exit is required.

Syntax:

break

Example:

#loop ends once a specified color is reached

colors = ["blue", "pink", "red", "green", "yellow"]

for x in colors:

if x == 'green':

break

print('Great color :', x)

print("Interesting loop!")

Run the program and see the result:

Great color : blue

Great color : pink

Great color : red

Interesting loop!

Continue Statement

The continue statement skips the statement(s) in the current iteration and passes program control to the next iteration.

Syntax:

continue

To illustrate, you can replace the 'break' statement in the above example with the 'continue' statement.

colors = ["blue", "pink", "red", "green", "yellow"]

for x in colors:

if x == 'green':

continue

print('Great color :', x)

print("An amazing loop!")

When you run the program, here's the output:

Great color : blue

Great color : pink

Great color : red
Great color : yellow

An amazing loop!

Notice that when it reached the color 'green', it skipped the print statement and went on to print the next item on the list.

Pass Statement

Pass is a null operation in Python. The interpreter reads the pass statement but does nothing. It is commonly used as a placeholder whenever a statement is required by syntax. Programmers will generally use a pass statement in place of codes that are yet to be written. This will allow them to test complete segments while avoiding error messages for incomplete segments.

Syntax:

Pass

Chapter 10

Python dictonary

A dictionary, or just dict, though containing sequential data as well, is an associative array mapping type with mapped keys as values. The data it contains may be in sequence, but they are not sorted.

The elements of a dictionary are mutable and can be of any other data type. Each is made up of a key:value pair-matched by a colon (:) and just as with lists and tuples, separated by commas. The syntax of a dictionary is an identified object made up of one or more elements enclosed in curly braces {}.

The syntax takes this format:

> **myDict = {key1:value1, key2:value2, key3:value3}**

Similar to lists, dictionaries are mutable and can contain mixed content, including tuples (assuming the values are all of the same type), lists, strings, integers, etc.

The point of the key:value pair model is that every key stored within the dictionary is unique. In effect, the dictionary is designed to store the values of a list of unique items or properties.

Given that the following things are true:

1. When adding to or creating a dictionary, all entries must be in a key:value pair format. If either the key or the value is missing, an exception will be given.

2. If a key:value pair is added to a dictionary, and the key already exists in the dictionary, the old key and value will be discarded for the new entry.

3. Values can be updated only when a key is provided.

4. key:value pairs are always deleted together – there is no way to delete just the value or just the key.

5. Lists cannot be used as keys.

Here are some common operations on dictionaries.

Create an empty dictionary:

```
>>> x={}
```

Create a dictionary:
```
>>> x=dict(name='john', age=35, height=6)
```

```
>>> print(x)
```

{'name': 'john', 'age': 35, 'height': 6}

Test if a key exists:

```
>>> if 'age' in x.keys():
```

```
 print('found it!')
```

found it!

Get a value for a key:

```
>>> y=x['height']
```

```
 >>> print('Height = ' + str(y))
```

Height = 6

List all keys:

```
>>> for y in x.keys():
```

```
 print(y)
```

name

age
height

Print keys and values:

```
>>> for y in x.keys():
```

```
v=x[y]

if type(v)!='str':

v=str(v)

print(y + '=' + v)

name=john

age=35

height=6
```

Update a value for a key:

```
>>> x['age']=40

>>> print(x)

{'name': 'john', 'age': 40, 'height': 6}
```

Delete a key:value pair

```
>>> del(x['height'])

>>> print(x)

{'name': 'john', 'age': 40}
```

Add a Key:Value pair

```
>>> x['height']=6

>>> print(x)

{'name': 'john', 'age': 40, 'height': 6}
```

Dumping all keys or values into a list:

```
>>> list(x.keys()) # keys as a list

['name', 'age', 'height']

>>> list(x.values()) # values as a list
```

['john', 40, 6]

Creating a dictionary

The most popular way to create a dictionary object in Python is to name an empty dictionary object in the same way we have created other object types throughout this book. Once the dictionary is created, you can add key:value pairs as necessary.

Creating a dictionary then adding key:value pairs

```
1 myDict = {}
2
3 myDict ["Name"] = "Jane"
4 myDict ["Age"] = 21
5 myDict ["City"] = "London"
6 myDict ["Hobbies"] = "Cycling", "Coding", "Cooking", "Gaming",
7
8 print (myDict)
```

In this exercise, we created an empty dictionary called myDict in the first line of the script. From the third to the sixth line, we added key:value pairs to the empty dictionary then, at the end, printed out the contents of the dictionary myDict.

Another way to create a dictionary is to assign key:value pairs to a named dictionary object as in exercise 27.

Creating a dictionary by assigning key:value pairs

```
1 myDict = {["Name"] = "Jane", ["Age"] = 21, ["Gender" = "F"]
["City"] = "London"}
2
3 print (myDict)
```

You will notice that it does not matter what order the key:value pairs are entered into the dictionary because keys and not indices access them, they are always printed in a different order.

One rule you must observe when creating a dictionary is that the keys must be unique, but the values do not need to be. The keys are immutable, while the values are maybe of mutable data types such as strings, numbers, or lists.

Accessing dictionary key:value pairs

Dictionary data is not sorted; hence they can be accessed independently without indexing as we did with strings, lists, and tuples. The dictionary is a compound object type that cannot be sliced or indexed.

Python uses complex algorithms that map the keys of a dictionary. This makes accessing, retrieving, and updating dictionary key:value pairs much faster than other sequential object types by this process known as hashing.

The keys are used to access the dictionary key:value pairs. The next exercise demonstrates how we can access the values of dictionary *weather*.

Accessing dictionary key:value pairs:

```
1 weather = {["Mon"] = "Cloudy", ["Tue"] = "Sunny", ["Wed"] =
"Rainy"}
2
3 print (weather["Wed"])
```

If you attempt to access a key:value pair of a missing key you will encounter an error *KerError: [Key]*

Updating a dictionary

You can add new key:value pairs to a dictionary and modify or delete the values of existing entries, as demonstrated in the next exercise.

Updating a dictionary:

```
1 weather = {["Mon"] = "Cloudy", ["Tue"] = "Sunny", ["Wed"] =
"Rainy"}
2
3 weather["Thu"] = "Hot"
4 weather["Wed"] = "Gloomy"
5 del weather["Mon"]
6
7 print (weather["Wed"])
```

In this exercise, we have created a dictionary called weather with day:weather type key:value pairs as you can see. In line 3, we have added a new key:value pair; in line 4 we update the value of the "Wed" key, and in line 5 we delete the key:value pair for "Mon". Does your script work as it should?

The **del** statement is used to remove a single item in the dictionary explicitly; to delete the entire dictionary, use **clear**.

Basic dictionary operations with in-built functions and methods

The table in your next exercise summarizes the vital operations you can carry out on a dictionary in Python at this stage. You will notice that we have already come across most of them earlier with the previous object types we have covered. Nevertheless, try all these operations with dictionaries to understand how each is applied.

Dictionary functions and methods

```
1 janedoe = {["ID"] = 7234, ["Height"] = "5.5 ft", ["Weight"] = "212
lbs"}
2 johndoe = {["ID"] = 2932, ["Height"] = "6.0 ft", ["Weight"] =
"190 lbs"}
```

Operation	Description	Exercise example
Compare cmp	Compares the key:value pairs of two dic-tionaries	cmp(johndoe, janedoe)
Length len	Returns the total length (number of key:value pairs) in the dictionary.	len(johndoe)
String str	Returns a printable string of the key:value pairs of the dictionary.	str(johndoe)
Clear dict.clear()	Removes all the key:value elements of the dictionary dict	johndoe.clear()
Copy dict.copy()	Returns a copy of the dictionary dict	johndoe.copy()
Items dict.items()	Returns a tuple format of dictionary dict key:value pairs	johndoe.items()
Keys dict.keys()	Returns a list of the dictionary dict's keys	johndoe.keys()
Values dict. values()	Returns a list of the dictionary dict's val-ues.	johndoe.values()
Update dict1. update(dict2)	Adds the key:value pairs of dictionary dict2 to those of dict1	johndoe. update(janedoe)

Chapter 11

Make your codes

Exercise 1
Dictionary Demo

Please click "Start > Programs > Python3.5 > IDLE (Python GUI)".

Write the following code to IDLE editor:

```
color ={0:"red", 1:"yellow", 2:"green", 3:"white"}

v = color.values()

for c in v:

 print (c)
```

Save the file and run the program by pressing F5 key.

(Run>Run Module).

Output:

```
 red

yellow

green

white
```

Explanation:

"color ={0:"red", 1:"yellow", 2:"green", 3:"white"}" is a Dictionary.

"color.values()" returns all values of dictionary "color".

The for-in loop repeats a given block of codes by a specified number of times.

"for c in v" loop repeats to execute "print (c)", "c" stores the values of each element.

Exercise 2
isalpha() Demo
Please click "Start > Programs > Python3.5 > IDLE (Python GUI)".

Write the following code to IDLE editor:

name = raw_input("Please enter your last name: ")

isLetter = name.isalpha() if isLetter:

 print ("OK! Valid Last Name!")

else:

 print ("No Good! Invalid Last Name!")

Save the file, and run the program by pressing F5 key.

(Run>Run Module).

Output:

(Assume inputting "Swift")

Please enter your last name: Swift

OK! Valid Last Name!

Explanation:

isalpha() return true if all characters are letters.

If a user enters a digital number or symbol, isalpha() will return false.

Here, the user enters "Swift", isalpha() returns true, because all characters are letters.

Exercise 3
Write & Read File

(Please create an empty text file "tryFile.txt" in the same directory with the following Python file) Please click "Start > Programs > Python3.5 > IDLE (Python GUI)".

Write the following code to IDLE editor:

f = open("tryFile.txt", "w")

f.write("I am learning Python programming!")

f.close

f =open("tryFile.txt", "r")

print(f.read())

f.close

Save the file, and run the program by pressing F5 key.

(Run>Run Module).

Output

I am learning Python programming!

Explanation:
"open("tryFile.txt", "w")" opens tryFile.txt in "w" mode.

"w" mode opens a file for writing.

 f.write("I am learning Python programming!") writes the specified

text to file object "f".

f =open("tryFile.txt", "r") opens tryFile.txt in "r" mode.

f.read() reads the data in file object "f".

Exercise 4
Import Module Demo
Please click "Start > Programs > Python3.5 > IDLE (Python GUI)".

Write the following code to IDLE editor:

program001.py

```
def red():

 print ("This flower is red")

def yellow():

 print ("This flower is yellow")

def green():

print ("This flower is green")
```
Save the file named program001.py, and close the file.

"program001.py" should be in the same directory with the following working file.

Please click "Start > Programs > Python3.5 > IDLE (Python GUI)".

Write the following code to IDLE editor:

```
# program002.py

import program001

program001.red()

program001.yellow()

program001.green()
```

Save the file named program002.py, and run the program by pressing F5, (Run > Run Module).

Output:

This flower is red

This flower is yellow

This flower is green

Exercise 5
Class & Object
Please click "Start > Programs > Python3.5 > IDLE (Python GUI)".

Write the following code to IDLE editor:

class Flower:

def __init__(self, name, color):

self.name = name

self.color = color

f = Flower("rose", "red")

print ("The flower's name is " + f.name)

print ("The flower's color is " + f.color)

Save the file, and run the program by pressing F5 key.

Output:

The flower's name is rose

The flower's color is red

Explanation:

"class Flower" creates a class "Flower".

"def __init__(self):" defines a constructor.

A constructor is used to initialize the variables.

"self" is a variable that refers to the current object "f".

f = Flower("rose", "red") creates an object "f", automatically calls def __init__(self, name, color), and passes two parameters "rose, red" to "name, color", initializes the variables "name" and "color".

Conclusion

This book is meant to help a beginner programmer learn Python. With this book, you should be able to write basic programs and even more sophisticated programs with multiple objects.

This book has been the perfect launchpad for a beginner looking to get the right foundation in object-oriented programming to advance to intermediate and advanced topics in programming using Python. Considering how far you have come, you are on the right track to becoming an expert in Python programming—whether you are pursuing it to advance your career or to become a proficient hobbyist coder.

I hope this book was able to help you to learn the fundamentals of Python Programming quickly and easily and inspire you to create your meaningful programs and practical applications.

The next step is to take your learning to the next level by taking advanced courses in Python programming and acquiring the skills needed to develop larger, more complicated, and highly useful programs that will harness the many powerful features of this programming language.

I wish you the best of luck!

PYTHON DATA SCIENCE

After work guide to start learning Data Science on your own. Avoid common beginners mistakes of coding. Approach Panda and NumPy to become a brilliant computer programmer.

Michail Kölling

Introduction

The purpose of it is to teach you the process of data science, while also providing you with all the fundamental skills and tools to support your learning process. This book is intended for complete beginners looking for a way to understand the basics of data science easily.

Learning data science with Python can be intimidating at times due to the requirements of programming and mathematical knowledge.
Results can often be challenging to communicate because they can be along string of numbers that aren't easily understood by beginners. You will learn some basic tools that can help you create interactive charts and make it possible for you to share your results with others.

Keep in mind that to benefit the most from this book, you should work through the examples presented in each section. If you have a difficult time understanding some of them, break them apart line by line, and slowly push through them until you understand the concepts. Each chapter will teach you about the tools you need, show you how to install them, and give you enough information so that you can work on your own as well. Make sure to practice everything you read because, without practical work, you won't succeed at fully understanding the theory.

There are a lot of options that we can work with when it comes to data science, and almost all businesses are going to be able to handle this kind of process and see some of the benefits. If you have been wanting to know more about your customers and what they are looking for from you and your business, then the data science process is going to be the best option to help you out.

To start this guidebook, we are going to take a look at what data science is all about, why it is important, and why we would want to work with this process in the first place as well. We will then take some time to learn the lifecycle of data science, and how we need to go through a series of steps like the finding the right data, preparing the data, coming up with the right model, and more.

Then we are going to spend some time taking a look at the basics that come with the Python language, and how we can use this to help with our data science project. There are a lot of great coding languages out there that we can work with when it is time to handle data science, but many agree that the power, the libraries, and the ease to use and learn of Python make it one of the best choices to handle with this idea. We will also spend some time looking at a few of the libraries that are going to work with when it comes to Python, including NumPy and its arrays, Seaborn, and Matplotlib to get all of the work done in no time.

This is just the start of some of the fantastic things that we can do when it is time to start on data science. We can spend our time looking at what machine learning is all about, the different types of machine learning, and how we can put it all together when it is time to sort through our data and find the right patterns and insights in the process.

There are a lot of benefits that we can see when it comes to working on data science. Many companies in a lot of different industries are going to work with this to ensure that we will be able to handle how to work with their customers, how to beat out the competition, and so much more. When you are ready to work with the idea of data science, and you want to work with all of the different parts that are found with it, then make sure to check out this guidebook to help you get started.

Chapter 1

What is the difference between data science and analysis

What is Data Science?

Data science is likely a term that you have heard about at least a few times. If you are running a company, and you have ever taken a look at some of the steps that you can take to make yourself more efficient and to reduce the risks. When it is time to make some big and important decisions, then you have most likely heard about data science from others who are in the same boat as you. But this doesn't explain that much about data science and what we can do with it. And that is where this guidebook is going to come into play.

As the world started to enter the era of big data, the need for the right storage to use with it was something else that seemed to grow like crazy as well too. This was one of the main challenges and concerns that happen with these industries, at least until a few years ago. The main focus because of this issue was that companies might be able to collect and use a lot of data for their needs, they didn't have an excellent place to store all of that data to work with later.

Now, thanks to some of the changes that are there in the technology that we have, this is no longer the big issue that it was in the past. And this means that we can make a few adjustments and work with more and more data in the process. And you will find that the secret sauce that is going to bring it all together and helps us not only to gather up the data that we need but will ensure that we can learn what is found in all of that data is going to be data science.

There are a lot of companies that are looking to get into the world of data science because they know all of the benefits that come with this as well. When we are ready to handle some of the data that is going on with all of this, we need to make sure that we are getting the right data, and that we understand all of the information that we are dealing with at the same time. But that is all going to be covered in the data analysis that we are doing along the way.

Why is Data Science So Important?

The first thing that we need to take a look at when we are doing some of our work here is why data science is so important, and why a company may need to work with the process of data science along the way. The first issue is the way that this data has been structured in our modern world, especially when it is compared to how it was done in the past. Traditionally, the data that companies were able to get their hands on was going to be smaller in size, and it was pretty much structured the whole time. This allowed us to work with simple business intelligence tools to analyze what is going on.

However, this is not the case any longer. Some benefits and negatives come with this, of course. It allows us the option to know more about a situation because we can gather up the data and understand more with more data. But often, this data is going to be unstructured, and that makes it harder to sort through and understand as well.

Unlike some of the data that was found in those traditional systems, the ones that were structured and easier to work with, today, we will find that most of our data is unstructured or at least semi-structured. This is going to make it harder to work with and can take longer. But because we can find more information to help shape the decisions that we are making, this is not necessarily a bad thing all of the time.

This data is going to be generated from a lot of different sources, including things like instruments, sensors, multimedia forms, text files, and even some financial logs along the way. Because of all these sources that we are getting the data from, it is essential to see that we are not able to work with some of the simple business intelligence tools because they are not capable of handling all the data. This is why it is important to work with data science to work with algorithms and analytical tools that are more advanced and complex as well. This ensures that we can really analyze and processes meaningful insights out of the data as well.

Based on the data that the car can gather, it can make decisions to help it drive, when it should speed up, go slower, when it should overtake, or even where to turn with the help of data science and to make use of advanced machine learning algorithms.

And we can even work with the idea of data science to help out with the predictive analytics. For example, we can work with something like weather forecasting. Data from things like satellites, radars, aircraft, ships, and more can be analyzed to help us build up some of the models that we have. These models are going to be useful when we can forecast the weather, while also being able to predict the occurrence of any natural calamities that we would like. It is also going to help us to take some of the right measures ahead of time when we see this, and can, in the process, help us save a lot of lives as well.

How Can I Use Data Science?

One of the first things that we will have questions when it comes to data science is the idea of how we can use it. It may seem like a beautiful thing to learn about and like we can work with it just for fun, but there are quite a few practical purposes that are going to come with using data science, no matter what industry you are in or how you plan to use it. Some of the different ways that we can rely on data science will include.

It can help with marketing. Marketing is all about data, and when we can use all of the big data that is needed for data science, we will find that we can learn more about our customers and how we can reach them to make a sale. There are different ways that a company will be able to use data science to help them get ahead of the game, and it can help with knowing how to reach the customers, placing heads in the right places for the right customers, and more.

Helps the company to learn more about their customers. As a company, the more that you can learn about your customers, the better off you will be. Learning about what your customers want out of your business, where your customers are located, their demographics, and how you can serve them better will ensure that they will continue to pick out your business, rather than working with someone else along the way. It can even help you to determine which products you are going to sell next.

It can help to reduce waste. All companies want to learn about and reduce the amount of waste that is going ton in their company. This waste can be resources, time, machine parts, and even part of the process of making the product. When we can cut down on some of this waste, it can help the company to become more efficient and will increase the profits that the company is going to experience.

When you can properly use data science, you will find that it is easier to cut out some of this waste and see the results that you would like.

Financial institutions use it to help them fight off fraud. Fraud can cost these financial institutions a lot of money overall. If they are not careful with how they handle their money and they don't learn how to watch out for legitimate transactions and the fraudulent ones, there are going to be some problems along the way. When the financial institution can come up with algorithms and programs that can recognize and stop fraud, it can end up saving them millions of dollars a year.

This is where data science can come in, as well. Using a lot of different factors, as well as training the algorithms on past transactions that were fraudulent, it is easier for one of these systems to figure out when a transaction is fraudulent or not. And the more times that the algorithm goes through the process, the better it is going to be at doing that work, and the fewer instances of fraud that are going to happen.

It can speed up loan applications. There are often a huge amount of loan applications that come into banks and other financial institutions regularly today. This is a lot for a loan officer to handle, and the resources of the financial institution to do on their own. Data science can come into this to help.

With the help of data science, the financial institution can go through the applications and figure out which loans are the best bets and not. You can set up a few of the different criteria that the application needs to meet, and then work from there. If the application meets some of the requirements, then it is going to be a good option to work with. The loan officer will get these and can make the final determination on it. But if the loan application doesn't meet the requirements, it will get ignored and not be seen at all. This helps to speed up the loan application process and can allow the loan officer a chance to keep up with their work and focus on the customers who will bring that financial institution money. It helps out in the medical field in a variety of ways. There are so many ways that the process of data science would be able to help out the medical field. To start with, we can see that data science is going to help out with doctors and finishing up their surgeries. With the use of machine learning and other algorithms that come with data science, doctors are going to be able to make the right incisions and get the surgery done with minimal issues and with less recovery time.

In addition, these algorithms are going to help doctors make a prognosis about their patients. With the ever-increasing workload that is on doctors and the limited time they have to be with each patient, having these can be beneficial. They will be able to use data science to look through some of the images that are available, such as scans and x-rays, and then get a diagnosis in no time at all.

And finally, we can even find data science in work when it comes to the administrative tasks that come in the medical field. These machines can talk to the customers, ask a few questions, and figure out the severity of the issue of the patient, and can direct them to the right location. For fields that are running low on staff to handle some of their patient needs, this can be helpful.

It helps a company learn more about their current competition and the industry they are in. If you want to beat out some of the competition that you have right now, then you need to find out as much information about your industry and your competition. You need to see what they are doing, how customers are responding to it, and how you can use this to your advantage.

When you have all of this information in place, you will find that it is easier to figure out what is working and what is not working. You can then jump right in and make some of the necessary adjustments to your business model. You may find a new way to reach your customers that no one else is working with. You may be able to make some modifications to a technique that someone else is working with that can improve your own business, as well.

Many manufacturing companies are going to work with data science because it allows them to make predictions that can save them money. First, you can use these kinds of algorithms to figure out when a part on a machine is likely to break, or when you need to do maintenance. Then you can schedule this to be done during the off-hours, ensuring that the machine is always up and running on time, and that production is not going to be halted while you get things figured out.

These algorithms can also work, in pretty much any business, when it is time to work with finding ways to cut down on some of the waste that is present. Every company is going to have some kind of waste, and figuring out how to reduce that waste, and take care of it, will make it so that you can offer the products at a competitive rate, while still making as much in profits as possible. It is as simple as working with data science to figure out where these wastes are and how you can keep them to a minimum.

When you are online doing some shopping, and you see that there is a recommendation tab on that website, we are seeing some of the work of data science and machine learning coming to life. These are so popular on many websites because they can make it easier for the customer to make some informed decisions on what they want to watch next or purchase next or something else. And businesses are going to enjoy them as well because, with these recommendation systems, it is more likely that the customer is going to make another purchase, which is going to increase the bottom line for that company.

Next on the list is going to be the process of speech recognition. If you have ever talked and asked a question to your smartphone, or you have worked with some of the popular devices like the Echo, Cortana, and more, then you can recognize how this feature is going to be fun and innovative. And it is run with some of the principles of data science.

In fact, some of the best examples that we are going to find when it comes to data science is this speech recognition. Using these features, even if you are not currently in a position to type out a message, you are still about to talk to the machine or the device and ask a question. However, this may not perform accurately, especially when we are in the beginning. This means that we may have to spend some time working with the program and teaching it how to recognize some of the things that we are saying. And this is the machine learning that is behind the process, where the machine, through experience and some time, will be able to learn how to recognize the speech of the user faster and more efficiently.

If you have ever worked with some of the websites that are out there that help out with price comparisons, then you have seen data science at work as well. At a basic kind of level, you will find that these are websites that will be driven with the use of lots and lots of data that they can get with the help of RSS Feeds and APIs. They can then use this information to figure out what the price of the same product from different websites and sources will be so you can make the best decision and save money. This can be used in many industries to help you compare prices and figure out what is best for you.

We can also take a look at how this kind of technology is going to work when we talk about something like airline route planning. This industry is one that is going to bear a lot of heavy losses if they are not careful. Except for a few companies, many are struggling to maintain the occupancy that they need and make some profits. And when we add in the higher prices of fuel right now, and the need to offer heavy discounts to many customers, the situation is slowly getting worse.

It wasn't too long before these airline companies started to work with data science to see how they can increase their profits and make more without scaring their customers away. This helped them to figure out some of the strategic improvements that they can make. Today, with the help of data science, these airline companies can:

Make better predictions about a flight being delayed.

Decide which class of airplanes they should invest their money in.

Whether they should land at the direct destination, or take a halt in between.

Help to drive some of the loyalty programs that customers can sign up for.

Two of the airline companies who have embraced these changes will include American Airlines and Southwest, and they are now some of the most profitable of the airlines out there.

And finally, we are going to look at delivery logistics to make sure that packages are delivered in time and that things don't get lost. Companies like UPS, FedEx, and DHL are going to use data science to help improve how efficient they are operational.

With the help of data science, these companies and more have been able to figure out the best routes to ship, the best times that they should deliver, and the mode of transportation that is the best for these as well. This helps them to have more cost efficiency and more benefits along the way as well. In addition, the data that these companies can generate with the installed GPS units can provide them with the data they need to explore more possibilities and to learn more with data science along the way.

There are so many benefits that we can see when it comes to using data science for a company. In many cases, if you are not willing to use data science at least a little bit, you will find that you will fall behind. No matter what kind of business problem you are trying to work on or what you would like to solve in your business, you will find that working with data science is one of the best and most effective methods to help you out.

Data Analysis

While we are on the topic of working with data science, we also need to take a look at some of the data analysis.]This is basically a subset of data science, and it is going to be where we will handle the data that we are gathering, which comes in from many different sources, and then using algorithms to help us figure out what all of this data means.

You can use all of the data that we want, and we can fill up a lot of data warehouses if we would like, but if you don't understand what the data is telling us, then the data is not going to matter all that much, and your company will not be able to use it. This is where we will be able to grab the process of data analysis and make it come into play for us.

To help us get started, data analytics is going to be the process or the science of taking the raw data that we have and then analyzing it to help us make some good conclusions about all of that information. Many techniques and the processes used with this have been automated into algorithms and other mechanical processes that can work over the data in its raw form before turning it into something that we can read through and understand better than before.

When the data analytics are used properly, it is going to be used to help us see some of the metrics and the trends that we may miss out on in some of the other situations out there because there is just so much data that we are gathering and holding onto. This information is then going to be what we can use to optimize processes to help increase how efficient a system or a business can be overall.

Now that we know a bit about the broad meaning of data analytics, it is time to get into some of the different parts of it, and how we can use it to our advantage. The term data analytics is going to be broad, and it includes many diverse types of data analysis. Any type of information that can be subjected to techniques of data analytics to get inside that can then be used by humans to improve something about their business will fall under this umbrella.

Let's look at an example of this. Many manufacturing companies are going to spend time recording the work queue, downtime, and run time for the different machines that they are working with. They will then take the data that contains this information, and use it to better plan how and when the workloads should happen. This helps the machines get as close to their peak capacity as possible, saving time and money in the process.

This is just one of the tasks that data analytics is going to be able to help out with, even though preventing bottlenecks in production is a good thing to pay attention to. Gaming companies are going to be able to use this process to set up the right reward schedules for players, which are done in a way that ensures the majority of players stay active in the game rather than dropping off and rarely using it. Another example is a content company. They can use the various parts of data analytics to keep their customers clicking, watching, or even reorganizing the content so that they can get the clicks and the views that they need.

As we are working through this process, we always have to keep in mind that the data analysis that we are working on here is a pretty complex process, and not one that we can just glance at and come up with the answers that we want. If you do this, then it is likely that you will end up missing out on important information, especially when you work with one of the larger sets of data.

Following the right steps along the way can make a big difference in what we are going to see with this data analysis. And some of the different steps that we can use here will include the following:

We start this process by determining the requirements of the data or how the data has been grouped. There are a lot of possibilities here, including the data being separated by things like gender, income, demographics, and age. The values of the data could also be numerical, or they may be divided up by category as well.

Then in the second step of this is the process of collecting our data. There are a ton of different sources where you can get all of this information. It could be from your employees, from sources in the environment, online sources like surveys and social media, and even from your computer system.

Once the data has been collected, and you are sure you have the data that you need, it is time to organize the data Since you are collecting it from a variety of sources, you have to make sure that it is organized in a manner that makes sense, and one that the algorithm will be able to read through quickly and find the trends to make predictions from when you get to that step.

You can choose what method you would like to use when you organize the information. You can work with a spreadsheet or try some kind of software that is good at handling data that is statistical.

Once you have been able to organize the data the way that you would like, it is time to clean it all up before the analysis happens. This means that the data scientist has to go through and scrub the data and check that there are no errors or duplications that are found in the information, or that the data is not incomplete. This step takes some time, but it ensures that everything is fixed and ready to go before you even start.

The key thing that we have to remember here is that it is going to be the science that we can use to use raw data, analyze it, and then make some good conclusions on this information as well. The processes and the techniques that are used in this kind of thing is going to be automated in many cases, and you will see that when we work with the right algorithm, it will be able to take all of that raw data and turn it into something that humans can consume. And the main reason that a business would want to use this kind of process, and to analyze the data, is because it is going to be so useful when it is time to optimize your customer service, your performance, and how you can help your performance.

Why Does the Analysis of Data Matter?

While we are here, we need to take a moment to look at why this data analysis is going to be so important, and why a business would like to go through these algorithms and more to learn from that data they have been able to gather in the first place. These companies find that they can use the insights and predictions that are in the data, but when there is such a large amount of data, and all of that data comes to them from a variety of sources, it is going to need a lot of work to sort through—too much work to try and do manually.

The process that of data analytics is something that can be helpful to any business no matter what industry they are in because it will help them to optimize their performance. It can also help them to work on their business model and can make it easier for them to identify some methods that are more efficient for reducing costs and getting things figured out.

In addition to all of this, a company will be able to take that data analysis and make decisions that are going to help propel them into the future. This analysis is also going to help them to learn more about some of the customer trends that are out there and can help you to offer new services and products that are going to work for your customers as well.

Choices in Data Analysis

The next thing that we need to spend some of our time here is to figure out what kinds of analysis are open for you to work with as well. There are a lot of variations that come with the data analysis, and you can pick the one that works the best for your needs. There are a number of these, but we are going to focus on some of the ones that you are most likely to use when you first get started on this whole process. The four basic types that a beginner in data analysis can focus on, and that most data scientists are going to work with will include the following:

•   Descriptive analytics. This is one that will take the time to describe what has happened in the data over a chosen period. You may look at things like whether the number of views has gone up, or if the sales for your company are higher or lower than they were in the previous month for a product.

•   Diagnostic analytics This is the one that will focus more on why something has happened or the root of how your business is doing. This one is helpful, but it will involve data inputs that are more diverse and a bit of hypothesizing in the process. For example, did you have a slow sales week because the weather was terrible and no one went out shopping? Or did something go wrong with one of your marketing campaigns, and that is why sales are struggling?

•   Predictive analytics. This one is going to be used to help predict what is most likely to happen soon, based on the information that we have at our disposal right now. What happened to the sales last year when the summer was warm? How many weather models are going to tell us that there will be a hot summer this year, and we should prepare for more of what we saw in the past?

As we can see, some differences show up with this, even though they are going to focus more on handling the data and helping us to gather some of the useful insights that are there from the data. The demand to handle this data and then perform these in an accurate and timely manner through the analysis is going to be higher, even though there are not enough professionals to handle all of this work currently.

Even without a professional with this, companies can learn how to make the data analysis work and can then use this to leverage a ton of data and learn from it. Companies are seeing all of the benefits of doing this, and they like that this is going to help them to make some smart decisions. Such decisions are driven by data so that they are going to be able to see a lot of benefits and see how to beat out the competition.

What Are the Benefits of a Data Analysis?

When it is time to work with data analysis, it will not take you too long to realize that there are a lot of benefits that are going to come with this overall as well. No matter what kind of company you are in and what your goals are, you will be able to receive a lot of these benefits in the process as well. This process may seem like it has a ton of steps and that you are going to spend too long working on it for it to be worth your time. But it can be so worth it if you take the time to learn about the data and all of the cool things that it can do for you. With this in mind, some of the benefits that you are going to receive when it is time to work with data analysis for your company, no matter what kind of company, will include:

•   It helps you to understand your customers better. All businesses want to understand their customers. This is the best way to make more sales and increase revenue. But how are you supposed to know what the customer wants, and what is going to convince them to come to your store compared to going over to a competitor? This data analysis can take information from customer surveys and customer habits and help you make more informed decisions to provide better customer service to increase sales as well.

•   It helps you to know what trends are going on that you should follow for your business. There are always trends that go on in any market, but these trends are often shifting and changing at really fast rates that are hard to keep up with. Using a data analysis can help you to catch on to some of the trends ahead of time, making it easier for you to meet the needs of your customers.

•   It helps you to know your product better. Sometimes, this data analysis can be used to help you know which products are doing the best and why. You may find out that one product is doing better than you thought, or that you should start selling more of a similar product to increase sales.

•   It can help make smarter business decisions overall. It is always best if you can have data and information behind all of the decisions that you make for your company. The data analysis helps you to comb through all the information and see what is there before you make any decisions about your company.

This data analysis process is going to be one of the best ways that you can beat out the competition. Companies who are willing to look through the data and are willing to see what insights and trends are there are the ones who will be able to find these things faster than the competition, and who will be able to win in their industry.

You will find that these benefits are going to help out your company, and are some of the main reasons why this data analysis can be so good for the whole company, and why it is something that is in such high demand for almost every industry that is out there. For some of the smaller companies that are out there, the ones who may not be choosing to work with this kind of process will find that they can still work with it on a local level and get some results as well.

Data analysis has numerous benefits, and being able to figure out how to make this happen, and what you can do to see some of the results when it comes to learning what is in that data, is going to be very important as well. Make sure to go through some of the steps that we talked about in this chapter. In the rest of this guidebook, and you will see that you can make this work for your needs as well.

Chapter 2

NumPy introduction

The n-dimensional Array

You can build complex data structures with them because they are powerful at storing data; however, they're not great at operating on that data. They aren't optimal when it comes to processing power and speed, which are critical when working with complex algorithms. This is why we're using NumPy and its ndarray object, which stands for an "n-dimensional array". Let's look at the properties of a NumPy array:

It is optimal and fast at transferring data. When you work with complex data, you want the memory to handle it efficiently instead of being bottlenecked.

You can perform vectorization. In other words, you can make linear algebra computations and specific element operations without being forced to use "for" loops. This is a large plus for NumPy because Python "for" loops cost a lot of resources, making it expensive to work with a large number of loops instead of ndarrays.

In data science operations, you will have to use tools, or libraries, such as SciPy and Scikit-learn. You can't use them without arrays because they are required as an input, otherwise, functions won't perform as intended.

With that being said, here are a few methods of creating a ndarray:

- Take an already existing data structure and turn it into an array.
- Build the array from the start and add in the values later.

- You can also upload data to an array even when it's stored on a disk.

Converting a list to a one-dimensional array is a fairly common operation in data science processes. Keep in mind that you have to take into account the type of objects such a list contains. This will have an impact on the dimensionality of the result. Here's an example of this with a list that contains only integers:

In: import numpy as np

```
int_list = [1,2,3]
```

```
Array_1 = np.array(int_list)
```

```
In: Array_1
Out: array([1, 2, 3])
```

You can access the array just like you access a list in Python. You simply use indexing, and just like in Python, it starts from 0. This is how this operation would look: In: Array_1[1]

Out: 2

Now you can gain more data about the objects inside the array like so:

In: type(Array_1)

Out: numpy.ndarray

In: Array_1.dtype

Out: dtype('int64')

The result of the dtype is related to the type of operating system you're running. In this example, we're using a 64 bit operating system.

Next, let's see how we can load an array from a file. N-dimensional arrays can be created from the data contained inside a file. Here's an example in code:

In: import numpy as np

cars = np.loadtxt('regression-datasets

cars.csv',delimiter=',', dtype=float)

In this example, we tell our tool to create an array from a file with the help of the "loadtxt" method by giving it a filename, delimiter, and a data type.

The Importance of the NumPy Arrays

One thing that you will quickly notice when it comes time to work with the different libraries that are supposed to work with Python is that many of them are going to be based on the NumPy array. This means that we will need to spend at least a little bit of time learning about these arrays and how we can make them work for some of our needs as well. These arrays are going to help to lead us in many of the other parts that we want to do with data science, so learning how to make them work, and what they can do is going to make a big difference.

The first thing that we need to take a look at is what the NumPy array is all about. Often we are going to work with what is known as a structured NumPy array. This is going to be an array of structures, which are going to be similar to what we see with the C language structure. We will also see that these arrays are going to be homogenous, which means that they are only going to be able to contain data that is the same type. So instead of creating an array that is an integer or a floating number, we can go through and create one of these arrays with some homogenous other structures as well.

Now, if you have spent some time working with the Python language, you may look at some of these arrays and wonder how they are going to be any different than what you can see with the Python list. There are going to be a few different reasons for this, and we are going to take a bit of time exploring these to gain a better understanding of what is going to happen with both the array and the list when we use them.

To start with, the array in NumPy is going to be more compact than what we are going to see with the lists in Python. A regular list of Python is going to take about 20 MB or more of data to handle, and this can go up if you are working with a longer or more complicated list on the process. But if you are working with a 3D array in NumPy and has a single-precision float in a cell, it is going to be about 4 MB. This can help us to get to the information a lot faster. And when you are already working with data analysis or a data science project that has a ton of information, the less space some of your other coding parts will take, the better off for you.

Also, you would also find that accessing the array versus the list in terms of reading and writing items is going to be a lot faster and easier to handle when you choose to work with the array. This will help you to get through some of the arrays that you would like to handle a little bit faster and will ensure that you are going to get things done faster. When you have at one of the data to get through, and you are working with machine learning, you will find that all of this can be useful in the long run.

Now, in the beginning, it may not seem like the difference in space or speed that comes with the Python lists and the NumPy arrays would be that big of a deal. But you will find that there are a ton of times when this is going to be super important to what you are trying to get done with some of your codes.

It may not matter that much if you are just working with a million cells, but it is going to matter when you are working with something a lot larger, like a billion cells. Neither approach is going to fit into the architecture that is based on 32-bit. Still, if you are working with a 64-bit, you can build with the NumPy and get it all done with about 4 GB of data while the Python when it is doing all of the works on its own, would need a minimum of 12 GB to get it done, and many people will say that it takes twice as much as this if not more. And we can imagine that the more space that we need to use, the more we will have to spend on the hardware to take care of it.

Not only is NumPy going to be more efficient like we talked about above, but you will also find that it is a lot nicer and more convenient to work with. When you work with this one, you are going to find that you can get a lot of matrix and vector options to work for you for free. This is going to be nice because it allows you to avoid some of the work that is unnecessary, but which you have to do to get some of the other parts of Python, like the lists to work. Add into this that you can efficiently implement them, and it is no wonder that so many people want to work with these arrays for some of their data analysis projects.

To take it a bit further, not only are you going to enjoy the convenience that comes with these arrays, but you will like how efficient they are, along with their functionality and the speed. When it comes to sorting through millions and even billions of data points overall, it is essential that we can do this in a fast and efficient manner along the way. This is something that the NumPy array is going to be able to help us with.

The first thing to look at here is going to be the functionality. You are going to be able to build up a lot of things when you are working with the NumPy array. For example, you can work with things like linear algebra, some of the basic statistics, fast searches, FFTs, convolutions, and histograms, to name a few. And how are you supposed to be able to handle some of the data science projects that you want to do without some of these important parts showing up as well?

And another thing that you will be able to notice and enjoy when it comes to working with the NumPy array is that it has a lot of speed. The speed may not be that noticeable when you are working on a smaller project that doesn't have a lot of data points attached to it. But when you are working with a big project with a lot of data points, you will quickly find that this is going to be something important and something that the NumPy array can deliver on.

Some of the other benefits that you will be able to receive when you decide to work with the NumPy array rather than the Python list with some of your data analysis projects will include some of the following:

The arrays that show up in NumPy are going to come out at a fixed size at creation. This is different than what we can see when it comes to the Python list that can change and grow dynamically. Changing the size of your array when it is done is going just to create a brand-new array that you can work with.

The elements that you are going to see with some of these arrays are going to tell us that they must be the same kind of data type. We can work with heterogeneous types as well sometimes, but this makes it impossible to do some of the mathematical operations that you want to do. And as this is going to make it so that you can't do some of the parts of data science that you want with the arrays, it is not usually recommended. However, because you are using the same types of objects in all of this, you will find that all of them are going to be the same size in the memory of the code that you are writing.

The arrays that we are working with are going to be facilitated advances mathematical and other types of operations when it is time to work on large numbers of data. Typically, these operations are going to be executed more efficiently, and often with less code than what we can see with some of the different built-in sequences that we are going to see with Python as well.

The final thing that you are going to notice when it is time to work with the NumPy library is that many of the other specialized libraries that work with Python, including those for deep learning, machine learning, data science, and data analysis, are going to be based on these NumPy arrays. It is hard to do any of the functions that you need concerning these topics if you do not have the NumPy array in place first, and to do this. We need to make sure that we have this library up and ready to go as well.

As we are already able to see here, there are a ton of benefits and uses that we are going to be able to see when it is time to work with one of these NumPy arrays. They are designed to handle a lot of different options when it comes to handling our data science project, and learning how to make them work the right way is going to be critical to how much success we are going to be able to see with this process overall. Make sure that when you want to work with some kind of data science project that you make sure to install and important the NumPy library. This is going to ensure that we can get the best results out of everything and will make it easier for us to get the results that we would like when the project is done.

NumPy Array Operations

Sometimes, when you work with two-dimensional arrays, you may want to add new rows or columns to represent new data and variables. This operation is known as array stacking, and it doesn't take long for NumPy to render the new information. Start by creating a new array: In:

```
import numpy as np

dataset = np.arange(50).reshape(10,5)
```

Next, add a new row, and several lines that will be concatenated:

In: single_line = np.arange(1*5).reshape(1,5)

several_lines = np.arange(3*5).reshape(3,5)

Now let's use the vstack method, which stands for a vertical stack, to add a new single line.

In: np.vstack((dataset,single_line))

This command line will also work if we want to add several lines.

In: np.vstack((dataset,several_lines))

Next, let's see how to add a variable to the array. This is done with the "hstack" method, which stands for horizontal stack. Here's an example: In: bias = np.ones(10).reshape(10,1) np.hstack((dataset,bias))

In this line of code, we added bias of unit values to the array we created earlier.

As an aspiring data scientist, you will only need to know how to add new rows and columns to your arrays. In most projects, you won't need to do more than that, so practice working with two-dimensional arrays and NumPy because this tool is engraved in data science.

What is the NumPy Library

Now it is time for us to take a look at one of the great libraries that we can work with when it comes to using Python and getting our data analysis to work well for our needs. NumPy is one of the first that we can look at, and it is going to be one of the best. It is going to be the basis that we can see with some of the other important libraries that we will discuss later on, or other data analysis libraries, so it is worth our time to take a look at it.

To start with, NumPy is a library that is used in Python. We can use it for several different reasons, including numerical as well as scientific computing if we need it. For the most part, though, it is going to be used to help us compute our array s quickly and efficiently. We will have it based and written out in the Python and the C language.

Even though this is a language that works for the C language as well, this is going to be a basic data analysis library that we are going to use with Python. The word NumPy is going to stand for Numerical Python. We are going to bring out this library to help us to process any of the homogeneous multidimensional arrays that we want to handle.

This library is going to be one of the core libraries that is used for different scientific computations. This means that it is going to have a powerful array of multidimensional objects, and it will integrate some tools that are useful when it is time to work with these arrays as well.

You will quickly find that when you work with the data analysis that we have been talking about that NumPy is going to be useful in almost all of the scientific programming that we try to do with Python, including things like statistics, machine learning, and bioinformatics. It is also going to provide us with some good functionality that we can work with, functionality that can work well will run efficiently and is well written in the process.

Understanding More About NumPy

This library is really basic, but it is still going to be important when it comes to handling some of the scientific computing that we want to do with Python. Plus, it will not take that long working with data science and data analysis before you find that this is going to be the library that other data analysis libraries are going to be dependent on.

Some of the other significant libraries are going to be dependent on the arrays in NumPy as their inputs and outputs. In addition to this, it is also going to provide some functions that are going to allow developers a way for developers to perform all of the basic and the advanced functions that they would like, whether we are talking about statistics or mathematics, especially when we are dealing with multidimensional arrays and matrices, without needing to use as many lines of codes to get it all done.

When we compare these arrays with the lists that we talked about earlier with Python, you will find that the arrays are going to be much faster. But Python lists do have an advantage over the arrays because they are more flexible as you are only able to store the same data type in each column when we are working with the arrays.

There are a few features that you are going to enjoy when it is time to work with the NumPy library. Some of the main features that you will enjoy the most will include:

The NumPy library is going to be a combination of Python and C language,

This is going to consist of arrays that are homogeneous and multidimensional. Ndarray is part of this as well, which will be n-dimensional arrays as well.

It is going to work on a lot of different functions for arrays if you would like.
It can also help us to reshape the arrays. It also allows Python to have a way to work as an alternative to MATLAB.

There are a lot of reasons why we would want to work with NumPy rather than having to pick one of the other libraries that are out there along the way. We will use the array in NumPy for the work that we are doing with Python instead of a list. And some of the reasons for this include it is convenient to work with, it is going to perform faster than other methods, and it is going to use less memory overall.

All of these are going to be important when we are trying to do some of the algorithms that we need in data analysis. And mostly, you will notice that the arrays are going to be the number one thing that we utilize when it is time to work with this library as well.

There are a few other things that we need to explore when it comes to how we can work with the NumPy library. First, the NumPy array is going to take up a lot less space than other options. On the other hand, we can create an array, and it is only going to take about 4 MB. If you need to use a lot of different arrays as you go through, and they are going to fit better on the space of your memory overall. Arrays are also going to be easier to access when you would like to read and write on them later on.

Also, the performance when it comes to speed, you will find that the NumPy arrays are going to be great. It is going to be able to perform a lot faster when it comes to computations than what we find with the Python lists. Because this library is considered open- sourced, it is not going to cost you anything to get started with. Then it also has the benefit of working with the popular Python programming language, which has high-quality libraries for almost all of the tasks that you want to accomplish.

All of these are great benefits to work with. You will find that it is a high-quality library that is going to help us to get things done. You can get it to match up with the libraries that you want, it is going to be free to work with, and it can handle a lot of the data analysis projects that you want to do. It is also an easy library that will connect some of the codes that are already existing in the C language over to the interpreter for Python so you can get your work done.

There are a lot of benefits that are going to come up when you want to work with the NumPy library, and you will find that it is going to be the basis for a lot of the codes and algorithms that you want to write out when you are working with your data analysis. Learning how to use this language and what it can do for you is going to make a world of difference in how much you can accomplish for the long- term, and it is worth your time to learn more about it as well to complete your project.

Chapter 3

Manipulation data with Pandas

Pandas

Pandas is built on NumPy, and they are meant to be used together. This makes it extremely easy to extract arrays from the data frames. Once these arrays are extracted, they can be turned into data frames themselves. Let's take a look at an example:

In: import pandas as pd

import numpy as np

marketing_filename = 'regression-datasets-marketing.csv'

marketing = pd.read_csv(marketing _filename, header=None)

In this phase, we are uploading data to a data frame. Next, we're regoing to use the "values" method to extract an array that is of the same type as those contained inside the data frame.

In: marketing _array = marketing.values

marketing _array.dtype

Out: dtype('float64')

We can see that we have a float type array. You can anticipate the type of the array by first using the "dtype" method. This will establish which types are being used by the specified data frame object. Do this before extracting the array. This is how this operation would look: In: marketing.dtypes

Out: ofloat64
1 int64
2float64
3 int64

4float64
5float64
6float64
7float64
8int64
9int64
10int64
11float64
12float64
13float64
dtype: object

Matrix Operations

This includes matrix calculations, such as matrix to matrix multiplication. Let's create a two-dimensional array.

This is a two-dimensional array of numbers from 0 to 24. Next, we will declare a vector of coefficients and a column that will stack the vector and its reverse. Here's what it would look like: In: coefs = np.array([1., 0.5, 0.5, 0.5, 0.5])

coefs_matrix = np.column_stack((coefs,coefs[::-1]))

print (coefs_matrix)

Out:
[[1. 0.5]
 [0.5 0.5]
 [0.5 0.5]
 [0.5 0.5]
 [0.5 1.]]

Now we can perform the multiplication. Here's an example of multiplying the array with the vector:

In: np.dot(M,coefs)

Out: array ([5.,20.,35.,50.,65.])

Here's an example of multiplication between the array and the coefficient vectors:

In: np.dot(M,coefs_matrix)

Out:array([[5.,7.],

[20.,22.],
[35.,37.],

[50.,52.],
[65.,67.]])

In both of these multiplication operations, we used the "np.dot" function in order to achieve them. Next up, let's discuss slicing and indexing.

Slicing and Indexing

Indexing is great for viewing the ndarray by sending an instruction to visualize the slice of columns and rows or the index.

Let's start by creating a 10x10 array. It will initially be two-dimensional.

In: import numpy as np

M = np.arange(100, dtype=int).reshape(10,10)

Next let's extract the rows from 2 to 8, but only the ones that are evenly numbered.

In: M[2:9:2,:]
Out:array([[20, 21, 22, 23, 24, 25, 26, 27, 28, 29],
[40, 41, 42, 43, 44, 45, 46, 47, 48, 49],
[60, 61, 62, 63, 64, 65, 66, 67, 68, 69],
[80, 81, 82, 83, 84, 85, 86, 87, 88, 89]])

Now let's extract the column, but only the ones from index 5.

In: M[2:9:2,5:]

Out:array([[25, 26, 27, 28, 29],
[45, 46, 47, 48, 49],
[65, 66, 67, 68, 69],
[85, 86, 87, 88, 89]])

We successfully sliced the rows and the columns. But what happens if we try a negative index? Doing so would reverse the array. Here's how our previous array would look when using a negative index.

In: M[2:9:2,5::-1]
Out:array([[25, 24, 23, 22, 21, 20],
[45, 44, 43, 42, 41, 40],
[65, 64, 63, 62, 61, 60],
[85, 84, 83, 82, 81, 80]])

There are other ways of slicing and indexing the arrays, but for this book, it's enough to know how to perform the previously mentioned steps. However, keep in mind that this process is only a way of viewing the data. If you want to use these views further by creating new data, you cannot make any modifications to the original arrays. If you do, it can lead to some negative side effects. In that case, you want to use the "copy" method. This will create a copy of the array which you can modify however you wish. Here's the code line for the copy method: In: N = M[2:9:2,5:]. copy()

Pandas are built on NumPy, and they are meant to be used together. This makes it extremely easy to extract arrays from the data frames. Once these arrays are extracted, they can be turned into data frames themselves. Let's take a look at an example:

In: import pandas as pd

import numpy as np

marketing_filename = 'regression-datasets-marketing.csv'

marketing = pd.read_csv(marketing _filename, header=None)

In this phase, we are uploading data to a data frame. Next, we're going to use the "values" method to extract an array that is of the same type as those contained inside the data frame.

In: marketing_array = marketing.values

marketing_array.dtype

Out: dtype('float64')

We can see that we have a float type array. You can anticipate the type of the array by first using the "dtype" method. This will establish which types are being used by the specified data frame object. Do this before extracting the array. This is how this operation would look:

In: marketing.dtypes

Out: 0float64
1int64
2float64
3int64
4float64
5float64
6float64
7float64
8int64
9int64
10int64

11float64
12float64
13float64
dtype: object

Matrix Operations

This includes matrix calculations, such as matrix to matrix multiplication. Let's create a two-dimensional array.

This is a two-dimensional array of numbers from 0 to 24. Next, we will declare a vector of coefficients and a column that will stack the vector and its reverse. Here's what it would look like:

In: coefs = np.array([1., 0.5, 0.5, 0.5, 0.5])

coefs_matrix = np.column_stack((coefs,coefs[::-1]))

print (coefs_matrix)

Out:
[[1. 0.5]
[0.50.5]
[0.50.5]
[0.50.5]
[0.51.]]

Now we can perform the multiplication. Here's an example of multiplying the array with the vector:

In: np.dot(M,coefs)
Out: array([5.,20.,35.,50.,65.])
Here's an example of multiplication between the array and the coefficient vectors:
In: np.dot(M,coefs_matrix)
Out: array([[5.,7.],
[20.,22.],
[35.,37.],
[50.,52.],
[65.,67.]])

In both of these multiplication operations, we used the "np.dot" function in order to achieve them. Next up, let's discuss slicing and indexing.

Slicing and Indexing

Indexing is great for viewing the nd-array by sending an instruction to visualize the slice of columns and rows or the index.

Let's start by creating a 10x10 array. It will initially be two-dimensional.

```
In: import numpy as np
M = np.arange(100, dtype=int).reshape(10,10)
```

Next let's extract the rows from 2 to 8, but only the ones that are evenly numbered.

```
In: M[2:9:2,:]
Out: array([[20, 21, 22, 23, 24, 25, 26, 27, 28, 29],
[40, 41, 42, 43, 44, 45, 46, 47, 48, 49],
[60, 61, 62, 63, 64, 65, 66, 67, 68, 69],
[80, 81, 82, 83, 84, 85, 86, 87, 88, 89]])
```

Now let's extract the column, but only the ones from index 5.

```
In: M[2:9:2,5:]
Out: array([[25, 26, 27, 28, 29],
[45, 46, 47, 48, 49],
[65, 66, 67, 68, 69],
[85, 86, 87, 88, 89]])
```

We successfully sliced the rows and the columns. But what happens if we try a negative index? Doing so would reverse the array. Here's how our previous array would look when using a negative index.

```
In: M[2:9:2,5::-1]
Out: array([[25, 24, 23, 22, 21, 20],
[45, 44, 43, 42, 41, 40],
[65, 64, 63, 62, 61, 60],
[85, 84, 83, 82, 81, 80]])
```

However, keep in mind that this process is only a way of viewing the data. If you want to use these views further by creating new data, you cannot make any modifications to the original arrays. If you do, it can lead to some negative side effects. In that case, you want to use the "copy" method. This will create a copy of the array, which you can modify however you wish. Here's the code line for the copy method:

```
In: N = M[2:9:2,5:].copy()
```

Data Munging with Pandas

Now that you're set up with all the tools you need, and with a clean environment, it's time, to begin with, the data science process is known as data munging. Sometimes known as data wrangling, this step is one of the most important ones in the entire data science pipeline. The basic concept behind it is that you need to process a set of data to be able to use it together with another set of data or to analyze it. Necessarily, you will make enough changes to an original dataset to make it more useful for your specific goals. This is a preprocessing step.

To understand this idea better, imagine that you have a set of data on which you need to apply a classification algorithm. However, you realize that you can't perform this step just yet because the dataset is a combination of continuous and categorical variables. This means that you have to modify some of these variables to match the correct format. The challenge here is that you are dealing with raw data, and you cannot analyze it just yet. First, you need to clean the data with various data munging techniques and tools.

In most real-world scenarios, you will be dealing with a great deal of data that is raw and cannot be analyzed just yet, unlike the datasets used for study and practice. This is why you need to clean the data, and it can take you a great deal of time. Many data scientists spend more time preparing the data instead of coding or running various algorithms. So how do we prepare our data? One of the most popular methods includes using the Pandas library, which is used for data analysis and manipulation, as mentioned earlier. The purpose of this library, in this case, is to allow you to analyze raw, real-world data a lot faster.

Keep in mind that the purpose of data munging is to gather enough information to be able to detect the pattern within it. Furthermore, data needs to be accurate to be useful to a data scientist or analyst to cut down on the time and resources needed to come up with meaningful results. With that in mind, the first step you need to take involves acquiring the data. After all, without data, you can't do anything. However, before you gain access to it, you need to understand that all data items are different and are not created equally. You will often have issues recognizing authentic data with an identified source. The second step is about joining the data once it has been extracted from every source. At this stage, the data needs to be modified and then combined to proceed at a later time with the analysis. Finally, we have the last step that involves cleaning the data. This stage is the main one. You will need to modify the data to obtain a format you can use. You might also have to perform optional steps like correcting noisy data or bad data that can negatively influence the results.

As you can already see, this step is essential, although tedious and time-consuming. However, you sometimes cannot avoid it. You will have to make sure that you have relevant, up to date information that doesn't contain any null values to select only the data you are interested in for analysis. Fortunately, Python, together with Pandas, are some of the most powerful tools you can use to aid you in data munging.

The Process
You can gather data in many ways. You can extract it from a database, from images, from spreadsheets, and any other digital source that holds information. This is your raw data, however. You cannot use it for a proper analysis because, among all that data, you also have missing information and corrupted data. You need to first bring order to chaos by using Python data structures to turn the raw information into an organized data set made out of properly formatted variables. This dataset is then processed with the help of various algorithms.

Next, you can examine your data to come up with an early observation that you will later test. You will obtain new variables by processing the ones you currently have and move up the data science pipeline with various techniques such as graph analysis and reveal the most valuable variables. You will now be able to create the first data model; however, your testing phase will tell you that you will have to apply any corrections to your data and therefore return to the data munging processes to rework each step. Keep in mind that, in most cases, the output you expect will not reflect the real output that you will receive. The theory doesn't always lead you in the direction you expect, and that is why you need to process many different scenarios and test to see what works.

Importing Datasets

Before we can do anything, we need the actual data. To import a dataset, we are going to use Pandas to access tabular information from various databases or spreadsheets. Essentially, this tool will build a data structure in which each row of the tabular file will be indexed, while also separating the variables so that we can manipulate the data. With that being said, we will work in Jupyter and type the following command to import Pandas into our environment and access a CSV file:

In: import pandas as pd

iris_filename = 'datasets-ucl-iris.csv'

iris = pd.read_csv(iris_filename, sep=',', decimal='.', header=None,

names= ['sepal_length', 'sepal_width', 'petal_length', 'petal_width', 'target'])

(Source: The Iris Dataset https://scikitlearn.org/stable/auto_examples/datasets/plot_iris_dataset.html retrieved in October 2019)

As you can see, the first step of this process is to import the tool we are going to use. Whether you are going to use Pandas or Scikitlearn, it is not enough to just have it installed on your system. You need to import it into your project to have access to its functions and features. Next, we created a new file and named it, while also defining the character that will act as a separator and a decimal. In this example, the new file will contain an open-source dataset that has been used to teach new data scientists and machine learners for years. The dataset is called Iris, and it contains 50 samples of three different species of Iris flowers. We also mentioned that we don't want to define a header because it is not needed in our example. What we did so far was to create a new data item named iris, which is a data frame when we discuss it in the context of working with Pandas. In this case, a data frame is the same as a Python list or dictionary, but with a set of added features. Next, we want to explore what the data item contains by typing:

In: iris.head()

This is a simple instruction without any parameters. By default, if we don't specify, we are going to access the first five rows from the file. If you want more, then you simply need to mention the number of rows you want to access by typing it as an argument between the parentheses of the function. Next, we want to read the names of the columns to see what kind of information they contain:

In: iris.columns

Out: Index(['sepal_length', 'sepal_width', 'petal_length',

'petal_width', 'target'], dtype='object')

As you can see in the output, what we have for now is an index of each column name. The structure of the output looks like a list. Now, let's obtain the target column:

In: Y = iris['target']

Y
This is what you should see as the output.

Out:
0 Iris-setosa
1 Iris -setosa
2 Iris -setosa
3 Iris -setosa
...
149 Iris-virginica

Name: target, dtype: object

The "Y" in this result is a series typical of Pandas. What you should know is that it is nearly identical to an array. However, it is only unidirectional. Furthermore, you will notice that the index class is the same as the one for a dictionary. Next, we are going to request to extract the list of columns by using the index:

In: X = iris[['sepal_length', 'sepal_width']]

Now we have the data frame, which is a matrix instead of a unidimensional series. The reason why it is a matrix is that we asked to extract several columns at once, and therefore we mainly obtained an array that is structured in columns and rows. Now let's also obtain all of the dimensions.

In: print (X.shape)
Out: (150, 2)
In: print (Y.shape)
Out: (150)

The result is now a tuple, and we can analyze the size of the array in either dimension.

These are the bare-bones basics of manipulating a new dataset and performing some basic exploration. Let's move on to the next step and preprocess the data so that we can use it.

Data Preprocessing

Now that you know how to load a dataset, let's explore the procedures you need to take to preprocess all the information within it. First, we are going to assume that we need to perform a certain action on several rows. To use any function, we first need to set up a mask. Take note that in this case, a mask is a collection of Boolean values that determine the selected line. The practical example will clear up this notion, so let's get to it:

In: mask_feature = iris['sepal_length'] > 7.0
In: mask_feature

0 False

1 False

...

146 True

147 True

148 True

149 False

As you can see, we have chosen only the lines which contain a sepal length value that is greater than seven. These observations are declared with a Boolean value. Next, we are going to apply a mask to modify the iris virginica target and create a new label for it:

In: mask_target = iris['target'] == 'Iris-virginica'

In: iris.loc[mask_target, 'target'] = 'MyLabel'

Wherever the old iris virginica label appeared, it will now be replaced with "MyLabel" as the new label. Take note that for this operation, we need to use the "loc" function to gain access to the data with the help of the indexes. Now let's take the next step and see the labels that are contained by the target column:

In: iris['target'].unique()

Out: array(['Iris-setosa', 'Iris-versicolor', 'New label'], dtype=object)

Now let's group all of the columns:

In: grouped_targets_mean = iris.groupby(['target']).mean()

grouped_targets_mean

Out:
In: grouped_targets_var = iris.groupby(['target']).var()
grouped_targets_var

With this step, we have grouped the columns by using the group by function. Take note that this is similar to the "group by" command that you have in SQL. In the next input line, we have also applied the mean function, which of course, calculates the mean value. Keep in mind that we can apply this method either to a single column or multiple columns at the same time. Furthermore, we can use the variance, count, or sum functions to gain different values. Take note that the result you obtain is also a Pandas data frame, which means you can connect all of these operations. In this example, we are grouping all data observations by labels to be able to analyze the difference between all the values inside the groups. But what if we also have time series to deal with?

In case you aren't familiar with time series, you should know that they imply the analysis of a collection of data entries that appear in order. This order is determined chronologically. In essence, you are dealing with a group of points that are distributed in time with an equal space dividing each one of them. You will frequently encounter time series because they are used in many fields, usually regarding statistical analysis. For instance, when you have to work with weather data, you will find a time series regarding the forecasting or the detection of sunspots.

The next challenge, however, is dealing with data entries that contain noise. Keep in mind that while these training datasets have been documented and processed for years, they tend to be very clean, and in fact, they require very little preprocessing and cleaning. However, in the real world, you will frequently deal with noisy data. In that case, the first thing we can do is use a rolling function, which looks like this:

In: smooth_time_series = pd.rolling_mean(time_series, 5)

For this process, we are applying the mean function once more. Keep in mind that you don't necessarily have to use the mean. You can also go with the median value instead. In addition, you will notice that we request only to access five samples. Next, we are going to use the apply function to perform some operations on our columns and rows. This is a function that can be used for multiple purposes, so let's start by determining how many nonzero items we have per line:

In: iris.apply (np.count_nonzero, axis=1).head()
Out: 0 5
1 5
2 5
3 5
4 5

dtype: int64

Finally, the applymap function is then used to perform operations on the elements themselves. Let's say that we need to obtain the value of the length for every single string representation inside every cell:

In: iris.applymap (lambda el:len(str(el))).head()

In order to obtain these values, the cells are casted to a string, and then we can determine the length.
Now that you have an idea about using Pandas for data preprocessing let's also discuss the topic of data selection with the help of the same tool.

Data Selection

What do we mean when we are referring to data selection? Let's assume that you have a dataset with an index column that you need to access to modify it and work with it. For the sake of this example, we are going to presume that the index starts from 100, like so:

n,val1,val2,val3
100,10,10,C
101,10,20,C
102,10,30,B
103,10,40,B
104,10,50,A

As you can see, the first row is row number 0, and its index value is 100. Once you import the file, you will see an index column, as usual; however, there's the possibility of changing it or using it by mistake. Therefore, it would be a good idea to split the column from the rest of the data to avoid making any mistakes when you are running low on coffee. We are going to use Pandas to select the column and break it apart from the rest:

In: dataset = pd.read_csv('a_selection_example_1.csv',

index_col=0) dataset

That's it! Now you can manipulate the values as usual, whether you select the values by index, column, or line locations. For instance, you can access the fourth value from the fifth line, which in our example has an index value equal to 105. Here's how the selection looks:

In: dataset['val4'][105]

You might be tempted to consider this to be a matrix; however, it isn't, so make sure not to make the confusion. In addition, you should always determine the column you want to access before you specify the row. This way, you won't make any mistakes when looking to gain access to a certain cell's value.

Preparing your data and learning some surface information about it can greatly help you along the line, so make sure always to dedicate some time for data munging and preprocessing. In the next chapter, we are going to continue going deeper to gain further insight into the data exploration and data science pipeline as a whole.

Chapter 4

Visualization with Matplotlib

How to Work with Matplotlib to Create Great Visuals

Another great library that we can work with, especially when we are spending some time working on our own visuals as we talked about before, is the matplotlib library. This is going to be a great option to work with when we handle some of the work that we want to do with a data science project and will ensure that we can take all of the data points, and all of the different predictions that we were able to get with our algorithms and some of the machine learning that we have from earlier, to help us with visuals so that we understand the data a little bit easier.

To start with, the Matplotlib is going to be one of the plotting libraries that is available to work along with the Python programming language. It is also going to be one of the components that come with the NumPy library that we talked about before, big data, and some of the numerical handling resources. Matplotlib uses an API that is more object-oriented to help embed plots in applications of Python as well.

Since Python is going to be used in machine learning in many cases, resources like NumPy and matplotlib are going to be used in many cases to help out with some of the modelings that we need to do with machine learning and to ensure that we can work with these technologies either.

The idea that we are going to get with this one is that the programmer can access these libraries to handle some of the key tasks that are inside of the bigger environment that we have with Python. It is then able to go through and integrate the results with all of the other elements and features of the program for machine learning, a neural network, and some of the other more advanced options that we would like to use.

You will find that some of the utility that we can see with this library, as well as with the NumPy is going to be centered around numbers. The utility of Matplotlib is going to be specifically done with visual plotting tools. So, in a sense, these resources are going t be more analytical rather than generative. However, all of the infrastructures that we can see with this library is going to allow for the programs of machine learning, when we properly use them, can give us the right results for human handlers as well.

With some of this information in mind, we need to look a bit more about the Matplotlib library in more detail. To start with, this is going to be part of the package from Python to help with 2D graphics. Learning how to work with this kind of library efficiently is going to be so important when you would like to handle some of the visuals and more that you want to do in a data science project.

What is Matplotlib?

This is going to be one of the best plotting libraries that you can use in Python, especially when you would like to handle things like 2D graphics. It can be used with a lot of other different places, like on the web application servers, Python shell, Python script, and some of the other toolkits out there that are graphical user interfaces.

There are going to be some toolkits that are available that will help to extend out some of the functionality that we are going to see with matplotlib and will ensure that we can do some more with this program in no time at all. Some of these are going to include us going through a separate download, and then others are going to be found with the source code of this library but will have to depend on a few other aspects that are not found in Python or this library. Some of the different extensions that we can focus on and can work with when it is time to extend out what matplotlib can do will include:

•   Basemap: This is going to be a map plotting toolkit that can be helpful if this is what you would like to work with inside of your project. It is a good option to use if you would like to work with political boundaries, coastlines, and even some map projections overall.

•   Natgrid: This is going to be an interface that goes to the natgrid library. This is best when we want to handle something like the irregular gridding of the spaced data that we have.

•   Mplot3d: This is going to be helpful when you would like to extend out the 2D functions of matplotlib into something that is more 3D in nature instead.

•   Excel tools; This library is going to provide us with some of the utilities that we need to exchange data with Microsoft Excel if we need it.

•   Cartopy: This is going to be one of the mapping libraries that we can work with that are going to help us with some of the definitions of map projections and some of the arbitrary point, line, polygon, and image transformation capabilities to name a few of the features that we can rely on.

There are a lot of the different options that we can work with along the way to handle some of the features of this library as well. It is good for handling most of the features that we would like to see, and most of the graphs that are going to be important when it comes to this kind of data science. For example, you may find that this library is going to work well when we want to handle things like pie charts, line graphs, histograms, bar graphs, area plots, scatter plots, and more.

If you need to create your chart or graph to go through some of the data that you are handling during this time, then working with the Matplotlib library is going to be one of the best options. It does lack some of the 3D features that you may need, so this is something to consider based on your data. But for some of the basic parts that you would like to add into the mix, and for most of the visuals that you would like to focus on, you will find that the Matplotlib library is going to be able to handle it in no time.

Chapter 5

Machine learning

What is Machine Learning

Now it is time for us to look at the basics that are going to come with machine learning and how we can use this for our needs. Think about a few of the situations that you have done in the past. For example, have you ever spent time shopping online? While you were the products that to purchase, did you ever notice when it would make recommendations for you, based on the product that you are looking at, or base don some of the purchases that you made in the past? If you have seen something similar to this on a website that you are shopping on, then you have been exposed to machine learning.

Another example is when you get a call from a bank or another financial company that will ask you to take out a new insurance policy or a loan. It is unlikely that this financial institution is going to waste their time calling everyone. This would take too long and would be a waste. Instead, they are going to use machine learning to help them figure out the best customers, the ones who are most likely to purchase their products before starting.

So, let's take a closer look at what machine learning is all about. Machine learning is going to be one of the parts of artificial intelligence that are going to focus mainly on machine learning from their experience. Then the machine can make some predictions based on the experience that has happened in the past.

What does machine learning do? It is going to enable the system, machines, computers, and more to make decisions, decisions that are based on data, rather than having the programmer do all of the codings to get this done. These programs or algorithms are going to be designed in a different manner than what we find in the past because they can learn and improve over time when we have been able to expose them to some new data. This is what is going to make them so strong and good at analyzing the data that you are working with along the way.

In the world that we work in today, these machines, or the robots, have to still be programmed before they are able to really start following any of the instructions that you would like. But what if, in the future, the machine is able to start learning on their own from work and experience as we do. This is not something that we can use right now, but it is an interesting part that we can consider to help us reach some of our goals with machine learning later on.

How Machine Learning Works for Data Science

Machine learning is an interesting option that is going to be able to work with data science to give us some of the information that we need. This option is going to have a network or system work based on experiences and examples, and that it can do all of this without being programmed on how to behave in every situation.

What this means is that instead of the programmer spending time writing out the codes they want, we will spend time feeding data into a generic algorithm. From there, the algorithm machine is going to be able to build up the logic based on the data that is given. There are a lot of parts that come with machine learning, and figuring out how we can work with this and more can ensure that we get the most out of this along the way as well.

There are already a lot of applications where we are seeing machine learning growing so much. If you have ever worked with a search engine to find something online, then we are familiar with some of the work that we can do with machine learning. If you have worked with some kind of voice-activated device, whether it is on your phone or one of those personal assistant devices, then you will find that you have worked with machine learning as well. And these are just the start of what we can do with machine learning as well.

In the future, this technology is likely going to go into new industries and provide us with new products and technology that we can't imagine today. It is already able to do so many things for us, and when we think about the future of this technology, as more and more people jump on it and learn how to use it, we are sure to see some amazing things. With this in mind, let's take some time to learn a bit more about machine learning and how we can use this for our needs as well.

What Does Machine Learning Do?

The algorithms that we can use with machine learning will be trained, with the help of the data we set aside for training, to create the model that we would like. When we put in some new input data to this algorithm, it is going to use some of the models as its basis for providing us with some of the predictions that we need along the way.

The prediction that the algorithm can give for us is going to be evaluated for accuracy. If we find that the accuracy is acceptable, then this algorithm with machine learning is going to be deployed. If we decide that the accuracy level is not good, then this algorithm will go through again and be trained until it reaches the accuracy that we would like.

There are a lot of ways that machine learning is going to be able to help us out. Many times, the analysis part of our data science project is going to happen with machine learning, and that can make a difference in the insights that we are going to find along the way as well. And with all of the great techniques and methods that we can use here as well will ensure that we are going to get the results that we need.

The Different Types of Machine Learning

The next thing that we need to spend some time on is the different types of machine learning that we can work with. There are three main types of machine learning that we can work with. These are going to include supervised learning, unsupervised learning, and reinforcement learning. We are going to take some time to look at each of these and see what we can do with each of them to help us reach our goals.

First, we need to take a look at what supervised learning is all about. When we are talking about supervised learning, we are talking about the one where we can use labeled data and examples to help the algorithm work. We can view this one like the algorithm being guided by a teacher. We are going to have a set of data that is going to act as the teacher, and the role of this teacher, or data set, is going to be the train the model or the machine that we are working with. Once we have been able to go through and train the model, we can use it to start making some predictions or decisions when the new data is provided to it later on.

Then we can work with the idea of unsupervised learning as well. This one is going to be a bit different than what we are used to with supervised learning, but it is going to add in some of the functionality that we are looking for when it is time to handle our work with machine learning. The models of unsupervised learning learn through a lot of observations; then, with the help of these observations, it can find some of the structures that we need in the data.

Once the model is given the set of data that we want to work with, it is automatically able to find some of the relationships and patterns that are in the set of data, usually through the process of creating clusters in it. What it is not able to do here is add in labels to the clusters at all. This means that it is not able to tell us that one group is apples, and another is mangoes, but it can separate them because they are quite a bit different.

Let's say that we had a bunch of images that we wanted to use mangoes, bananas, and apples. With unsupervised learning, this is going to take a look at the relationships and patterns that are found in those images and will create some clusters while dividing up the set of data into those various clusters. If you find that the new data is fed into the model after it is all done, then it is going to take that new data and add it into one of the created clusters that you have.

And finally, we can work with the idea of reinforcement learning. On the outside of this, before we dive into it too much, we are going to find that reinforcement learning looks a lot like what we are going to see with the unsupervised learning that we talked about above. But the main difference is that reinforcement learning is going to rely more on the idea of trial and error to help the algorithm to learn.

As we can see, there are a lot of parts that are going to come with the machine learning that we can work with. And this is going to be a really important option that we can focus on when it comes to data science. If you are looking to work on a data science project of any kind, and you need some models or algorithms that are going to help us to sort through the data and give us the insights and patterns that we need, then you have to spend some time working with the machine learning that we did before.

Machine Learning and How It Fits with Data Science

Machine learning can be an important part of the Data Science process, as long as we use it properly.

Remember, as we go through this process, that part of Data Science is working on data analysis. This helps us to take a lot of the data we have collected along the way, and then actually see the insights and the predictions that are inside of it. To make this happen, we need to be able to create our models (that can sort through all of the data), find the hidden patterns, and provide us with our insights.

To define these models, and to make sure that they work the way that we want, we need to have a variety of good algorithms in place, and this is where Machine Learning is going to come into play quite a bit. You will find that with the help of Machine Learning, and the variety of algorithms that are present in Machine Learning, we can create models that can go through any kind of data we have, whether it is big or small, and provide us with the answers that we need here.

Machine learning is a process that we can use to make the system or the machine we are working with think in a manner that humans do. This allows the algorithm to go through and find hidden patterns in the same manner that a human would be able to do, but it can do it much faster and more efficiently than any human could do manually.

Think about how hard this would be to do manually for any human, or even for a group of people who are trying to get through all of that data. It could take them years to get through all of that data and find the insights that they need. And with how fast data is being generated and collected, those predictions and insights would be worthless by the time we got to that point anyway.

Machine learning can make this process so much easier. It allows us to have a way to think through the data and find the hidden patterns and insights that are inside for our needs. With the right Machine Learning algorithm, we can learn how the process works, and all of the steps that are necessary to make this happen for us. With this in mind, it is time to take a closer look at Machine Learning, and all of the parts that we need to know to make this work for our needs.

How Does Machine Learning Work with Data Analysis?

Now that we know a little bit more about how machine learning works and why it is important, it is time for us to take a look more specifically at how machine learning can come in and help us out with our data analysis. There are so many reasons why we can use machine learning when it comes to the data analysis, so it is important to take some time to look at how we can use it as well.

Machine learning is going to be the underlying process for all of the algorithms that we want to create along the way. No matter how simple or how complex your algorithm will be, a lot of the coding and the mechanics that come with it are going to be run by the machine learning that we will talk about in this guidebook. And with the help of Python, you can make some amazing algorithms that help us to sort through the data.

So, if you are hoping to go through this process of data analysis to sort through your data and understand what is found inside of it, then you need to learn a bit about machine learning ahead of time. The good news with this one is that machine learning is going to be able to work well with the Python language that we talked about above, ensuring that we can get it done with a simple coding language, even though the ideas that come with machine learning are going to be a bit more complex overall.

Supervised Machine Learning

The first type of learning that we need to take a look at here is known as supervised machine learning. This is going to be the most basic form of machine learning that we can work with, but it will provide us with some of the different parts that we need to keep things going well and can help us to train our algorithms quickly and efficiently.

To start, supervised learning is simply going to be the process of helping an algorithm to learn to map an input to a particular output. We are going to spend or time on this one while showing lots of examples, with the corresponding answers, to the algorithm in the hopes that it will find the connections and learn. Then, when the training is done, the algorithm will be able to look at new inputs, without the corresponding output, and give us the right answer on its own.

This whole process is going to be achieved when we work on a labeled data set that was collected earlier. If the mapping is done correctly, the algorithm is going to be able to learn successfully. If it is not reaching the goals here, then that means we have to go through and make some changes to our algorithm to help it learn well. Supervised machine learning algorithms, when they are trained well, will be able to make some good predictions for the new data they get later on in the future.

This is going to be a similar process that we would see with a teacher to student scenario. There is going to be a teacher who can guide the student to learn well from books and other materials. The student is then going to be tested and, if they are correct, then the student will pass. If not, then the teacher will change things up and will help the student to learn better, so that they can learn from the mistakes that they made in the past so that they get better. This is going to be the basics that come with using supervised machine learning.

Unsupervised Machine Learning

The second type of machine learning that we can work with is known as unsupervised learning. This is going to be a method that we can use in data analysis because it will enable the machines to go through and classify both the tangible and intangible objects, without having to go through and provide the machine or the system with any information about of time about the objects.

The things or the objects that our machines are going to need to classify are going to be varied, such as the purchasing behaviors of the customer, some of the patterns of behavior of bacteria, and even things like hacker attacks or fraud happening with a bank. The main idea that we are going to be able to see with this kind of learning is that we want to expose our machines to large volumes of data that are varied and then allowing the algorithm to takes time to learn and infer from the data. However, we need to be able to take the time to teach the program how it can learn from that data.

It is pretty common for a computer system to need to learn how to make sense of large volumes of data, both the unstructured and the structured types, and then learn what insights are inside. In reality, it may be almost impossible to provide prior information about all of the data types that a system could receive over a period of time, and working with this kind of machine learning can help to make things happen, even when you are not able to train your machine ahead of time to teach it.

Keeping all of this in mind, we will find that supervised learning is not going to be all that suitable in every case, such as when the systems we are working with need to have a constant amount of information about data that is new. For example, hacking attacks on a bank or a financial system are going to go through and change their patterns and their nature frequently. Supervised learning would struggle with keeping up, but unsupervised learning is going to be more appropriate to handle this.

In these cases, and more, unsupervised learning is going to be able to go onto a system and quickly learn from all of the data from the attack to keep up. Then it can infer and learn some more insights about potential future attacks, while also suggesting some preemptive actions to work with along the way.

There are a lot of times when we will want to work with unsupervised learning. Any time that you want to work with a program or a machine that needs to do at least a little bit of learning on its own to get things done, then unsupervised learning is going to be the right option to focus on.

Reinforcement Machine Learning

The third type of machine learning that we need to take a look at is known as reinforcement machine learning. This is going to be a bit different compared to what we saw with the other two options, but there are a lot of times when we can use this kind of learning to help us out with sorting through our data, including our data analysis. Let's dive into the basics of reinforcement machine learning and how we can use it for our needs.

To start, the reinforcement learning, in the context of artificial intelligence, is going to be a type of dynamic programming that can train algorithms, based on the idea of the reward when the algorithm gets the right answer, and a type of punishment when it gets the wrong answer.

One of the algorithms that use reinforcement learning, or the agent, is going to be able to learn how to interact with the environment that is going on around it. The agent or the algorithm is going to receive some kind of reward when it performs correctly. But when it performs incorrectly, it is going to get some kind of punishment or penalty in the process. The agent, through these rewards and penalties, is going to learn, without any kind of intervention from a human, by maximizing its reward and then figuring out the best way to minimize the penalty that it is going to deal with.

The algorithm is going to be successful with this when it has a chance to learn the right way to behave, and the wrong way to behave. When it learns, through the rewards, the right way to behave, it will continue with those actions or those guesses to get more rewards. And when it does get a penalty for doing something wrong, it is going to remember this as well and will learn how to avoid these along the way as well.

Reinforcement learning is going to be one of the approaches that we can use with machine learning, and the inspiration for it is going to be found in behaviorist psychology. We can view this in a manner that is similar to how a child can learn a new task. This learning is going to have some contrasts to how the other machine learning options will approach a situation because this particular algorithm is not going to be explicitly told how it should perform a task. It has to learn and go through this problem all on its own.

As an agent, which could be something like a program that is set up to play chess or a self-driving car, is going to interact with the environment that is all around it, and it is going to receive a type of reward state depending on how well it can perform. So, if the game can successfully win the game of chess, then it will receive a reward.

This goes the other way as well. If the agent does not perform in the manner that it should, whether that means that it doesn't win the game when it should or does something else that is wrong based on the programming, then it is going to get a penalty of some sort. In the case of the game, it is going to be checkmated rather than winning, and it can learn from that in the process.

The agent, through more practice and over time, is going to be able to make some good decisions to maximize its rewards and minimize the number of times it gets a penalty through dynamic programming. The advantage of working with this kind of approach, especially when we work with artificial intelligence, is that it is going to allow our AI program to learn without the programming having to go through and spell out exactly how an agent should complete its tasks.

As we can see, there are a lot of different parts that come together with the idea of machine learning, and being able to explore some of these and what we can do with the three main types of machine learning is going to be important based on how we want to use this in our own data analysis. Take some time to look more closely at how we can utilize all of the types of machine learning for our own needs and move from there into using it to help pick out the algorithm we need to see success.

Conclusion

Thank you for reading this book. The next step is to get started by seeing how data science is going to be able to work for your business. You will find that there are a lot of different ways that you can use the large amount of info that you have access to, and all of the data that you have been able to collect over time. Collecting the data is just the first step to the process. We also need to make sure that we can gain all of the insights and predictions that come out of that information, and this is where the process of data science is going to come into play.

This guidebook has taken some time to explore what data science is all about and how it can help benefit your company in so many ways. We looked at some of the tasks that data science can help out with, what data science is and how to work with the life cycle of data, the future of data, and so much more. This helps us to see some of the parts that come to data analysis, and even how beneficial gathering and using all of that information can be to grow your business.

But this is not the only step that we can work with. We also need to take this a bit further and not just collect the data, but also be able to analyze that data and see what information it holds. This is a part of the data science life cycle, but it deserves some special attention because, without it, the data would just sit there without being used.

Data science is a great thing to add to your business, and it can help you to make sure customer satisfaction is high, that waste is low, that you can make more money and can even help with predictions in the future, such as what products you should develop and put out on the market. But learning all of this is not something that just happens on its own. Working with data science and adding in some Python language and the different libraries that are included with it can make the difference. When you are ready to work with Python data science to improve many different aspects of your own business and to beat out the competition, make sure to check out this guidebook to help you get started with it right away.

When you are ready to learn more about what data analysis can do for you, and how you can work with this data analysis to get the best results, along with the Python language and machine learning, then it is time to take a look at what this guidebook has to offer! More and more tools will become available for Data Analysis, and some of them will not need the analyst.

The staffing required for the Data Analysis will keep on expanding, and people from scientists to analysts to architects to the experts in the field of data management will be needed. However, a crunch in the availability of big data talent might see the large companies develop new tactics. Some large institutes predict that various organizations will use internal training to get their issues resolved. A business model having big data in the form of service can be seen on the horizon.

Many companies are jumping on board and learning more about how to work with data science and what all this process can do for them. And with the help of this guidebook, you will be able to do some of the same as well. When you are ready to jump on board and learn more about data science and how you and your business can benefit from this process, make sure to check out this guidebook to get started.

Data science is taking over the business world, and many companies, no matter what industry they are in, have found that this kind of process is exactly what they need to not only collect the data they have but also to clean it and perform an analysis to find the insights and predictions that are inside. When data science is used properly, and we add in some Python to help create the models and more that is needed, we are going to be able to find the best way to make business decisions that improve our standing in the industry.

There are a lot of different parts that come with data science, and being able to put them all together can help us to do better with helping our customers, finding new products to bring to market, and more. And with the help of this guidebook, we can hopefully find the best ways to beat out the competition and see the results that will work for us. It takes some time, and a good data analysis with the right algorithms from Python, but it can be one of the best ways to make some smart and sound decisions for your business.
Many companies are going to use the ideas of data science to get as many benefits as possible. Each company will be able to use this differently and will find that it can help them add to their bottom line, increase profits, and reach their customers in new and innovative manners. When you're ready to learn more about how data science works, and all of the different parts that come with it, make sure to check out this guidebook to get started.

SQL Coding for Beginners

After work guide to start learning SQL on your own. Surprise yourself by discovering how to manage, analyze and manipulate data with simple tips and tricks.

Michail Kölling

Introduction

SQL is a programming language that stands for 'Structured Query Language,' and it is a simple language to learn, considering it will allow interaction to occur between the different databases that are in the same system. This database system first came out in the 70s, but when IBM came out with its prototype of this programming language, then it started to see a growth in popularity, and the business world started to take notice.

The version of SQL that was initially used by IBM, known back then as ORACLE, was so successful that the team behind it eventually left IBM and became its own company. ORACLE, thanks to how it can work with SQL, is still one of the leaders in programming languages, and it is always changing so that it can keep up with everything that is needed in the programming and database management world.

The SQL is a set of instructions that you can use to interact with your relational database. While there are a lot of languages that you can use to do this, SQL is the only language that most databases can understand. Whenever you are ready to interact with one of these databases, the software can go in and translate the commands that you are given, whether you are giving them in form entries or mouse clicks. These will be converted into SQL statements that the database will already be able to interpret.

If you have ever worked with a database-driven software program, then it is likely that you have used some form of SQL in the past. Likely, you didn't even know that you were doing this, though. For example, there are a lot of dynamic web pages that are database driven. These will take some user input from the forms and clicks that you are making and then will use this information to compose a SQL query. This query will then go through and retrieve the data from the database to act, such as switch over to a new page.

To illustrate how this works, think about a simple online catalog that allows you to search. The search page will often contain a form that will just have a text box. You can enter the name of the item that you would like to search using the form, and then you would simply need to click on the search button. As soon as you click on the search button, the web server will go through and search through the database to find anything related to that search term. It will bring those back to create a new web page that will go along with your specific request.

For those who have not spent that much time at all learning a programming language and who would not consider themselves programmers, the commands that you would use in SQL are not too hard to learn. Commands in SQL are all designed with a syntax that fits in with the English language.

At first, this will seem complicated, and you may be worried about how much work it will be to get it set up. But when you start to work on a few codes, you will find that it is not that hard to work with. Often, just reading out the SQL statement will help you to figure out what the command will do. Take a look at the code below:

As you embark on this journey to learn SQL, you must understand that the secret to becoming an expert on any programming language is practice. The more you practice, the better you will become! Practice hard; remember the fundamentals and focus on innovation!

Many companies are going to spend their time working with a database of some kind. We live in a world where technology and data are around us all of the time, and being able to use that data can make the difference. It can help us to learn more about our customers, know how to reduce the waste that we are finding. It can make it easier for us to beat out the competition and provides us with an excellent way to make smart business decisions overall.

This is where the SQL language is going to come into play. Other coding languages can handle some of our needs when it comes to coding and looking through databases, but the SQL option is often one of the best ones that we can choose. We will find that this is a language that we can work with when we want to create the tables for our databases, put things together in our databases, and so much more.

When you are ready to learn more about the SQL language and what it can do for you and the work that you can do with some of your databases, without being too difficult of a language to learn more about, make sure to check out this guidebook to help you get started.

Chapter 1
What is SQL

What is MySQL?

MySQL is a tool (database server) that uses SQL syntax to manage databases. It is an RDBMS (Relational Database Management System) that you can use to facilitate the manipulation of your databases.

If you are managing a website using MySQL, ascertain that the host of your website supports MySQL too.

Here's how you can install MySQL in your Microsoft Windows. We will be using Windows because it is the most common application used in computers.

Structured Query Language or SQL is a computer programming language that is typically used for storage, retrieval, and manipulation of data that is stored in the relational database. This is the standard computer programming language used for RDBMSs (Relational Database Management Systems) like Oracle, MySQL, and MS Access, in addition to many others. With that said, the version used by each of these systems may vary. For instance, Oracle uses PL/SQL, and MS SQL Server makes use of T-SQL.

IBM's Ted Cod, who is popularly known as the father of relational databases, gave the concept of the relational model for databases in 1970, and that is when it all began. It was four years later in 1974 that SQL appeared. This was just an idea, which got conceptualized in the form of System/R in 1978 and was released by IBM. The ANSI standard and prototype of relational databases was first released in 1986, which is popularly known as Oracle. IBM is credited for this release too.

Why SQL?

SQL has many advantages, which makes it a standard and popular programming language for databases. These advantages include –

SQL programming language can be used for accessing data in RDBMSs.

It can also be used for describing data.

The definition of data and its manipulation are also activities that SQL support.

SQL can be used with other programming languages by embedding SQL modules into other languages' code, pre-compilers, and libraries.

It is possible to create and drop databases using this programming language.
It can be used for setting permissions on views, tables, and procedures.
Lastly, it can be used for creating views, procedures, and functions.

The Process

Whenever you give a command to the system, the SQL process starts. The system determines the best way to perform the task, which is interpreted by the SQL engine. The different components involved in the process are as follows –

Optimization Engines

SQL Query Engine

Classic Query Engine

Query Dispatcher

The SQL Query engine is earmarked for handling SQL queries and does not manage logical files. The classic query engine handles these files and non-SQL queries. The SQL Architecture is illustrated in the image shown below.

Commands

Some of the basic SQL Commands that you will use and encounter during interactions with relational databases have been listed below. They will be explained in detail later in the book. Typically, commands in SQL are categorized into three categorized, namely DDL (Data Definition Language), DML (Data Manipulation Language), and DCL (Data Control Language). The commands that are classified under DDL category are as follows –

Create
This command is used for creating an object, table, or view.

Alter
This command is typically used for modifying an existing database object. In most cases, this object is a table.

Drop
The objects, tables, and views created using create can be deleted or removed using the drop command.
The next set of commands is commands that fall under the category of DML or data manipulation language. These commands are as follows –

Select
This command is used for retrieving a set of records from one or more than one table.

Delete

This command is used for deleting records.

Update

This command is used for modifying or updating records.

Insert

This command is used for inserting records.

The last category of commands falls under DCL or data control language. These commands are as follows –

Grant

Users can be granted privileges using the grant command.

Revoke

The privileges given to users can be taken back using the REVOKE command.

SQL is an exciting option that we can work with for some of our needs. SQL, or Structured Query Language, is a programming language that has become standardized in the designation of data management and storage. Because of this, a person with a little know-how can easily manipulate, parse, and create any type of data.

SQL Query Types

In the programming world, a question is formally referred to as a query. A query within a database can be two types, action or selection. With an action query, extra tasks are requested about information like deletion, refreshing, and addition, and a select query helps to recover information.

A query can be a helpful device when it comes to a database as they are called regularly by a client by way of a structure. A client uses them to obtain information after looking for it in tables, conduct many different calculation types by relying on necessities, and take part in a variety of database activities.

Luckily for those involved, Microsoft Access allows for the implementation of several types of queries, but where the main types include the total, parameter, activity, and select queries. You can easily refer to them as another piece of the database – similar to a macro or table.

When the time comes for a query to be manufactured in a database, you can utilize two different ways for it:

You can have the SQL queries scratch made by yourself, or

You can use Microsoft Access's Query Wizard

Query Language

A query language is used in databases to create queries, and the standard that all others go by is the Microsoft Structured Query Language. Beneath this SQL umbrella, there are just a handful of language variations available, and these include NuoDB, Oracle SQL, and MySQL. Distinct databases also have question dialects such as XQuery, Data Mining Extensions, Neo4j's Cipher, and Cassandra Query Language (CQL) that are incorporated by the NoSQL databases and diagram databases.

Select Query

This query type provides only a tiny amount of difficulty when making an inquiry, and consequently, this makes it the most commonly used in all databases of Microsoft Access. This utilization is what could choose the information that comes out of one of our table series that will then rely on that required information.

Lastly, the client is who chooses the criteria to be told to databases so that the use of the criteria can found a determination. After calling a select query, a table is created that allows you to change information to one record at a time.

Action Query

As soon as you call an activity question, activity occurs in the database that is based on what the query indicated. This allows several things to be incorporated, including creating new records, refreshing them, erasing lines, or creating a new table.

An action query is well-known throughout the information world due to their ability to change several records at once instead of just the normal one record, as we see in a "select query."

These are the four action query types available:

Append Query

This allows the addition of set consequences to an existing table.

Update Query

This allows for the refreshing of a table's field.

Make Table Query

This does exactly what its name suggests; a table is made based on queries set consequences.

Delete Query

This will erase a hidden table's records from a query set result.

Parameter Query

When used in conjunction with Microsoft Access, a "parameter query" can use a variety of queries to achieve your desired outcome. Because of this, when a query like this is used, you can send parameters to another query such as select or activity queries. These can be a condition or esteem so that the query will know what needs to be completed explicitly. With them being picked regardless of having an exchange box, the end-user will be able to enter any value in a parameter whenever they run a query. All a parameter query is just a select query that has been altered.

Aggregate Query

An aggregate query is a unique type of query. It can make changes to other queries (like the parameter, activity, or choice) just like a parameter does it, but is against a parameter passing to a different query that gets aggregated with other things that are chosen among other groups.

A summation is ultimately made within a table property that you choose. It can be turned into measurable sums, like a standard deviation or midpoints.

Getting ready to code

Just like any other programming language, you need to understand the essence of the language you are trying to learn before diving into it. Make a clear note about the advantages of SQL and note down common errors that you may get encountered with.

Make a list of necessary applications to be installed and check system requirements for all of that software.

Installing MySQL applications

MySQL is one of the tools that Microsoft offers for countless organizations and small businesses. There are several costly certification courses available for a better understanding of the management of these databases. Here in this book, we coherently explain to you the installation procedure after explaining the types of SQL Server editions that are available.

Type of SQL server software versions:

Microsoft offers a wide range of software availabilities for better deployment of the services. It is useless to buy huge resources if there is no enough data. It also doesn't make sense to rely on fewer resources for huge data, as there will be continuous downtime, which may irritate your service users. For this exact reason, MySQL is available in different types, as described below.

Express

This is a small comprehensive edition where it consists of simple resources and workbench tools that are needed to start running for an individual or a small enterprise.

Standard

Standard version is usually recommended for small business that has moderate data to be handled. It can quickly monitor the operations and processes data faster when compared with the express edition.

Enterprise

Enterprise version is one of the most used SQL servers all around the world. It has a wide range of capabilities and can be used by moth medium and large companies. It consists of a lot of services, such as reporting, analysis, and auditing. Enterprise version costs a lot more than the standard versions due to its complex nature.

Developer

This version of the SQL server is mainly used by developers to test and manipulate the functionalities in an environment. All the developers use this version to experiment with the logical entity they are dealing with. You can easily convert the license of your developer version to an enterprise version with a click .

Web
This version of the SQL server is primarily developed to deal with web applications. A lot of medium hosting services use this version to store small amounts of data.

What are the components that are in SQL software?

SQL Server software consists of various components that need to be installed. Here are some of the most used SQL server managers.

Server management system
This is the most critical component where every server that is present is registered, created, managed, or erased if needed. This is a working interface for database administrators to interact with the databases that are operating.

Server configuration manager
This component helps us to give customized information about network protocols and parameters in detail.

SQL Server profiler
This is the component that helps you monitor all the activities that are running through the system.

What to consider before installing the software?

1. Do thorough research about the software you are installing. You can further refer to the documentation or online resources to check minimum system requirements and components information.

2. Learn about components. Get a good understanding of different components such as analysis, reporting that SQL enterprise version offers. Nowadays, many industries must analyze and report the findings as a database administrator.

3. Learn about authentication modes that are present and do good research about them.

Starting and Stopping Oracle database instances

The process of starting an Oracle database instance is divided into three steps: starting the instance, loading the database, and opening the database. Users can start the database in different modes according to actual needs.

The following will explain several STARTUP modes listed in startup syntax, respectively.

1.NOMOUNT model

The code and running results are as follows:

SQL> connect system/sample instance as connect;

2.MOUNT mode

This mode starts the instance, loads the database, and keeps the database closed.

When starting the database instance to MOUNT mode, the code and running results are as follows.

SQL> shutdown {Enter the condition}

3.OPEN mode

This mode starts the instance, loads, and opens the database, which is the normal startup mode. Users who want to perform various operations on the database must start the database instance using OPEN mode.

Start the database instance to OPEN mode, and the code and running results are as follows.

SQL> startup

Like starting a database instance, shutting down the database instance is also divided into three steps, namely shutting down the database, uninstalling the database, and shutting down the Oracle instance.

The SQL statement for the shutdown is here:

SHUTDOWN [Enter the parameter here]

1.NORMAL approach

This method is called a normal shutdown. If there is no limit on the time to shut down the database, it is usually used to shut down the database.

The code and running results are as follows:

SQL> shutdown normal;

Database shutdowns immediately with the syntax.

2.TRANSACTIONAL approach

This method is called transaction closing. Its primary task is to ensure that all current active transactions can be committed and shut down the database in the shortest possible time.

3.ABORT mode

This method is called the termination closing method, which is mandatory and destructive. Using this method will force any database operation to be interrupted, which may lose some data information and affect the integrity of the database. Apart from using the database because it cannot be shut down using the other three methods, this method should be avoided as much as possible.

Launching MySQL workbench

MySQL Workbench is a visual database design software released by MySQL AB, whose predecessor was DB Designer of FabForce. MySQL Workbench is a unified visualization tool designed for developers, DBA, and database architects. It provides advanced data modeling, flexible SQL editor, and comprehensive management tools. It Can be used on Windows, Linux, and Mac.
To use it in windows, click on the SQL server studio and select the option workbench to open the interface. If you are using Linux and Mac, you need to enter the command 'workbench' after entering into the SQL instance.

How to install MySQL on Microsoft Windows
Go to the MySQL website
Go to www.mysql.com and browse through the applications to select MySQL. Ascertain that you obtain the MySQL from its official website to prevent downloading viruses, which can be harmful to your computer.
Select the 'download' option
Next, click on the download option. This will bring you to the MySQL Community Server and the MySQL Community Edition. Click 'download.'

Choose your Windows' processor version
Choose your Windows processor version by perusing the details given on the page. Choose from the 'other downloads' label. You can choose either the 32-bit or 64-bit.

Click the download button for the Windows (x86, 32-bit), ZIP Archive, or the Windows (x86, 64-bit), ZIP Archive, whichever applies to your computer.

Register on the site
Before you can download your selected version, you will be requested to register by answering the sign-in form for an Oracle account.

You don't have to reply to the optional questions. You can also click on the 'no thanks' button.

There is another option of just downloading the server without signing up. Still, you will not be enjoying some freebies such as being able to download some white papers and technical information, faster access to MySQL downloads and other services.

Sign in to your MySQL account
After registering, you can sign in now to your new account. A new page will appear, where you can select your area through the displayed images of flags. Afterward, you can click the download button and save it on your computer.

This can take several minutes.

Name the downloaded file
After downloading the file, you can name your MySQL file and save it on your desktop or C drive. It's up to you, whichever you prefer.

Install your MySQL Server
Click the file to open it and then click 'install' to install MySQL on your computer. This will open a small window in which your computer will ask if you want to open and install the program. Just click the "OK" button.

Browse your MySQL packages
The MySQL Enterprise Server page will appear giving you some information about what your MySQL package contains.

There are packages offered for a small fee, but since we're just interested in the community server, just click 'next' until you reached the 'finish' button.

Uncheck the box 'Register the MySQL Server now.'

After the Wizard has completed the set-up, a box appears asking you to configure and register your MySQL Server. Uncheck the 'Register the MySQL Server now' box, and check the small box for the "Configure the MySQL Server now.'
Then click 'finish.'

Click' next' on the Configuration Wizard box

A box will appear, and you just have to click next.

Select the configuration type

A box will appear asking you to select your configuration type. Tick the small circle for the 'Detailed Configuration,' instead of the 'Standard Configuration.' Click the 'next' button.

Select the server type

There will be three choices; the Developer Machine, the Server Machine, and the Dedicated MySQL Server Machine.
Select the Server Machine because it will have medium memory usage, which is ideal for a beginner like you, who is interested to learn more about MySQL.
The Developer Machine uses minimal memory and may not allow you the maximum usage of your MySQL.
On the other hand, the MySQL Server Machine is for people who work as database programmers or full-time MySQL users. It will use all of the available memory in your computer, so it is not recommended for you.

Select the database usage

For database usage, there are three choices, namely; Multifunctional Database, Transactional Database Only, and Non-Transactional Database Only. Choose the Multifunctional Database because your purpose is for general purposes.
The Transactional and non-transactional are used for more specific purposes.
Click the 'next' button at the bottom of the display box.

Select the drive for the InnoDB datafile

If you do not want to use the 'default' settings, you can select the drive from your computer, where you want to store your InnoDB datafile. Choose the drive you prefer and then click 'next.'

Set the number of concurrent connections to the server

This will indicate the number of users that will be connecting simultaneously to your server. The choices are; Discussion Support (DSS)/OLAP, Online Transaction Processing (OLTP), and Manual Setting.
It is recommended that you choose the option, DSS/OLAP because you will not require a high number of concurrent connections. OLTP is needed for highly loaded servers, while the manual setting can be bothersome to be setting it now and then.
After setting this, click 'next.'

Set the networking options

Enable the TCP/IP Networking by checking the small box before it. Below it, add your port number and then check the small box to Enable Strict Mode to set the server SQL mode.

Click 'next.'

Select the default character set

The most recommended is the Standard Character Set because it is suited for English and other West European languages. It is also the default for English.

The other two choices, namely, Best Support For Multilingualism and the Manual Default Character Set, are best for those who have other languages other than English.

Tick the small circle before the Standard Character Set and click 'next.'

Set the Windows options

Tick the two choices displayed, which are; Install As Windows Server and Include Bin Directory in Windows Path. This will allow you to work with your MySQL from your command line.

Selecting the Install As Windows Server will automatically display the Service Name. The small box below the Service Name must be checked too.

Click 'next.'

Set the security options

Set your password. The box will indicate where you can type it.

Click 'next.'

Execute your configurations

All you have to do is to click 'execute,' and your computer will configure by itself based on your specifications.

Once the configuration is complete and all the boxes are checked, click 'finish.'

Set the verification process

· Go to the start menu and type cmd and press enter. This will take you to the command panel.

· Type the following: mysql -u root -p
Press 'enter'.

Take note that there is a space between **mysql** and the **dash** symbol, and between u and **root**. Also, there is a space between root and the **dash** symbol.

· The command panel will ask for your password. Type your password and press ENTER.

· A MySQL prompt will appear.

· You can type any SQL command to display the databases. Remember to add the semicolon at the end of your SQL statement.

· Close your command panel for the meantime.

Congratulations!! You have successfully installed and configured MySQL on your machine. It is time for action now.

Using your MySQL can motivate you to learn more about other related applications such as PHP and similar products.

What is essential is for you to learn the basics of SQL first.

Some of the Commands That You Can Get Started With

Now it is time for us to dive into some of the fun things that we get to do with this kind of coding language. We are going to look at some of the commands that we can do when it comes to working with the SQL language and how we can search through our databases and see what information is inside as much as possible. In this chapter, we are going to take a look at how we can work with SQL and some of the basic commands that we can use to make this work for our needs.

These commands are helpful because they will make it easier to work with the different parts that we want in that database. We will find that some of these are going to be easy commands to work with, and then from there, we can move on to some of the commands that are more difficult and complicated so that we can see some of the power that it comes to working in this kind of language.

When it is time for you to learn some of the more basic commands that are available in SQL, you will find that the best way to deal with them is to divide them up into six separate categories. All of these categories are going to be based on what you can use them for the inside of your chosen system. Below are going to be the six options of categories of commands that will work in the SQL language to help you to get things done with your codes.

Data Definition Commands

The first type of commands that we are going to look at is known as DDL, or data definition language. This is one of the aspects that is found inside of the SQL language that is going to make it easier for us to generate objects in the database before we go through and arrange them the way that we would like. For example, you would then be able to use this part of our SQL system to help s to delete or add objects to the table that

we are making. Some of the different
commands that will work with the DDL category here will include:

The drop view

The drop index

Alter the index

Create the index

Alter the table in some manner
Create the table Drop the table.

Data Manipulation Language

The second part that we are going to take a look at here is going to be known as the DML or the data manipulation language. This is going to be the aspect of SQL that we can use when we would like to be able to modify some of the information about the objects that are found in the database that you are using. This is going to make it easier to delete the objects, update these objects, or insert something new inside of the database. This is going to give us a lot of freedom when we want to make sure that the right changes to our information in the database are added in without having to make a new part of the table for this database.

Data Query Language

Now we need to move on to the Data Query Language or the DQL as you are most likely to hear it called. This language is going to be one of the most powerful aspects that you are going to see with SQL, especially when you are working with a more modern database system for your business.

This one can be nice because you will only need to handle one easy command to choose what you want off of the database, and the command is the Select command. You can work with the Select command to help run some queries when they are needed inside of any relational database. If you would like to have it so that the results that come out are going to be more detailed, then it is possible to go through and add in some options or clauses to get this to all work out for you.

Data Control Language

Next on the list is going to be the DCL or the Data Control Language. This is going to be a command that you will be able to choose to work with any time that you want to have some control over the people who can be on that database or who can access it. The DCL command is used in some cases to generate the database objects related to who has access to see this information. This could include who will have the right to distribute privileges of access to the data. This is a good thing to use if your business is dealing with a lot of sensitive information and you only want a few people to be able to get ahold of it. Some of the commands that you may find useful to use when working with the DCL commands include:

Revoke

Grand

Alter password Create synonym

Data Administration Commands

When you are working with the data administration commands, you are going to find that it allows you some power over the database that others are not able to have. You will be able to analyze, and when needed, audit the operation that is going on in the database. In some cases, you will be able to use this to assess the overall performance of that database with the help of these specific commands.

This is going to be what can help to make these the right commands to work with when you would like to go through the system and fix some of the bugs that may be showing up in some of the work that you are doing. You will be able to work with these commands to get rid of these so that the database can work properly.

Two options come with these data administration commands, and these include start audit and stop the audit. One thing that we do need to keep in mind when working with the database administration is that it is going to be different than the data administration when you are working with the SQL language. The database administration is going to make it easier for you to manage what is going on with the database, including some of the commands that can be used with SQL. It can also have some more specifics than the data administration when it comes to implementing the SQL language that you want.

The Transactional Control Commands

These are the good commands that you can use in SQL any time that you want to keep track of as well as manage the transactions that will happen inside the database. If you sell a product of any kind on your website, for example, you will need to use the transactional control commands to help keep track of these commands, keep track of the amount you are making, and to keep track of all the other things that you will need when working with those transactions. There are a few things that you will be able to do with these transactional control commands including:

Commit—this one is going to save all the information that you have about the transactions inside the database.

Savepoint—this is going to generate different points inside the groups of transactions. You should use this along with the Rollback command.

Rollback—this is the command that you will use if you want to go through the database and undo one or more of the transactions.

Set transaction—this is the command that will assign names to the transactions in your database. You can use it to help add in some organization to your database system.

As we can see, as we go through this process, all of these commands are going to be important to what we want to get done within the code that we are writing out. These can help us to get some of the specific results that we are looking for inside of our database.

And we will be able to take a bit more time to explore these and learn more about them as we go through this guidebook so that we can get a more in-depth look at what they are all about and how we can use them for some of our own needs as well. But this is a great way for us to get an introduction to what they are all about and how we can use them for some of our own needs as well.

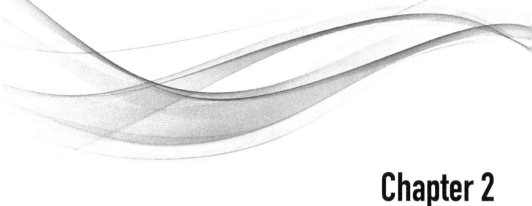

Chapter 2

Control Flow Tools

Now that we know how to write basic stored routines let us move on to a slightly more advanced concept.

For instance, suppose we want to pay 2 months bonus for employees with a salary below 3000, but a 1-month bonus for employees with salary above that?

To achieve the above, we need to use control flow tools. These include IF, CASE, and LOOP statements.

In this section, we'll be using a lot of examples to illustrate the concepts discussed. Ready?

IF statement

Let's start with the IF statement. The syntax for the IF statement is as follows:
IF condition 1 is met THEN do task A;

ELSEIF condition 2 is met THEN do task B;

ELSEIF condition 3 is met THEN do task C;

ELSE do task Z;

END IF;

The IF statement first checks if the first condition is met. If it is, it'll perform task A. If it is not, it'll move on to the first ELSEIF statement. If this condition is met, it'll perform task B. If it is not, it'll move down the ELSEIF statements until it finds a condition that is met. If no conditions are met, it'll perform task Z.

There can be as many ELSEIF statements as needed.

Also, both the ELSEIF and ELSE statements are optional. You do not need to include them if there are no other conditions to check.

However, if you omit the ELSE statement and there exists a case that is not fulfilled by any of the IF and ELSEIF statements, MySQL will give you an error.

Let's look at some examples of the IF statement now.

Example 1

```
DELIMITER $$
CREATE FUNCTION if_demo_A(x INT) RETURNS VARCHAR(255) DETERMINISTIC
BEGIN

IF x > 0 THEN RETURN 'x is positive';

ELSEIF x = 0 THEN RETURN 'x is zero';

ELSE RETURN 'x is negative';

END IF;

END $$

DELIMITER;
```

This IF statement first checks if the input (x) is greater than zero. If it is, it returns 'x is positive'.
If it is not, it checks if x equals zero. If it is, it returns 'x is zero'.
If both the first two conditions are not met, it moves on to the ELSE statement and returns' x is negative'.

To run this function, we write

```
SELECT if_demo_A(2);
```

We'll get 'x is positive'.

If we change the input from 2 to 0 or -1, we'll get 'x is zero' and 'x is negative' respectively.
Example 2

```
DELIMITER $$CREATE FUNCTION if_demo_B(x INT) RETURNS VARCHAR(255)
DETERMINISTIC

BEGIN

IF x > 0 THEN RETURN 'x is positive';

ELSEIF x = 0 THEN RETURN 'x is zero';
```

END IF;

END $$

DELIMITER ;

This example is similar to the previous one except that we omitted the ELSE statement. If we run the function now, we'll get the following outputs: SELECT *if_ demo_B(2);*

Output:

x is positive

SELECT if_demo_B(-1);

Output:

Error Code: 1321. FUNCTION if_demo_B ended without RETURN

You can see that if we pass a value to the function that it is unable to process (a negative number in this case), the function returns an error.

CASE statement

Next, let's move on to CASE statements.
The CASE statement is very similar to the IF statement and can often be used interchangeably. In most cases, choosing between IF and CASE is a matter of personal preference.

The syntax is:

CASE case_variable

WHEN value_1 THEN do task A;

WHEN value_2 THEN do task B;

...

ELSE do task Z;

END CASE;

Or

CASE

WHEN condition 1 is met THEN do task A;

WHEN condition 2 is met THEN do task B;

...

ELSE do task Z;

END CASE;

Let's look at some examples.

Example 1

```
DELIMITER $$

CREATE FUNCTION case_demo_A(x INT) RETURNS VARCHAR(255)
DETERMINISTIC

BEGIN

CASE x

WHEN 1 THEN RETURN 'x is 1';

WHEN 2 THEN RETURN 'x is 2';

ELSE RETURN 'x is neither 1 nor 2';

END CASE;

END $$

DELIMITER ;
```

Calling the function:

```
SELECT case_demo_A(1);
```

Output:

x is 1

```
SELECT case_demo_A(5);
```

Output:

x is neither 1 nor 2

Example 2

```
DELIMITER $$

CREATE FUNCTION case_demo_B(x INT) RETURNS VARCHAR(255) DETERMINISTIC

BEGIN

CASE

WHEN x > 0 THEN RETURN 'x is positive';

WHEN x = 0 THEN RETURN 'x is zero';

ELSE RETURN 'x is negative';

END CASE;

END $$

DELIMITER ;
```

This second example uses the second syntax and tests x for a range instead of a single value.

Calling the function:

```
SELECT case_demo_B(1);
```

Output:

x is positive

```
SELECT case_demo_B(-1);
```

Output

x is negative

WHILE statement

The next control flow statement is the WHILE statement. This statement allows us to specify a task to be done repeatedly while a certain condition is valid.

The syntax is:

[name of while statement :] WHILE condition is true DO

-- some tasks

END WHILE;

Example

```
DELIMITER $$

CREATE FUNCTION while_demo(x INT, y INT) RETURNS VARCHAR(255)
DETERMINISTIC

BEGIN

DECLARE z VARCHAR(255);

SET z = '';

while_example: WHILE x<y DO

SET x = x + 1;

SET z = concat(z, x);

END WHILE;

RETURN z;

END $$

DELIMITER ;
```

Here, we first declare a local variable z and initialize it to an empty string (an empty string is a string with no content).

Next, we declare a WHILE statement. A WHILE statement can be labelled (but labelling it is optional). Here we label it while_example.

Next, the WHILE condition checks if x is smaller than y. (Both x and y are input parameters to the function.)

While x is smaller than y, the WHILE statement does the following:

First, it increases x by 1.

Next, it uses the concat() function to concatenate z with the new value of x. Finally, it assigns the result back to z.

Recall that concat() is a built-in MySQL function that joins two strings together. If one (or both) of the values is a number (like in our example), it converts them to strings before joining them together.

After the WHILE statement, we simply return the value of z.

If you run the function using the following statement:

SELECT while_demo(1, 5);

you'll get
2345

as the output.

This is because when the loop starts, x = 1 and y = 5. As x is smaller than 5, the WHILE statement increases x by 1 (x = 2 now) and concatenates the result with z. Hence, z = '2'.

Next, the loop repeats itself. It increases x by 1 again (x = 3 now) and concatenates the result with z.

z becomes '23'.

These tasks of increasing x by 1 and concatenating the result with z are performed repetitively until the condition x < y is no longer true.

REPEAT statement

Next, let's look at the REPEAT statement. A REPEAT statement is also used to perform repetitive tasks.

It repeatedly performs some tasks until the UNTIL condition is met. The syntax of a REPEAT statement is: [name of repeat statement :] REPEAT

-- do some tasks

UNTIL stop condition is met

END REPEAT;
Example

DELIMITER $$

```
CREATE FUNCTION repeat_demo(x INT, y INT) RETURNS VARCHAR(255)
DETERMINISTIC

BEGIN

DECLARE z VARCHAR(255);

SET z = '';

REPEAT

SET x = x + 1;

SET z = concat(z, x);

UNTIL x>=y

END REPEAT;

RETURN z;

END $$

DELIMITER ;
```

This REPEAT statement repeats two tasks (SET x = x + 1 and SET z = concat(z, x)) until the x >= y condition is met.
If you run the function with the following statement

```
SELECT repeat_demo(1, 5);
```

You'll get the same output as the previous WHILE statement:

2345

As you can see, a REPEAT statement is very similar to a WHILE statement.
The main difference is that a REPEAT statement performs some tasks while a specified condition (in the UNTIL clause) is not met. On the other hand, a WHILE statement performs some tasks while a specified condition is met.
In addition, another important difference is that **a REPEAT statement will always perform the tasks at least once**. This is because the check (e.g., UNTIL x>=y) is done AFTER the tasks are completed.

Hence, if you run the following statement
SELECT repeat_demo(5, 1);

you'll get 6 as the result because even though the REPEAT condition (UNTIL x>=y) is already met, the two tasks inside the REPEAT statement are executed at least once since the check is done after the tasks are completed.

Clear?

LOOP statement.

Last but not least, let's move on to the LOOP statement. This statement is very similar to the WHILE and REPEAT statements, except that it does not come with a condition to exit the loop.

Instead, we use the ITERATE or LEAVE keywords to exit it.
The syntax of a LOOP statement is:

[name of loop statement :] LOOP

-- some tasks

END LOOP;

Let's look at a few examples.

Example 1

```
DELIMITER $$

CREATE FUNCTION loop_demo_A(x INT, y INT) RETURNS VARCHAR(255)
DETERMINISTIC

BEGIN

DECLARE z VARCHAR(255);

SET z = '';

simple_loop: LOOP

SET x = x + 1;
IF x > y THEN

LEAVE simple_loop;

END IF;
SET z = concat(z, x);

END LOOP;
```

RETURN z;

END $$

DELIMITER ;

Here, we declare a loop called simple_loop. Providing a name for a LOOP statement is often necessary as we need the name to use the LEAVE or ITERATE statements later.

Within the loop, we do the following:
First, we increase the value of x by 1.
Next, we check if x is greater than y. If it is, we leave the loop.
To leave the loop, we write
LEAVE simple_loop;

LEAVE is a keyword in MySQL to indicate that we want to exit the loop. We must provide the name of the loop to exit. In our example, we are exiting simple_loop.
If the LEAVE condition is not met, we remain in the loop and concatenate z with x.
If you run the function now with the following statement
SELECT loop_demo_A(1, 5);
you'll get
2345
as the output.

Example 2
Besides using the LEAVE keyword, we can also use the ITERATE keyword. In contrast to the LEAVE keyword that exits the loop completely, the ITERATE keyword-only skips one iteration of the loop.

Let's look at an example:

DELIMITER $$

CREATE FUNCTION loop_demo_B(x INT, y INT) RETURNS VARCHAR(255) DETERMINISTIC

BEGIN

DECLARE z VARCHAR(255);

SET z = '';

simple_loop: LOOP

SET x = x + 1;

IF x = 3 THEN ITERATE simple_loop;

ELSEIF x > y THEN LEAVE simple_loop;

END IF;

SET z = concat(z, x);

END LOOP;

RETURN z;

END $$

DELIMITER ;

Here, we added one more IF condition to our LOOP statement. This IF condition uses the ITERATE keyword.

If you run the function using the following statement,

SELECT loop_demo_B(1, 5);

you'll get

245

as the output.

The iteration x = 3 is skipped because of the condition

IF x = 3 THEN ITERATE simple_loop;
Clear?

Good!

With this example, we've come to the end of the chapter.

IF statement

In Python, you can use various condition statements. However, you have to ascertain that you follow the Python syntax rules and indentation. One of these rules is to provide an indentation after the 'if' and 'else' statements when you enter their codes. Simply press the tab once to provide the indentation.

Anyway, the program will assist you in determining errors in your Python syntax. If there's an error, it will display the errors and what's wrong with them. You can also press for help if you're lost in the sea of Python lingo.

Therefore, relax and enjoy the experience.

Functions.

The 'IF ELSE' statements, which execute codes, are generally used to compare values, or determine their correctness. 'if' is expressed, if the condition is 'true', while 'else' is expressed when the condition is 'false'.

General code is:

```
if expression:
Statement/s
else:
Statement/s.
```

Example:

Assign a base statement first. Let's say you're teaching chemistry to freshmen college students, and you want to encourage them to attend your tutorials. You can compose this Python code:

```
hours = float(input('How many hours can you allot for your chemistry tutorials?'))

if hours < 1:

print ('You need more time to study.')

else:

print ('Great! Keep it up!')

print ('Chemistry needs more of your time.')
```

CASE statement.

Ruby language is common in organizations for web application development. Ruby on Rails is a framework that allows for rapid development, and business teams focus on other business processes instead of coding functions from scratch. This framework provides a separator known as MVC structure (Model-view-controller). The MVC provides support in separating data, user interface, and business functions.

On the other hand, Python has the most popular MVC frameworks known as Django web framework for web application development. Also, Python is famous beyond the domains of web applications. For example, the Pandas library is useful for data preparation. Other libraries such as NumPy and stats-model are also supportive in this case. Matplotlib is a powerful Python library for data visualization. Tensorflow is famous for machine learning tasks and projects. Besides, SciPy is another open-source library for Python, which is used for scientific computing and solving math functions that used to make engineering students sweat.
WHILE statement.

The *while* statement is the main looping statement and is mostly used whenever simple iterations are required.

Its structure is as follows: Counter = 10

while counter>0:

print counter

counter = counter-1

print 'Backward counting from 10 to 1'

This simple *while* loop will keep on checking the *while* condition again and again until the condition becomes false. Until the condition becomes false, every time the cycle goes through the loop. Then after the condition becomes false, the interpreter resumes the recent activity and continues with the program statements just after the loop. The following diagram illustrates the flow of while controls.

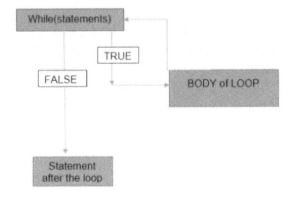

LOOP statement.

As defined in the previous chapter, it is a symbol used to represent repeated (iterated) word/s or sentence/s in Python programming. Anything that is being repeatedly used can employ a loop (a piece of code). Hence, it facilitates the task that you would want to accomplish.

Types of loops.

The *'while' loop* – this is used to implement a piece of code repeatedly.

Example:
Let's say you have these values: a – for individual numbers; t – for sum of the numbers:

a=1

t=0

And you want the user to 'Enter numbers to add to the total.', you write the code for the 'while; loop this way: print ('Enter numbers to add to the total.')

print ('Enter x to quit.')

(Now use the 'while' function to allow the action to become repetitive.)

while a ! = 0:

print ('Current Total: ' , t)

a = float(input("Number? '))

a = float (a)

t+ = a

print ('Grand Total = ' , t)

This is how your code will look like.

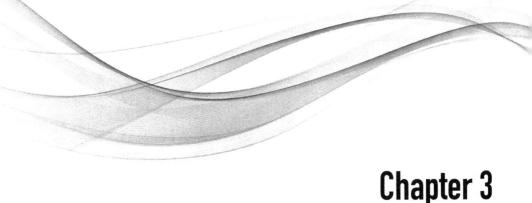

Chapter 3

Tool and Database Structure

MySQL

The open-source SQL database is MySQL. It supports different platforms like Unix, Linux, Mac OSX, and Microsoft Windows. Although the core version of My SQL is free, you may have to pay for some of the premium features. Moreover, MySQL comes coupled with a SQL database server, which is fast, robust, and multi-threaded.

MySQL's development started in the year 1994, and scientists David Axmark and Michael Widenius are credited for the first internal release of the DBMS in 1995. The windows version of the DBMS came much later in 1998. Initially, the MySQL project was owned by MySQL AB. The ownership of the project changed to Sun Microsystems in the year 2008, after which the version 5.1 of MySQL was released. Key features of this database management system include –

Flexibility

High Availability

Scalability

High Performance

Web Strength

Robust Transactional Support

Data Warehouse Strength

Comprehensive Application Development

Strong Data Protection

Open Source Freedom

Management Ease

Lowest Total Cost of Ownership

24 x 7 Support

MS SQL Server

Microsoft came up with its relational database management system in the form of MS SQL Server, which works on ANSI SQL and T-SQL, as its primary query languages. Sybase released the first version of this DBMS in the year 1987. Sybase collaborated with Aston-Tate and Microsoft for porting SQL Server to OS/2 and released SQL Server 1.0 in 1989, after which Aston-Tate dropped out of SQL development, and Microsoft released SQL Server 2000. Key features of MS SQL Server include –

High Availability

Database snapshots

High Performance

Database mirroring

Service Broker

CLR integration

Ranking functions

DDL triggers

XML integration

Isolation levels based on row version

Database Mail

TRY...CATCH

Oracle
Oracle is one of the most popular and largest multi-user DBMSs available in the market today. As the name suggests, Oracle is owned and created by 'Oracle Corporation'. The key feature of Oracle is that it efficiently manage its resources, which in entirety is that database that is accessed by many clients over the network.
Considering the fundamental architecture of Oracle, it is deemed best for client-server computing. Moreover, it supports many platforms like Unix, Windows, Linux, and Mac OSX. The journey of oracle began way back in 1977 when Ed Oats, Bob Miner, and Larry

Ellison founded 'Software Development Laboratory'. Oracle became the first commercial SQL database management system when its Version 2.0 was released in the year 1979.

It was in the same year that the name of the company was changed to Relational Software Inc. (RSI). Because most of the development work undertaken by this company was related to Oracle, its name again changed in 1982, and it got its current identity of Oracle Corporation.

It was in the subsequent years that Oracle got its multi-faceted features. For instance, the cross-platform version of Oracle or Oracle Version 3.0 was released in 1983, while features like concurrency control were added in versions 4.0 and 5.0. Key features of Oracle include –

Read Consistency

Concurrency

Quiesce Database

Locking Mechanisms

Self-managing database

Portability

ASM

SQL*Plus

Resource Manager

Scheduler

Materialized views

Data Warehousing

Table compression

Bitmap indexes

Analytic SQL

Parallel Execution

Partitioning

Data mining

MS Access

MS Access is a basic database management system from Microsoft and is used at the entry-level, which makes it also one of the most popular Microsoft products ever. Other reasons for its popularity include its inexpensiveness and ability to create robust solutions for small projects. Besides this, Microsoft's flagship feature of highly intuitive and easy-to-use graphical interfaces also adds to the reputation of the product.

It is important to mention here that MS Access makes use of Jet-SQL, which is a variant of SQL. This dialect of SQL is specifically used by the Jet database engine, which is used by MS Access for database operations. The first version of MS Access was released in 1992, and it has seen many improvements and additions over the years. Presently, MS Access is available as part of the MS Office product by Microsoft. Key features of this database management system include –

MS Access allows users to create forms, reports, tables, and queries. Moreover, the user can connect all these tools with the help of macros.

Data can be imported from and exported to different formats that include Oracle, ODBC, Outlook, and Excel, in addition to several others.

MS Access supports a special format called the Jet database Format or MDB. This format allows the storage of the application and its data in the same file. This file can be used to transfer the complete application even if the user is in a disconnected environment.

There is support for parameterized queries, which can be referenced by .NET or VB6 programs via ADO or DAO.

MS Access can also be interfaced with MS SQL Server's desktop version, which can be used as an alternative to the existing database engine of this DBMS.

It is important to understand that MS Access is not a client-server DBMS, and thus, it does not implement stored procedures, transaction logging, or database triggers. It is, in fact, a file server-based database.

Types of SQL Tools

There are different kinds of SQL tools in the market. When choosing these tools, you need to consider various factors. These include:

What You Want to Manage - For instance, in case you want to administer SQL server instances, it's advisable to purchase Azure Data Studio.

Creation and Maintenance of Database Code - You need to select SQL Server Data Tools (SSDT).

Querying SQL Server with a Command-Line tool - you can choose MySQL-CLI.

Writing T-SQL Scripts-You should apply visual studio code and MySQL extension.

This section aims to appraise the commonly used tools in SQL server management as follows:

Interbase

This is a robust tool that is fast and embedded with the SQL database. It comes with business-grade safety, disaster recovery, and the ability to handle change smoothly. The tools have the following features:

Adheres to SQL standards - The tools are compatible with all SQL standards, recognizes Unicode, and are suitable for any global character.

Provides multiple Unicode, live alerts, and change view tracking.
Lightweight - it is suitable for the current CPU and may be used in a variety of systems.

Quick recovery - it is suitable for rapid disaster recovery.

dbForge Studio for SQL server
This is one of the best IDE tools which performs a variety of functions, including server management, administration, data reporting, analysis, and others. The tool has the following features:

Able database management

Has high-quality coding support

High-quality SQL server reporting

protection-it provides the best information protection.

dbWatch
This tool offers database administration full support and is used for various databases, including Oracle, SQL Server, Azure, and others. The tool is used for maintenance purposes in different environments, including hybrid and cloud. It has the following characteristics:

Assists in monitoring performance and generation of important reports.

Enables routine memory minimization for the SQL server.

Assists in DB administration with a short message and electronic mail additions.

Support-it provides various support services, including multisite and data cluster assistance.

Bulk install and bulk alerts-they are used when you're handling the bulk installation and alert services.

SQL Sentry
This is one of the best tools that offer SQL database monitoring services. It can handle ever-growing business workloads. Due to the increasing need for high-performance data, many companies are using this tool. The SQL sentry has the following features:

AssistsAssists in the collection and presentation of performance metrics.

Analysis and tuning capabilities-the tool has a functionality that enables SQL query analysis and high tuning capabilities.

It is highly rated as the best DBA solution.

Adminer

This is a data management tool that provides various solutions. These include the management of databases, tables, columns, relations, and others. The tool is sold as a one PHP file and supports various databases on different systems, including MS SQL, Oracle, and MYSQL. You can download various versions as files. Adminer has various qualities, including:

Performs a listing of data tables with various functions, including sort, search, and others.

It has a variety of customization options.

It indicates procedures and destroys them.

DBComparer

This is a database comparison device that analyses and offers insights on database structures that are easy to use. The tools enable you to compare different objects, including tables, foreign keys roles, and others. DBComparer has different features like:

Routinely contrast various database structures.

It provides different choices for evaluation.

It's an in-build visual tree for the spontaneous representation of differences.

EMS SQL Manager Lite for SQL Server

This tool is used for creating SQL database objects and allowing various editing tasks to be done. The tool has the best user-interface and loaded with useful functionalities. It can replace SSMS.

Support features - the tool supports a variety of SQL features, including Azure SQL database, Unicode, and others.

Provides tools for query building - the tool provides both visual and text devices for query development.

Comparison - the database tool helps in comparing and synchronizing various database structures.

Loaded with SQL-debugger - the tools come with an SQL-debugger that tracks processes, functions, and scripts.

Firebird

This is an efficient SQL tool that works well with Windows and Linux. Firebird has various features, including:

Complete support for processes - the tool has full support for various procedures, including standard transactions, many access ways, support for incremental backups, and others.

Application of complex technology - the tool applies the latest technology like FB25 and FB30. This means that it offers high-quality services.

Support of cloud - The tool recognizes cloud infrastructure.

Squirrel SQL

This tool supports the management of Java databases. Through this tool, you can view the SQL database and provide commands. The tool works on different databases, including IBM, SQL, Oracle, and others. Its key features include:

Popup menu - through this menu, you can perform various functions such as editing.

Display of object tree - this shows you the season window.

Charts - it displays charts of tables and how they are connected.

SQLite Database Browser

This tool is sourced openly and helps in creating and editing various files in the database. SQLite Database Browser has various features, including:

Creation and modification of database - through this tool, you can create and edit various databases, tables, and others.

SQL commands - the tool has a log that displays all SQL commands that have been issued and how they've been used, Creates simple graphs – the tool can plot a graph from the data on the table.

DBeaver

This tool is openly sourced and used by database administrators and managers to support various databases like MySQL and IBM. The key role of the tool is to create and modify databases, SQL scripts, the exportation of data, and others. The tool has various features, including:

Creation of data-ability to create and modify data.

Plugins-the tool is offered with various plugins.

DB Visualizer

This is an open-source universal database tool that helps in the management of various

databases such as Oracle, Sybase, Informix, and others. The tool has a browser that navigates through database objects. It helps in the formation and modification of database objects. The core features of DB Visualizer include:
Management of particular database objects.

Forms and modifies various processes and functions.

It provides schema assistance.

Working with the Queries.

When you do set up the query that you would like to use, you will find that you are sending out an inquiry to the database that you already set up. You will find that there are a few methods to do this, but the SELECT command is going to be one of the best options to make this happen, and can instantly bring back the information that we need from there, based on our search.

For example, if you are working with a table that is going to hold onto all of the products that you offer for sale, then you would be able to use the command of SELECT to find the best selling products or ones that will meet another criterion that you have at that time. The request is going to be right on any of the information on the product that is stored in the database, and you will see that this is done pretty normally when we are talking about work in a relational database.

Databases

The meaning behind the word "database" has changed so much in the past couple of decades that it barely preserves its definition. To some people, a database refers to any number of data items contained in a book or list. To others, it refers to a repository of structured data or records, which can be accessed through a computer system. We will focus on the second definition, which also includes SQL. Keep in mind that in this case, a record refers to the representation of an item. For instance, you are running your own business, and therefore you will create one record for every unique client. These records will contain a number of characteristics that describe the object. For example, you can include data such as names, phone numbers, addresses, and so on.

A database, however, doesn't contain only data. It also includes metadata, which has the purpose of defining the information's structure inside the database. Why is this important? Because if you know how the data is organized, then you can access it, manage it, maintain it, and modify it. All of this means that a database is self-describing, as it contains information on the connections between the data objects. The metadata is reserved inside what's known as a data dictionary. The dictionary is what describes the components of a database, namely the table, the rows, columns, and so on. On a side note, you should know that flat-file systems do not contain metadata. This means that the programs that handle these files need to have some form of an equivalent integrated. The size of a database varies as well, depending on the number of records it contains. For instance, you can have anywhere between a dozen data objects and millions. For now, you don't have to worry about any such limitations. However, databases can be categorized in three different ways:

•Personal databases are the smallest. They are stored on the user's personal computer and are characterized by a basic data structure.

•Group databases, on the other hand, are more complex. They are intended to be used by a department or team, which means that they contain a great deal more data than a personal database. This means that they also need to be accessed from multiple devices at the same time.

Finally, we have the enterprise version of a database. They are vast, complex, and need the most reliable equipment to be safely stored and maintained.
As you can see, you can categorize a database by looking at three attributes: how large it is, how many people need to have access to it, and what kind of technical equipment it requires.

Database Management Systems

To manage a database and any applications that have access to it, we need to use a database management system. Keep in mind that a database is nothing more than a structure designed to contain information. We need a tool that actually creates that structure and then allows us to access, maintain, or modify the data inside it. There are many such programs available for free or at a specific cost.
Not all data management systems are created equally, however. The one you need depends on your goal and your requirements. For instance, some of these programs are designed to operate on professional, enterprise-grade equipment and handle massive databases. On the other hand, some of them are intended to work on basic, personal use laptops. However, keep in mind that these tools sometimes need to function at the same time on different hardware settings running different operating systems. Furthermore, we also have the cloud to consider as a storage option. Nowadays, you can gain public online storage through services offered by organizations such as Amazon and Microsoft. The cloud is one of those terms you will often hear in any tech field due to the massive increase in computer processing power and storage capabilities that many businesses require today. What you should know for now in case you don't, is that the cloud is an assembly of computers that make their resources available to anyone via the Internet. This means that anyone can access these services from the comfort of their home instead of physically connecting to a data center. In this case, a data management system with cloud capabilities can provide you with the functionality you need to manage your databases remotely.
Database management systems ensure the flow of data between the user and the system is always the same no matter the type of system and the size of the database.

Database Types

The very first database models were built using a hierarchy-based structure. This lead to a number of problems, including the fact that such databases were not easy to modify and maintain due to their inflexibility. The structural issue and various redundancy problems have led to the development of a network type database. Its purpose was to eliminate such imperfections. They indeed offered the advantage of a near lack in redundancy; however, to achieve this quality, another sacrifice had to be made. The structure of a network model database was highly complex and therefore led to another set of problems.

An answer to these technical issues was soon offered with the development of the relational database. The structure was simple and minimal redundancy was one of its main features. With the creation of this new database type, SQL entered the stage. Its purpose was to turn the relational databases into something revolutionary and send the other models into obscurity.

The Relational Database

With a new type of database, a new database management system was needed. This is how Oracle came to be: a new answer given by a small startup company. At this point, relational databases entered the mainstream. This made possible the ability to modify the structure of this model without changing the design of the programs used on the other database types. For instance, to create more columns inside the database table, all you needed to do was add them to it without any other time-consuming modifications. The applications that relied on the database did not require any changes.

Another powerful advantage was the fact some data could be stored in one table while other data could be in a different table. Neither of these tables had to be connected in any way. Therefore, you could change the information in one of them without having a negative effect on the other.

The Object-Relational Database

Both the relation model and the object model offered an array of advantages. Fortunately, the developers at the time thought about the possibility of profiting from the power of object-oriented databases, as well as the compatibility offered by the relational model. This is how the object-relational database came to be. In essence, it takes the relational model we already discussed, and it adds to it the functionality of the object model.

The object-oriented characteristics have been implemented using SQL and therefore allow all database management systems to adapt to becoming object-relational database management systems. Keep in mind that they still retain compatibility with the original relational model. Since the 90s, the relational database has been gradually expanded by introducing more and more object-oriented features as the programming techniques and languages continued to develop. However, at the heart of this type of database, the relational model remained true while it received a number of extensions over the years.

Relational databases started dropping in popularity in favor of the standard SQL databases we use today. Modern problems required complex SQL solutions that could only be provided by the object-oriented features.

Chapter 4

Tables

Creating Your First Database and Table Using Command Line

You can as well use SQL commands and statements to create databases and tables. The same applies to SQL Server Management Studio like the above guide, but commands and statements are used to give instructions to the system to perform a given function. As to build your first database, you use the command' SELECT DATABASE (database name)' and hitting the execute button to create the program. The message on the screen should, therefore, be 'Command(s) completed successfully," showing that your database has been created.

As to use the database, run the command 'USE (database_name),' which tells the query window to run the new database program. On the other hand, creating a new table entails running the command 'CREATE TABLE (table_name).' Entering data follows the command 'INSERT DATA INTO (table_name), VALUES (table_name),' and repeating the same process for all the datasets you have. The same also allows for viewing the data you saved and includes the command format 'SELECT * FROM (table_name). All the above commands are the critical ones when it comes to maneuvering through different SQL databases. As such, it is always essential to learn about each SQL basic commands to execute programs readily.

Create tables

The following are the simple steps:

Enter the keywords CREATE TABLE.

These keywords will express your intention and direct what action you have in mind.

Example: CREATE TABLE.

Enter the table name.

Right after your CREATE TABLE keywords, add the table name. The table name should be specific and unique to allow easy and quick access later on.

Example: CREATE TABLE "table_name"

The name of your table must not be easy to guess by anyone. You can do this by including your initials and your birthdate. If your name is Henry Sheldon, and your birth date is October 20, 1964, you can add that information to the name of your table.
Let's say you want your table to be about the traffic sources on your website; you can name the table"traffic_hs2064"

Take note that all SQL statements must end with a semicolon (;). All the data variables must be enclosed with quotation marks (" "), as well.

Example: CREATE TABLE traffic_hs2064

Add an open parenthesis in the next line.

The parenthesis will indicate the introduction of the columns you want to create.

Example: CREATE TABLE "table_name".

(

Let's apply this step to our specific example.

Example: CREATE TABLE traffic_hs2064

(

In some instances, the parentheses are not used.

Add the first column name.

What do you want to name your first column? This should be related to the data or information you want to collect for your table. Always separate your column definitions with a comma.
Example: CREATE TABLE "table_name"

("column_name" "data type",

In our example, the focus of the table is on the traffic sources of your website. Hence, you can name the first column, "country".

Example: CREATE TABLE traffic_hs2064

(country

Add more columns based on your data.

You can add more columns if you need more data about your table. It's up to you. So, if you want to add four more columns, this is how your SQL statement would appear.

Example: CREATE TABLE "table_name"

("column_name1" "data type",

"column_name2" "data type",

"column_name3" "data type",

"column_name4" "data type");

Let's say you have decided to add for column 2 the keyword used in searching for your website, for column 3, the number of minutes that the visitor had spent on your website, and for column 4, the particular post that the person visited. This is how your SQL statement would appear.

Take note:

The name of the table or column must start with a letter; then, it can be followed by a number, an underscore, or another letter. The number of the characters shouldn't exceed 30.

You can also use a VARCHAR (variable-length character) data type to help create the column.

Common data types are:

Date – date specified or value.

Number (size) – you should specify the maximum number of column digits inside the open and close parentheses

char (size) – you should specify the size of the fixed-length inside the open and close parentheses.

varchar (size) – you should specify the maximum size inside the open and close parentheses. This is for variable lengths of the entries.

Number (size, d) – This is similar to number (size), except that 'd' represents the maximum number of digits (from the decimal point) to the right of the number.

Hence if you want your column to show 10.21, your date type would be:

number (2,2)

Example: CREATE TABLE traffic_hs2064

(country varchar (40),

keywords varchar (30),

time number (3),

post varchar (40));

Add CONSTRAINTS, if any

CONSTRAINTS are rules that are applied for a particular column. You can add CONSTRAINTS if you wish. The most common CONSTRAINTS are:

"NOT NULL" – this indicates that the columns should not contain blanks

"UNIQUE" – this indicates that all entries added must be unique and not similar to any item on that particular column.

In summary, creating a table using a SQL statement will start with the CREATE TABLE, then the "table name", then an open parenthesis, then the "column names", the "data type", (add a comma after every column), add any "CONSTRAINTS".

Deleting Tables
Deleting tables, rows, or columns from your database is easy by using appropriate SQL statements. This is one of the commands that you must know to be able to optimize your introductory lessons to SQL.

Here are steps in deleting tables:

Select the DELETE command

On your monitor, choose the DELETE command and press the key. Downloading Windows MySQL Database, MySQL Connectors, and MySQL Workbench can facilitate your process.

Expert SQL users may laugh and say that these steps should not be included in this book. But for beginners, it is crucial to state specifically what steps should be done. Imagine yourself learning a new language; Russian, for example, and you'll know what I mean.

Indicate from what table

You can do this by adding the word"FROM" and the name of the table

DELETE FROM 'table_name"

Indicate the specific column or row by adding "where"

If you don't indicate the "where" all your files would be deleted, so ensure that your statement is complete.

Example: DELETE FROM 'table_name"

WHERE "column_name"

Hence, if you want to delete the entire table, simply choose:

DELETE FROM "table_name";

where time = (10)

DELETE from traffic_hs2064

where time = (5);

Complete your DELETE statement by adding the necessary variables

Example: DELETE FROM "table_name"

WHERE "column_name"

OPERATOR "value"

[AND/OR "column"

OPERATOR "value"];

Deleting the wrong tables from your database can cause problems, so, ascertain that you have entered the correct SQL statements.

Inserting Data into a Table

You can insert new data into an existing table through the following steps.

Enter the keywords INSERT INTO

Select the keywords INSERT INTO. The most common program, which is compatible with SQL, is windows MySQL. You can use this to insert data into your table.

Add the table name

Next, you can now add the table name. Be sure it is the correct table

Example: INSERT INTO"table_name"

Using our table:

Example: INSERT INTO traffic_hs2064

Add Open parenthesis

You can now add your open parenthesis after the table name and before the column_ names. Remember to add commas after each column.

Example: INSERT INTO"table_name"

(

Using our own table:

Example: INSERT INTO traffic_hs2064
(

Indicate the column

Indicate the column where you intend to insert your data.

Example: INSERT INTO"table_name"

("column_name",. . . "column_name"

Close the columns with a close parenthesis

Don't forget to add your closing parenthesis. This will indicate that you have identified the columns accordingly.

Example: INSERT INTO"table_name"

("first_columnname", ..."last_columnname")

Add the key word values

The keyword values will help your selection be more specific. The list of values follows this. These values must be enclosed in parentheses too.

Example: INSERT INTO"table_name"

("first_columnname", . . ."last_columnname")

values (first_value, . . . last_value

Add the closing parenthesis
Remember to add the close parenthesis to your SQL statement. This will indicate that the column does not go any further.

Example: INSERT INTO "table_name"

("first_columnname", . . ."last_columnname")

values (first_value, . . . last_value)

Add your semicolon

All SQL statements end up with a semicolon, except a few.

Example: INSERT INTO"table_name"

("first_columnname", . . ."last_columnname")

values (first_value, . . . last_value);

Take note that strings must be enclosed in single quotation marks, while numbers are not.

Using our sample table, you can come up with this SQL statement:

Example: INSERT INTO "traffic_hs2064"

(country, keyword. time)

values ('America', 'marketing', 10);

You can insert more data safely without affecting the other tables. Just make sure you're using the correct SQL commands or statements.

Dropping a Table
You can drop or delete a table with a few strokes on your keyboard. But before you decide to drop or delete a table, think about the extra time you may spend restoring it, if you happen to need it later on. So, be careful with this command.

Dropping a table is different from deleting the records/data in the table. When you drop a table, you are deleting the table definition plus the records/data in the table.

Example: DROP TABLE "table_name"

Using our table, the SQL statement would read like this.

Example: DROP TABLE traffic_hs2064;

DROPPING your table is easy as long as you can create the proper SQL.

Using the ALTER TABLE Query

There will be several times you need to use the ALTER TABLE command. This is when you need to edit, delete or modify tables and constraints.

The basic SQL statement for this query is:

Example: ALTER TABLE "table_name"

 ADD "column_name" data type;

You can use this base table as your demo table:

Traffic_hs2064

Country	Searchword	Time	Post
America	perfect	5	Matchmaker
Italy	partner	2	NatureTripping
Sweden	mate	10	Fiction
Spain	couple	3	News
Malaysia	team	6	Health
Philippines	island	5	Entertainment
Africa	lover	4	Opinion

If your base table is the table above, and you want to add another column labeled City, you can create your SQL query this way:

Examples: ALTER TABLE Traffic_hs2064

ADD City char(30);

The output table would appear this way:

Traffic_hs2064

Country	Searchword	Time	Post	City
America	perfect	5	Matchmaker	NULL
Italy	partner	2	NatureTripping	NULL
Sweden	mate	10	Fiction	NULL
Spain	couple	3	News	NULL
Malaysia	team	6	Health	NULL
Philippines	island	5	Entertainment	NULL
Africa	lover	4	Opinion	NULL

You can also ALTER a table to ADD a constraint such as NOT NULL.

Example: ALTER TABLE Traffic_hs2064

MODIFY City datatype NOT NULL;

This will modify all entries that are NOT NULL.

You can also ALTER TABLE to DROP COLUMNS such as the example below:
Example: ALTER TABLE Traffic_hs2064 DROP COLUMN Time;

Using the second table with this SQL query, the resulting table will be this:

Traffic_hs2064

Country	Searchword	Post	City
America	perfect	Matchmaker	NULL
Italy	partner	NatureTripping	NULL
Sweden	mate	Fiction	NULL
Spain	couple	News	NULL
Malaysia	team	Health	NULL
Philippines	island	Entertainment	NULL
Africa	lover	Opinion	NULL

You can ALTER TABLE by adding a UNIQUE CONSTRAINT. You can construct your SQL query this way:

Example: ALTER TABLE Traffic_hs2064

ADD CONSTRAINT uc_Country UNIQUE (Country, SearchWord);

In addition to these uses, the ALTER TABLE can also be used with the DROP CONSTRAINT like the example below.

Example: ALTER TABLE Traffic_hs2064

DROP CONSTRAINT uc_City;
Here are examples of CONSTRAINTS.

NOT NULL

This constraint indicates that the NOT NULL values should not be present in the columns of a stored table.

CHECK

This will ensure that all parameters have values that have met the criteria.

UNIQUE

This ascertains that all values in the columns are distinct or unique.

PRIMARY KEY

This indicates that the values in two or more columns are NOT NULL and simultaneously UNIQUE.

FOREIGN KEY

This will ascertain that the values of columns from different tables match.

DEFAULT

There is a specified DEFAULT value for columns. This may appear as blanks or appear as NULL.
Make sure you use these constraints properly to make the most out of your SQL queries.

Table

Tables are objects that are used by RDBMSs to hold data. Typically, a table is a collection of rows and columns that contain data entries. This is the simplest form of data storage. An example of how tables look like is shown below. This table has employees' data for a company. The fields of data included consist of ID number, name, gender, and salary.

ID Number	Name	Gender	Salary
20156	James	Male	1200
20157	Andy	Female	1250
20158	Rebecca	Female	575
20159	Andrew	Male	1100

Chapter 5

Learning Function

Built-In Functions & Calculations

Regarding SQL, a built-in function can be defined as a portion of programming that accepts zero or any other input and returns an answer. There are different roles of built-in functions. These include the performance of calculations, obtaining of the system value, and application in textual data manipulation. This part aims at examining the various SQL built-in functions, categories of functions, pros and cons of functions and types of built-in functions.

Types of SQL Functions

The SQL functions are grouped into two groups: aggregate and scalar function. Working on Group by, the aggregate functions run on different records and deliver a summary. Scalar functions, on the other hand, run on different records independently.
These are as follows:

Single Row Functions

They provide a one-row return for any queried table. They are found in select lists, START WIH, WHERE CLAUSE, and others. Examples of single-row functions include numeric_, data_mining, Datetime_, conversion_ and XML_functions.

Aggregate Function

When you apply this kind of function, you see a single row returns based on different rows. The aggregate function exists in Select lists, ORDER BY, and HAVING CLAUSE. They go hand in hand with Group by Clause and SELECT statements. Many of them do not pay attention to null values. Those that are usually used include AVG, EANK, MIN, SUM, and others.

Analytic Function

They are used to compute an aggregate value that is found on specific groups of rows. When you run this function, it delivers many rows for every group. The analytic functions are the last one to be run in a query. Examples of analytic functions include analytic-_ clause and Order-by-Clause.

Model Functions

These are found in SELECT statements. Examples of model functions include a CV, present, and previous.

User-Defined Function

They are used in PL/SQL to offer functions that are not found in SQL. They mostly used in sections where expressions occur. For instance, you can find them in the select list of Select statements.

SQL COUNT Function

It is used to provide the number of rows in a table.

Categories of Functions

Functions are classified according to the role they play on the SQL database. The following are some of the function categories available:

Aggregate Functions

They do a calculation on a specific set of values and deliver a single value. The aggregate values are used in the SELECT LIST and HAVING clause. The aggregate functions are referred to as being deterministic. This means that they return the same value when running on the same input value.

Analytic Function

They calculate an aggregate value according to a group of rows. They return many rows for different groups. The analytic functions can be used to perform different computations like running totals, percentages, and others.

Ranking Functions

They provide a ranking value for each portioned row. These kinds of functions are regarded as nondeterministic.

Rowset Functions

They're used to return an object that can be applied.

Scalar Functions

They work on a single value to return the same. There are various kinds of scalar values. These include configuration function, a conversion function, and others.

a) Configuration Functions—They offer information about the present configuration.

b) Conversion Functions—They support data changing.

c) Cursor Functions—They provide information concerning cursors.

d) Date and Time Data Type—They are concerned with operations as regards date and time.

Function Determinism
Functions that are found in SQL servers are either deterministic or nondeterministic. Deterministic functions provide the same answers when they are used. Nondeterministic functions, on the other hand, offer different results when they are applied.

SQL Calculations
There are various mathematical functions built-in the SQL server. The functions can be classified into 4 main groups, including Scientific and Trig Functions, rounding functions, signs, and random numbers. Although there are numerous mathematical functions within each class, not all of them are used regularly. The various classes are highlighted and explained below:

Scientific and Trig Functions
Under this category, there are various subclasses found under it. These include P1, SQRT, and SQUARE. P1 function is used to compute the circumference and area in circles. How it works: *SELECT 2 *10*. SQRT connotes square root. This function is used most of the time. The function recognizes any number that can be changed to float datatype. Example: *SELECT SQET (36)* Returns 6.SQUARE means that you multiply any number by itself. The concept of the Pythagoras theorem is useful here. This means that *A*squared+*B*squared=*C*squared. This can be performed as **SELECT SQRT (SQUARE (A) + SQUARE(B)) as C**.

Rounding Functions
Under this class, there are various subcategories, which include the CEILING and FLOOR. The ceiling function is helpful when dealing with a float or decimal number. Your interest is to find out the highest or lowest integer. Whereas the CEILING is the best highest integer, the floor represents the lowest integer. The ROUND function is applied when you want to round a number to the nearest specific decimal place. This is expressed as ROUND (*value, number of decimal places*).

Signs
Some occasions require that you obtain an absolute figure of a number. For instance, the absolute value of -7 is 7. The absolute number doesn't contain any sign. To assist you with this task, it's essential to utilize the ABS function.

COS (X)
This function recognizes an angle expressed as radian as the parameter. After an operation, you get a cosine value.

SIN (X)
This function notices a radian angle. After computation, it gives back a sine value.
Sign
You can use a sign function when you want a negative, positive, or zero value.

The Importance of SQL Built-In Functions and Mathematical Applications
The build-in functions are sub-programs that help users to achieve different results when

handling the SQL database. These applications are used several times when you want to manipulate or process data. The SQL functions provide tools that are applied when creating, processing, and manipulating data. The benefits of SQL in-build and math functions are as follows:

Manipulation of Data

The in-built tools and maths functions play a significant role in data manipulation. Manipulating massive data may be difficult if you do it manually. This is especially when the data is massive. Therefore, these functions play a significant role in ensuring that your data is manipulated fast as per your demands.

Assist in The Processing of Data

To benefit from data, you must process it. You may never have the ability to process big data manually. Therefore, the built-in SQL functions and maths applications assist you in processing your database.

Simplifies Tasks

In case you're a programmer, you can attest to the fact that these functions and formulas make your work ease. You can work fast when you apply these in-build functions and formulas. Due to these tools, you'll accomplish many projects within a short time.

Increase Your Productivity

Using the in-built functions enhance your productivity as a programmer. This is because the functions enable you to work quickly on different projects. In case you were to handle data manually, you may take much time before you accomplish a task, which ultimately injures your productivity. However, the built-in functions and calculations allow quick execution of tasks.

Time-Saving

Because functions are written once and used several times, and they save much time. Besides timesaving, the functions offer support to modular programming.

They Enhance Performance

When you apply functions, you enhance the performance of your database. This is because the functions are prepared and inserted before usage.

Enhances Understanding of Complicated Logic

The handling of the SQL database is a complex tax. Therefore, functions enable you to decompose data into smooth and manageable functions. In this way, you find it easy to maintain your database.

Cost-Effective

Because the functions are in-build in the SQL database, you can use them many times without the need to invest in new ones. In this connection, therefore, they reduce the cost of operating and maintaining your SQL database.

Downsides of In-Built Functions

The SQL in-built functions have various limitations, including:

Testability-

When using the in-built functions, it's challenging to test their business philosophy. This is a big challenge, especially when you want the functions to support your business philosophy. You may never understand whether the functions are in line with your business vision and mission.

Versioning

It's challenging to establish the kind of version that is used in the SQL build-functions. You need to understand whether any new versions can probably provide the best service.

Errors

In case there are errors within the in-build functions that you don't know, they may disrupt the program. This may prove costly and time-wasting.

Fear of Change

In case there is change, you may not understand how it will affect your SQL built-in functions. The world of technology keeps changes, and this change may affect the in-built functions.

The SQL in-built functions and calculations are essential as they enable a programmer to execute a task fast with minimal errors. The calculations in the in-built database make it possible to process and manipulate data.

Stored functions

You can create and utilize your user-defined functions.

Use a keyword to define a function.

The function should be defined first, making use of the word 'def', and then the name of its function.

When you want to define a function, you can use the general code below:

def functionname (arg1, arg2, arg3)

statement1

statement2

statement3

Press 'enter' twice to access results.

Take note: arg stands for argument.

Example:

You are an employer, and you want to print the numbers (num) of your employees. Thus, you defined 'employee' as the name of your file.

def employee(num)

print ("num")

See image below:

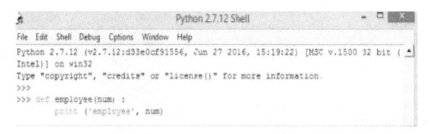

When you press ENTER, and input a number, the function will keep going until you decide to stop. So, the function can work repetitively. See image below:

```
Python 2.7.12 Shell                                    -
File  Edit  Shell  Debug  Options  Window  Help
Python 2.7.12 (v2.7.12:d33e0cf91556, Jun 27 2016, 15:19:22) [MSC v.1500 3
Intel)] on win32
Type "copyright", "credits" or "license()" for more information.
>>>
>>> def employee(num) :
        print ('employee', num)


>>> employee (101)
('employee', 101)
>>>
>>> employee (301)
('employee', 301)
```

You can also create the Python syntax this way:

def employee(num)

print 'employee', num

Press 'enter' twice, and then you can begin entering the numbers. The program will print it ad infinitum. See image below:

Functions can have no arguments, or have a couple of arguments. The arguments can be numbers or strings.

You can also make use of the keyword 'return' to 'return' results (the 'return' key indicates that answers to the computation specified will be 'returned' – (displayed in the results).

Example:

If you want to obtain the average of the grades of students in 4 subjects, you can create the code this way: You can use this code for as long as you don't exit the shell. If you want to save it, you can create a New File so you could save it.

def grades(a,b,c,d) :

  return ((a+b+c+d)/4)

See image below:

When you or the student enters his grades following the syntax/statement, the 'return' results would be the computed value already. See image below:

```
Python 2.7.12 Shell

File  Edit  Shell  Debug  Options  Window  Help
Python 2.7.12 (v2.7.12:d33e0cf91556, Jun 27 2016, 15:19:22) [MSC v.15
Intel)] on win32
Type "copyright", "credits" or "license()" for more information.
>>>
>>> def grades(a,b,c,d) :
        return ((a+b+c+d)/4)

>>>
>>> grades(80,79,81,84)
81
>>> grades(77,85,87,77)
81
>>> grades(90,88,86,85)
87
>>> grades(88,80,79,85)
83
>>> |
```

The student has to type in the shell, after the arrows (>>>), following the given format:

grades(80,90,85,75)

Through this method, you can compute the grades of your students-ad Infinitum.
Keep in mind that you have first to define (def) the function before your code can work, and print the results.

Remember to add the colon (:) after your def statement. You must also separate the arguments by commas.

In default parameters, the initially assigned value is printed, when the user doesn't enter any value.

In multiple parameters, an asterisk (*) can be used to indicate this.

Be adventurous and discover the joy of knowing how to make your codes work with Python.

Chapter 6

Queries and Subqueries

While we have spent a little bit of time taking a look at some of the commands and queries that we can use when it comes to working in the SQL language, it is time for us to go more in-depth about these queries and what they can do for some of our needs along the way as well.

When we are working on our business database, and it is all set up the way that we would like, it is going to be possible that at one point or another, you will want to search to make sure you can find the perfect information inside of all that. This is going to make it easier for us to find the easier information and results that we want. But we do have to make sure that the database is set up in the right manner so that we can use the right commands and see that it is fast and accurate in the process.

Think of this like when someone comes to your website, searching for that particular product that they would like to purchase.

Do you want them to get stuck on the website that is slow, and have them see results that have nothing to do with the item they wanted? Or would you like a fast search that was helpful and will encourage the person to make that purchase? Of course, for the success of your business, you are more likely to want the second option, and we can take a look at how to set up your database and work with queries to make this happen.

Queries

A query, as it sounds, is simply a question or request for data, values from a database. One can simply send in a question based on the set of information contained, and expect reply based on the data the tables in a database contains; the sent questions are the queries. A query could either be a select query that serves as a data retrieval query or an action query that requires more operations to be carried out on the data set, such as deletion, updating, or insertion. The query has languages that are used in making requests from a database, and the standard is Microsoft Structured Query Language (SQL). However, there are several other extensions of the language under the SQL umbrella, which includes Oracle SQL, MySQL, and NuoDB. There are, however, different ways to query, but once the basics are understood, the question formats become adaptive.

It is important to remember that a database stores information in tables, which is made up of rows that contains the data and columns telling the database what to store. To help ask a well-defined and directional question, there is a need for knowledge about the following: What column is the data supposed to be gotten from? What table holds the required information?

What is it to be selected? What fields are necessary for the particular question?

Are there influencing conditions for the selection?

In SQL, some keywords match the knowledge statements above. When the SELECT command is sent, it defines which database to get information from, the FROM command determines which table(s) to look at, and the WHERE command requests special conditions which are required for processing of such data.

A close to a great example of how the query works is the web search. However, they do not require keywords or positional parameters, as in the case of SQL Languages. Once texts are typed into a search engine, such as Google, Yahoo, or Bing, there is a request for information on a specific topic, and the request is finalized upon the selection of "ENTER". Afterward, the search engine deploys an algorithm to determine the best results basing on the search engine's set significance, which is not accessible to the public.

Types of search queries include Navigational searches that direct searches that are intended to find a particular website/blog, Informational searches that are designed to span across broad subject matters like comparisons, and Transactional searches which aims at completing a transaction/purchase.

The Relationship Between Index, Views, and Queries

The index, view, and query are all tied to one point of a database. *The query* happens to be at the top of the chart as it is the request that brings forth a *programmed view* which searches through an *index* for results to present.

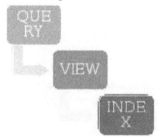

The chart above is a simple diagrammatic explanation as to how they are related. Once a query is initiated, a view that was programmed to respond crawls through the index, searching for the data set required to respond and gets directed to the information that is being required. This information is then sent back to the view, which in turn gives a response to the query displaying only the specific information that is related to the query and with general access. The synergy of the view and the index form an indexed view, which is beneficial as the processes are now more reduced, given that the various views are now linked to specific and tailored indexes.

Subqueries

The first concept you need to explore is that of the subquery. As the name suggests, a subquery is embedded into a query. It's, in fact, a query within a query. In most cases, its purpose is to perform a logical test or a calculation that will yield a result that can then be passed through the query. It may sound somewhat confusing at first, but its syntax is easy to understand. All you need to do is write the subquery in-between parentheses and implement it where it's needed.

One of the simplest examples of its application is using it to return several data items and then process them as a table inside the "from" statement of the parent query. Also, you can write a scalar subquery which yields one value and then implements it within a statement that can filter the rows with the help of various statements, such as WHERE. These two situations are where we use subqueries the most. With that in mind, let's take a look at an example of a subquery within an update table. We will have several subqueries generated by the update information and the conditions that we set to determine the rows we want to update. These subqueries will search for the values that correspond with the columns from two tables.Here's the SQL code: UPDATE table_1

SET mycolumn = (SELECT mycolumn

FROM table_2 WHERE table_1.mycolumn = table_2.mycolumn)

WHERE EXISTS (SELECT mycolumn

FROM table_2 WHERE table_1.mycolumn = table_2.mycolumn); In this example, we have a query that contains two subqueries. The syntax is the same for both of them. First, we write the SELECT statement within parentheses. This is our first subquery, and it is set inside a "set" clause. This is what generates the values needed for the update. Then we have the other subqueries set inside the "where exists" clause. The SELECT statement is again used to filter the data items that require the update.

On a side note, these two subqueries are referred to as correlated subqueries. This means that they depend on a component, like a table name, from the parent query. In our example, the subqueries depend on table_1 that is part of the main update operation. Keep in mind that uncorrelated subqueries do not have a reference to the elements within the parent query.

Filtering Using Subqueries

You have already worked using the WHERE operation to filter your query results. In case you don't remember, you used it together with various conditionals that look something like "WHERE salary > 2000". However, in this case, you know the value you need to use to create the condition. You will often not be so lucky to have this information, so what can you do in this case? Subqueries are your answer. You can use one to generate several values that you can use in your WHERE statement.

Let's say you want to determine which cities in Europe hold the top 10% of the population. In other words, you want to find out the 90th percentile. Normally, you might be tempted to write two queries to figure out the 90th percentile and to filter by city. However, you can achieve all of this with the help of a subquery.Here's how it looks in code: SELECT loc_name

city_eu_abbreviation

```
p0010001

FROM eu_cities_2010

WHERE p0010001 >= (

SELECT percentile_cont(.9) WITHIN GROUP (ORDER BY p0010001) FROM eu_
cities_2010)

ORDER BY p0010001 DESC;
```

The query itself is something you are already familiar with. However, we introduced the WHERE condition, which we use to filter the p0010001 column, but it doesn't contain the value you'd expect. After the greater or equal than the comparison operator, we have another query that implements the percentile_cont function we discussed in an earlier chapter. This function is used to create the value we need, namely the 90th percentile. Once it's generated, we can then use it inside the parent query.

Keep in mind that subqueries are only useful when writing a SELECT query. You can use the same kind of subquery you wrote with the WHERE clause but inside a DELETE statement. This way, you can delete anything you want from a table. It might sound like a slightly more complicated way of removing something but consider having half a billion rows in a database. It is massive, and it would take your system a lot of time to query all that data. However, you could split the information into bite-size chunks by copying the table and deleting only the rows or data items that aren't necessary.

Using Subqueries to Create Derived Tables

A subquery that returns you some data allows you to turn it into a table. This can be achieved by writing the subquery into a FROM statement. Keep in mind that the data itself is a collection of rows and columns, and by using the data from them, we create what is known as a derived table. This type of table is no different from other tables, which means that you can join it with other tables or query it further. The question is, when would you use this method of creating a table?

If the results are similar, then you have evenly distributed information. However, if there are significant differences between the two values, then you have outliers affecting the data. Now let's say you want to learn the median and the average population of European cities. Finding these values is one process, and then comparing them is another process. Both of these operations can be done together at the same time by writing a subquery inside the FROM statement.

Here's how all of this looks like in code:

```
SELECT round(calcs.average, 0) AS average,

calcs.median,
```

round (calcs.average - calcs.median, 0) AS median_average_diff FROM (

SELECT avg (p0010001) AS average,

percentile_cont(.5)

WITHIN GROUP (ORDER BY p0010001) :: numeric (10, 1) AS median from eu_cities_2010

)

AS calcs;

In this example, we have a self-explanatory subquery. We apply the percentile_cont and avg functions to calculate the median and average values of the population. Next, we reference our subquery as the parent query's table. The median and average values are then returned in the parent query, which approximates the result. The final result after running the query should look something like this: average median media_average_diff 98233 25857.0 72376

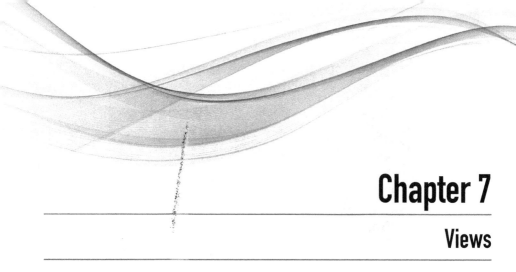

Chapter 7

Views

Views are virtual tables consisting of rows and columns which are separated explicitly to service the result of queries sent. It could also be said to be a composition of the data in a table in the form of a predefined SQL query. They are saved on the database for easy access following the **SELECT statement**. It can join data from multiple tables resulting in a newer and easier view. However, for views to exist as a stored set of data values, it has to be indexed. It serves as a protective layer and a security feature that grants people access to specific data without exposing the underlying base tables.

To create a view, we can choose columns from one or more tables in the database. The view can have either all the table rows or just a few of them based on a specified condition. With views, you can structure the data in a way you find natural to you. You can also control the way data is accessed and changed by presenting a user with what they are supposed to see or change. Views are the right way of summarizing data from various tables to generate reports.

Creating Views

To create database views in SQL, we use them CREATE VIEW statement. We can create a view from a single table, multiple tables, or from another view. For the users to create a view, they must have permission to do so.

The CREATE VIEW statement takes the syntax given below:

CREATE VIEW viewName AS

SELECT column_1, column_2.....

FROM tableName

WHERE [condition]; The parameter viewName is the name of the view to be created. The tableName is the name of the table from which the view is to be created while the condition is the condition to be used for filtering the table records during the creation of the view.

Consider the students' table with the following data:

```
mysql> select * from students;
+-------+----------+-----+
| REGNO | NAME     | AGE |
+-------+----------+-----+
|  3420 | Nicholas |  18 |
|  3201 | John     |  18 |
|  3200 | Mercy    |  19 |
|  3203 | Joel     |  21 |
|  3204 | Cate     |  19 |
+-------+----------+-----+
5 rows in set (0.00 sec)

mysql>
```

The following example shows how we can create a view from the above table. The view will have only the name of the student and their age:

CREATE VIEW students_view AS

SELECT name, age FROM students;

The statement should execute successfully, as shown below:

```
mysql> CREATE VIEW students_view AS
    -> SELECT name, age
    -> FROM students;
Query OK, 0 rows affected (0.57 sec)

mysql>
```

The view has been given the name students_view with only two columns from the table. The view has only two columns, name and age. Now that the view has been created, you can query it in the same way you query a table. The following command shows this: *SELECT * FROM* students_view; The command returns the following result:

```
mysql> SELECT * FROM students_view;
+-----------+-------+
| name      | age   |
+-----------+-------+
| Nicholas  | 18    |
| John      | 18    |
| Mercy     | 19    |
| Joel      | 21    |
| Cate      | 19    |
+-----------+-------+
5 rows in set (0.20 sec)

mysql>
```

The view has two columns from the table, just as we had stated.

WITH CHECK Option

We can use this option together with the CREATE VIEW statement. The purpose of the WITH CHECK options is to make sure that all the INSERTs and UPDATEs meet all the conditions created in the view's definition.

If the conditions are not met, the INSERT or UPDATE operation will return an error. In the example given below, we are showing how you can create the above view but this time with the WITH CHECK option: *CREATE VIEW* students_view *AS*

SELECT name, age *FROM* students

WHERE age > 18

WITH CHECK OPTION; When you create the above view, only the records where the age is above 18 will be added to the view. You can drop the previous view by running the following command: drop *view* students_view; Now, recreate the view by running the above command. It should run successfully, as shown below:

```
mysql> CREATE VIEW students_view AS
    -> SELECT name, age
    -> FROM students
    -> WHERE age > 18
    -> WITH CHECK OPTION;
Query OK, 0 rows affected (0.10 sec)

mysql>
```

Now, run the select command on the view to see the records it has:

*SELECT * FROM* students_view; The command will return the following result:

```
mysql> SELECT * FROM students_view;
+---------+-------+
| name    | age   |
+---------+-------+
| Mercy   |    19 |
| Joel    |    21 |
| Cate    |    19 |
+---------+-------+
3 rows in set (0.06 sec)

mysql>
```

You can see that only the records that meet the specified condition where it's added to the view.

Views can be built on top of single or multiple tables, as well as upon pre-existing views. Views could also be deleted as much as created. However, some specific conditions are required to have been met before any update could be made, they are: · The SELECT statement used to create the view must not include a GROUP BY clause or ORDER BY clause.

· The SELECT statement must not have the keyword "DISTINCT".

· The View must ensure it has NOT NULL values.

· The view must not be created using nested or complex queries.

· The view must be created from a single table, given that any view created using multiple tables does not allow for an update.

· The FROM clause may not have multiple tables.
· The CREATE OR REPLACE VIEW statement are available to add or remove relevant fields from a view.

· The SELECT clause must not contain summary functions.

· The SELECT clause must not contain set functions.

· The SELECT clause must not contain set operators.

· The WHERE clause must not contain subqueries.

· Calculated columns cannot be updated.

· All NOT NULL columns from the base table must be part of the view for the INSERT query to work.

Some of the advantages of views include:

Restricted Modification: This way, only those with access to the table can initiate major edits such as INSERT, UPDATE, and DELETE.

Saved Database Space: Here, the query doesn't always have to refer to tables. Hence incessant tables are not created as actual data are not stored.

Additional Security: Since selected columns and details are exposed to the public upon the request of a query, there is more security for other sensitive details contained in a table.

How to add a view

Views are uniquely identified and created using the following SQL statement.

CREATE VIEW {Enter the parameters here}

Here we will explain different parameters that go with this statement. Follow along!

1) Name of the view - With this parameter, you can select a name for your defined view.

2) List the name of the columns - By using this parameter you can give names for all of the columns present in your view. Give the names in a list form so that the DDL statement can recognize the format.

3) Encryption - By using this parameter, you are giving additional security to the view that you are trying to create. This encryption parameter increases the security of the database system.

4) Schema - For layman's introduction, the schema is a set of rules that are combinedly used in a database. Even views can be included in this schema definition. However, if you are trying to drop or change the contents of the view that is schema restricted, then you may face errors. So, always bind scheme only when you are sure of it.

5) Metadata - This parameter will help you create a referenced metadata information for all of your view content. All the column names and content will,be enlisted and can help you to check quickly if necessary.

By this, we have got a good understanding of views. In the next section, we will discuss some of the unique advantages of views. Follow along!

Advantages of Views

1) Views are mostly used for restricting values in the columns and rows. Views have options to access one or more parts of the table. This gives a unique advantage for views

over other database concepts.

2) Views can also be used to get rid of other advanced database operations such as joins. Without creating complex join operations, you can just use views to achieve results.

3) You can control the range values of the columns you are dealing with. Views are also a well-advanced layer for database security.

If you are not comfortable with SQL statements, you can use the SQL server management system to create views. All you need to do is to select your desired tables and columns and define a statement to create a view. It is handy but limited by its operations.

How to create an updatable view

Views are special database objects and can often be updated using the ALTER statements. Altering views can result in several disruptions in the system. For this reason, it is advisable to see views as advanced system operation. Here we will describe it in detail. The SQL statement for altering a view:

ALTER VIEW {Enter parameters here}

You can even use the SELECT statement to select the columns that you wish to change. All the advanced SELECT operations can be used to get results.

How to drop a view

Dropping views is a difficult topic to discuss because of the complexities it is accustomed to. If you use this DDL statement, the view selected is deleted from the system. The trick is all the views that are enclosed with the view you are trying to erase will also be deleted. The adverse linkage of views is very tough to deal with.

Here is the SQL statement:

DROP VIEW {enter view name here}

Note:

For suppose, if tables that are used for creating views are dropped, then they will not result in destroying the views. Views are primary entities that can exist without any primary data involved.

Modify Views from the SQL studio

You can easily use the manager to modify the view, and its operation steps are as follows: (1) In the "Microsoft SQL Server Management Studio" window, expand the corresponding server, double-click the "Database" node, select the corresponding database, click the "View" icon, select the view to modify in the details pane on the right, click the right mouse button, and select the "Design" command in the pop-up shortcut menu.

(2) In the open view designer window (which is similar to the window appeared before), the user can modify the definition of the view according to the method of creating the view.

(3) After the modification is completed, click the "Save" icon to save the modification to the view.
However, this process is quite overwhelming and can be cumbersome when dealing with huge modifications. In the next section, we will discuss modifying views using the ALTER statement.

Using DML statements for views

ALTER VIEW statement in SQL can modify views. The syntax of the ALTER VIEW statement differs from that of the CREATE VIEW statement by only one ALTER word.

Here is the syntax:

ALTER VIEW {View name} {Enter parameters}

This shows that the ALTER VIEW statement is very similar to the CREATE VIEW statement. If the original view definition was created with CHECK OPTION, then these options can only be modified if they are also included in ALTER VIEW.
Note: ALTER VIEW statements do not support adding, deleting, or changing the type of one or more individual columns in a current view.

The ALTER VIEW statement does not appear to add functionality to the data definition language. ALTER VIEW statement does not provide a shortcut to change the definition of the view. As mentioned earlier, this statement is the same as the CRATE VIEW statement in all other aspects except the name (ALTER instead of CREATE).

Therefore, when modifying a view, you can also use the DROP VIEW statement to delete the existing view, and then use the new structure to execute the CREATE VIEW statement to recreate the view.

However, using ALTER VIEW statements does have advantages over executing DROP VIEW/CREATE VIEW statements sequentially. When a view is deleted through the DROP VIEW statement, the database management system automatically deletes any triggers created on the view.

Then, when the view is recreated, the system neither restores the trigger on the view nor GRANT any access to the username (or role) that has permission to the original view.

Similarly, if you modify a view by executing the DROP VIEW statement and then executing the CREATE VIEW statement to recreate the view, you must also reenter the codes of all triggers on the original view and grant access to the view to users, roles, and accounts that are allowed to use the original view.

On the contrary, if the ALTER VIEW statement is executed to make the same modification to the view definition, the DROP VIEW statement does not need to be executed, and the triggers and permissions granted on the original view will remain on the new view.

Adding Data through Views

In addition to displaying table data through a view, you can also use INSERT statements to add data to the view's base table through a view. When adding data using INSERT statements on a view, the following rules must be met.

(1) When using the INSERT statement to insert data into the data table, the user must have the right to insert data.

(2) Since the view only refers to some fields in the table, the values of the fields referenced in the view can only be explicitly specified when inserting data through the view. For those fields that are not referenced in the table, you must know how to fill the data without specifying a value.

(3) Views cannot contain combinations of multiple field values or contain results using statistical functions.

(4) A view cannot contain the DISTINCT or GROUP BY clause.

(5) If WITH CHECK OPTION is used in the view, the clause will check whether the inserted data meets the conditions set by the SELECT statement in the view definition. If the inserted data does not meet this condition, the SQL Server will refuse to insert the data.

(6) You cannot use data modification statements for multiple underlying tables in one statement. Therefore, if you want to add data to a view that references multiple data tables, you must use multiple INSERT statements to add it.

Here is the syntax:

INSERT {Name of the view} {Data values}

Simplify Complex Queries through Views

Writing multi-table joins in SQL is common because almost all queries include extracting and correlating data from two or more tables. Therefore, it is much easier to create and use join table views than to reenter the same complex query repeatedly.

Moreover, many administrators who are not familiar with SQL and do not have time to learn SQL in-depth only know how to write simple single table queries.

By using views to combine data from multiple tables, administrators will have a single table containing data from several tables. They can use a single table SELECT statement to obtain the required data from the database, thus greatly simplifying the use of complex SQL statements.

Encrypt Views

After the view is created, the system stores the definition of this view in the system table comments. You can view the definition text of the view by executing the system stored procedure sp_helptext or directly opening the system table.

SQL Server provides a WITH ENCRYPTION clause to protect the definition of views, which can prevent other users from viewing the code of views or hiding the source code when SQL is published.

Here is the syntax:

CREATE VIEW {Enter encryption here}

Restrict User Access to Columns through Views

Views are virtual tables and can be used in almost any place where table references are allowed. However, views are not physical tables stored on the hard disk like other tables and indexes in the database. Views consist of SELECT statements that extract data from rows and columns of one or more base tables (or other views). One of the real benefits of using views is the ability to hide some tables that other users do not want to see.

Database security

Database security is usually divided into four core concepts, namely encryption, tracking, authentication, and authorization.

Encryption

Encryption is a process in which all the data we are dealing with is changed into random unusable data using different encryption algorithms. This encrypted algorithm can only be dealt with if you have the required keys for decryption. Databases such as SQL servers usually use advanced encryption algorithms for security purposes.

Authentication

Authentication is a procedure in which a database validates the credentials of the users and presents his instance data. Authentication is a complex process and has advanced in technicality as years flow. Authentication is usually done using secret codes known as passwords. Some of the advanced database systems will ask you to provide magnetic cards or fingerprints for authentication.

Authorization

After authentication servers, check the resources and will provide instances that you are authorized. Authorization is essential if you are dealing with a lot of administrators. Sometimes you may want to revoke access for a particular user for whatever reason it may be. Authorization revokes can make this happen without any hiccups.

Change tracking

Advanced industries usually use tracking systems to track their employees. Any employee with any malicious intent can be easily caught using this feature because tracking systems note down every SQL query statement that is being performed. All the statements are documented and can be easily seen by users with advanced privileges.

The security model of SQL

The security model of SQL is pretty basic and deals with three major characteristics, as explained below.

Principals

Principals are the user entities that have access to a particular resource in the database. For example, USER A has principal permission to the databases, and USER B doesn't have permission to the databases. SQL has made easy of the security feature by creating Microsoft groups. It is easy for administrators to grant permissions using groups.

Securables

Even after permitting groups, SQL security can help to restrict who can access what. For example, an organization programmer can't access the back-end server information, whereas Security analysts can look at both Backend and frontend servers. All the securable entities can be defined using schema. Any conflict in schema results in program errors leading to data loss.

Permissions

Permissions are individual permissions to every filegroup and file that is present. This is an advanced security feature Linux offers for every user that is present. Using this function can recursively result in good security standards.

Creating and deleting a role

To facilitate the management of databases, SQL Server refers to the concept of role, which is an aggregation of certain permissions. The role is used in many management systems today and can be said to be the basis for SQL Server to divide permissions. Roles are similar to groups. As long as managers assign permissions to roles, users inherit a certain role to achieve the purpose of assigning permissions. Using roles can not only divide permissions quickly but also change permissions conveniently. Therefore, it not only increases the security of the database but also facilitates the database managers.

Division of roles

The roles in SQL Server are divided into two categories, namely:

- Server-level roles.

- Role at the database level.

Although they are both called roles, the meanings represented by these two roles are different. The following are detailed descriptions of the meanings represented by these two roles, respectively.

Server-level roles and permissions

Server-level roles can also be called "fixed server roles". The main reason for this is that server-level roles cannot be changed (including cannot be added). In SQL Server, it has already defined roles, with a total of 9 roles. You can view it in the Object Resource Manager under SQL Server Management Studio.

Database-level roles

The role at the database level is divided into two parts, one is a predefined "fixed database role" in the database, and the other is a self-created "custom database role". A total of 10 roles can be viewed in specific databases.

How to create a role?

The creation role here refers to the creation of database roles. The predefined roles in the database may not meet the needs of actual work. At this time, database managers must create roles that meet the actual business needs.

Here is the step by step way to create a role:

1) Open the SQL server management studio and look for the instances that you are going to need.

2) Enter the database you need to work on in SSMS Object Explorer.

3) Right-click the [Security] node to open the function list item.

4) In the pop-up function list, enter [New] and select the list function of [Database Role]. After selecting Database Role, the dialog box for creating a new database role will pop up.

5) Fill in the details required for creating a role such as a name and other details and click Finish to complete the database role.

Once the database role is created, it can be permanently stored in SQL Server. When an actual business needs it, it can assign existing roles to specific users at any time.

Assigning a role to a database user can be done when creating a user or a role, or it can be modified on a user that has already been created. These special functionalities are known as privileges which we will be discussing next.

Granting and revoking a privilege

A role can be seen as a combination of privileges. When a user has a certain role, it inherits the set of privileges that the role has. Also, SQL Server allows developers to use DCL (Data Control Language) to control privileges.

You can grant and revoke privileges using certain statements. Here we will discuss them in brief for your better understanding.

GRANT

By using this statement, you can allow all your roles to certain users. If this privilege is not given, then it is difficult to operate as you expected.

Here is the SQL statement:

GRANT {Enter parameters} USER {Enter usernames}

REVOKE

By using this statement, you can stop the privileges or special permissions that you have given to the user before. By this statement, you can cut down the user access easily to maintain security in the system.

Chapter 8

Trigger-DML

Sometimes there are cases when certain SQL operations or transactions need to occur after performing some specific actions. This is a scenario that describes an SQL statement triggering another one to take place. A trigger is simply an SQL procedure compiled in the database that executes certain transactions based on previously occurring transactions. Such triggers can be performed before or after executing a DML statement (INSERT, DELETE, and UPDATE). Moreover, triggers can validate the integrity of data, maintain consistency of information, undo certain transactions, log operations, read and modify data values in different databases.

Creating a Trigger - Once a trigger has been created, it cannot be altered or modified anymore (you can just either recreate or replace it). How a trigger works depend on what conditions are specified – whether it will be executed all at once when a DML statement is performed, or it will be run multiple times for each table row that is affected by the given DML statement. A threshold value or a Boolean condition can also be included, which will trigger a course of action when the specified condition is met.

The standard syntax for creating a trigger is:

CREATE TRIGGER TRIGGER_NAME

TRIGGER_ACTION_TIMETRIGGER_EVENT

ON TABLE_NAME

[REFERENCING OLD_OR_NEW_VALUE_ALIAS_LIST]

TRIGGERED_ACTION

TRIGGER_NAME - the trigger's unique identifying name TRIGGER_ACTION_ TIMETRIGGER_EVENT - the specified time or duration that the set of triggered actions will occur (either before or after the triggering event).

TABLE_NAME – the database table for which the DML statements have been specified

TRIGGERED_ACTION – indicates the actions to be performed once an event is triggered

Dropping a Trigger

The basic syntax for dropping or destroying a trigger is the same as dropping a table:

DROP TRIGGER TRIGGER_NAME;

Chapter 9

Data Types

SQL Server and Database Data Types

To be able to hold data in certain columns, SQL Server and other relational database management systems utilize what is called "data types."

There are different data types available, depending on what data you plan to store.

For instance, you may be storing currency values, a product number, and a product description. Certain data types should be used to store that information.

The majority of the data types between each RDBMS are relatively the same, though their names differ slightly, like between SQL Server and MySQL. There are a lot of data types, though some are more frequently used than others. The following is a list of common ones that you may find or work with.

The AdventureWorks2012 database will be used as an example.

VARCHAR

This is an alphanumeric data type, great for holding strings like first and last names, as well as an email address, for example. You can specify the length of your varchar data type like so when creating a table, VARCHAR(n). The value of 'n' can be anywhere from 1 to 8,000, or you can substitute MAX, which is 2 to the 31st power, minus 1. However, this length is rarely used.

When designing your tables, estimate the length of the longest string plus a few bytes to be on the safe side. If you know that the strings you will be storing will be around 30 characters, you may want to specify VARCHAR(40) to be on the safe side.

This data type is flexible in a sense to where it will fit only the characters entered into it, even if you don't insert 40 characters like in the example above.

However, there is a bit of overhead with storage, as it will add 2 bytes to your entire string. For instance, if your string is 10 bytes/characters in length, then it will be 12 in all actuality.

NVARCHAR

Much like the varchar data type, this is alphanumeric as well. However, it also stores international characters. So this is a good option if you end up using characters and letters from another country's language.

The other difference between VARCHAR and NVCARCHAR is that NVARCHAR's values

go up to 4,000 instead of 8,000 like VARCHAR. Though they are the same in how they are defined in length like so: NVARCHAR(n) where 'n' is the length of characters.

Exact Numerics

Various number data types can be used to represent numbers in the database. These are called exact numbers.

These types are commonly used when creating IDs in the database, like an Employee ID, for instance.

Bigint – Values range from -9,223,372,036,854,775,808 to 9,223,372,036,854,775,807, which isn't used so frequently.

Int – most commonly used data type and its values range from -2,147,483,648 to 2,147,483,647

Smallint – Values range from -32,768 to 32,767

Tinyint – Values range from 0 to 255

In any case, it's best to pick the data type that will be the smallest out of all of them so that you can save space in your database.

Decimal

Much like the exact numeric data types, this holds numbers; however, they are numbers, including decimals. This is a great option when dealing with certain numbers, like weight or money. Decimal values can only hold up to 38 digits, including the decimal points. Let's say that you wanted to enter $1,000.50 into your database. First, you would change this value to 1000.50 and not try to add it with the dollar sign and comma. The proper way to define this value per the data type would be DECIMAL(6,2).

Float

However, this is more of an Approximate Numeric, meaning it should not be used for values that you do not expect to be exact. One example is that they are used in scientific equations and applications.

The maximum length of digits that can be held within a column while using this data type is 128. Though it uses the scientific notation and its range is from -1.79E + 308 to 1.79E + 308. The "E" represents an exponential value. In this case, its lowest value is -1.79 to the 308th power. Its max value is 1.79 to the 308th power (notice how this is in the positive range now).

To specify a float data type when creating a table, you'd simply specify the name of your column and then use FLOAT. There is no need to specify a length with this data type, as the database engine itself already handles it.

Date

The DATE data type in SQL Server is used quite often for storing dates, of course. Its format is YYYY-MM-DD. This data type will only show the month, day, and year and is useful if you only need to see that type of information aside from the time.

The values of the date data type range from '0001-01-01' to '9999-12-31'. So, you have a lot of date ranges to be able to work with!

When creating a table with a date data type, there's no need to specify any parameters. Simply inputting DATE will do.

Datetime

This is similar to the DATE data type, but more in-depth, as this includes time. The time is denoted in seconds; more specifically, it is accurate by 0.00333 seconds.

Its format is as follows YYYY-MM-DD HH:MI: SS. The values of this data type range between '1000-01-01 00:00:00' and '9999-12-31 23:59:59'.

Just as the DATE data type, there is no value or length specification needed for this when creating a table. Simply adding DATETIME will suffice.

If you're building a table and are deciding between these two data types, there isn't much overhead between either. Though, you should determine whether or not you need the times or would like the times in there. If so, then use the DATETIME data type, and if not, use the DATE data type.

BIT

This is an integer value that can either be 0, 1, or NULL. It's a relatively small data type in which it doesn't take up much space (8-bit columns = 1 byte in the database). The integer value of 1 equates to TRUE, and 0 equates to FALSE, which is a great option if you only have true/false values in a column.

Chapter 10

9 Common Mistakes and How to Avoid Them

Although SQL is a simple computer programming language, you may find it hard when working with massive data. It is essential to ensure that you write high-quality statements before you start working on moderate and huge tables. As you engage in writing your statements for various sites, you need to avoid the following mistakes:

Repetition of Data

Repetition of the same set of data in different tables is referred to as data redundancy. It's essential to ensure that each table has different kinds of data set and avoid repeating it. To make sure you don't repeat the same data in different tables, it crucial that you abide by normalization rules. If you repeat, you create confusion. For instance, you may have a table that has a client's mobile number. Since the mobile number belongs to the client, it can quickly identify them. It'll be wrong to create an order table and add the client's mobile number again. To avoid this mistake, it's essential to store your data in a single location and apply relationships existing between the primary and foreign key in handling your data.

Avoid Using Too Many Cursors

The use of too many cursors when performing your SQL is bothersome. It's essential to desist from applying too many loops when undertaking your SQL procedures. Although loops are a common feature in programming, they're ineffective in SQL. Instead of using them, you can apply effectively presented SQL statements. In case you occasionally use cursors, it's important to minimize them.

Using of AND and OR operations

Sometimes, you may fail to adhere to a logical order when writing your queries. The way you apply the AND and OR statements may change your information. It's essential to apply the right parenthetical structures or arrange your statements in the right pre-determined sequence.

Spelling Mistakes

SQL is a machine language and may be harsh if you misspell the words. For instance, instead of typing the word SELECT, you write SELCT. You need to desist from making this mistake by ensuring that you type the words correctly using capital letters. You also need to create borders that separate your main words from other words and table columns.

Missing Brackets and Single Quotes

These grammatical structures are applied many times in SQL programming. They come in pairs. The errors that many people make is that they either forget using these structures or don't apply them properly. For instance, you may use an opening bracket {(} and forget the closing one {)}. SQL also requires that you enclose text figures in single quotes. In case you don't have a quote, SQL may not understand where your text starts and stops. To stop committing these mistakes, it's essential to remember that brackets and quotes come in pairs and always observe this rule when dealing with them.

Commas and Semi Colons

These punctuation marks are applied in SQL for different purposes. Whereas commas are used when separating lists, semicolons are applied to signal to end of an expression. To avoid these mistakes, ensure that you place a comma in the front. Semicolons are optional and may or may not be used.

Not Minding Your Syntax

Syntax means the way words come together to form phrases and sentences after that. In case you don't arrange your words well, you'll not make a sensible statement. Likewise, in case you don't apply the right syntax, your database may not understand what you're saying. This may result in poor performance.

Assuming That Your Clients Understand What They Need

When clients call you, do not assume that they fully understand their database problem. It's essential to let them know that you're a professional in that area, and you'll assist them in discovering the problem and fixing it.

Avoiding Feedback

Although you'll be inclined to listen more to the managers who offered you the job, it's equally important to listen to the end-users of the program. So, apart from listening to managers, it's also important to listen to the users of the program like the clerks.

Conclusion

The next step is to start working with some of the different parts that you can do with the help of the SQL language. Many medium and large companies are going to work with a database of some sort. Whether you use this to hold onto data that you will use later on to make some big decisions, you hold onto information about your customers, hold onto things about some of the products that you sell, or you use the database for some other reason, you will quickly find that there are so many uses for working on these databases. Since many of these databases can be so large and have so many parts that come together in it, it is hard to imagine that we are going to be able to look through it manually to find everything that we need. This can sometimes make it difficult to do, and we will find that the SQL language is going to come in and help us. With some simple commands, simple enough that even those who have never worked with any kind of coding at all, will be able to pull up the different parts that they want out of the database.

There are so many times when a company will need to work with a database to get the results that they want, to hold onto the right information to show the customers, and even to hold onto the information about the customer for future use. When we can combine these databases with the SQL language, we will find that it is so much easier for you to handle and manage the database that you are working with. When you are ready to learn more about the SQL language and how it will help you with all of your database needs, make sure to check out this guidebook to help you get started.

SQL is like an emerging new skill that is quite vital to businesses. Just like basic literacy is important for any job out there, mastery of SQL skills is increasingly becoming important for anyone that wants to succeed in the business sector.

At last, you have reached the end of your journey, and you are ready to begin a new one! You have mastered the fundamental concepts behind SQL and know how to put them in the application. You have learned a new set of skills that you can adapt and use in several fields such as business, information technology, or engineering.

Many businesses will want to create, modify, and work with one of these databases for some of their own needs. It allows them to keep track of their customers, to make sure that their orders are placed in the right, to show off some of the products that they want to sell, and more. There are a lot of reasons to work with a database, but it will not take long to figure out that they can grow large, and you need some method to help keep the management of that database in line along the way.

This guidebook is meant to help you to get all of that done and more. We took a look at many of the commands, codes, and other parts that you need to make sure that your database is going to behave the way that you want. Even if you haven't been able to do much work with the databases in the past, you will find that with the tips and tricks and codes that we handle in this guidebook, you will be able to get some of the work done that you would like on that database. Your management skills of that information will go through the roof.

SQL is the fundamental programming language for databases, and you must be a pro at it if you work in the field of databases or are planning to become one. This book contains all the basic information you require to get started with SQL and shall build the right foundation for advanced courses in SQL. We hope this book helped you in your strive to learn the SQL programming language.

C++ PROGRAMMING

After work guide to master C++ on your own. Build your coding skills and learn how to solve common problems. Transform your passion in a possible job career as a computer programmer.

Michail Kölling

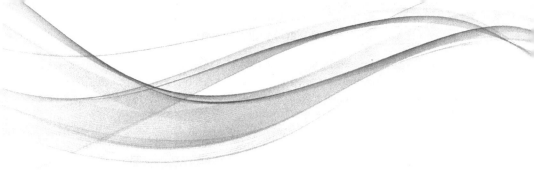

Introduction

Welcome to the wonderful world of programming, the chapters contained in this book will give you a basic understanding of programming in C++. By its final chapter, you will be able to create a complete program on your own, using C++.

This guide is aimed at newcomers to C++. If, however, you are entirely new to programming, I recommend first reading our primer to programming. It covers all the concepts, terms, programming paradigms, and coding techniques that a complete novice needs to know.

This guidebook is going to take some time to look over all of the things that we can do with the C++ language, and how beneficial learning this language can be.

This object-oriented programming course in C++ language presents learners with the concepts and techniques necessary to design, develop and implement a robust program model effectively. As a learner, you will be able to grasp practical knowledge on how to apply the fundamental concepts of object-oriented analysis and design and solve various problems in your day to day activities.

C++ is a computer programming language widely used for general-purpose programming. It is an extension of C-language. The basic understanding of C++ can be acquired from C. That's why both computer languages are represented as C/C++. Bjarne Stroustrup developed this multi-paradigm language in 1979.

In today's world, many operating systems use C++ as their basic language. Some system drivers, browsers, and games are based on C++ programs. It is a free form, compiled, and statically typed programming language. Many professionals believe that C++ is the most efficient language to achieve the desired results.

Learning code is ultimately the language of the future. We have all heard something close to that at some point in our lives.

By the time you reach the end, you should have no problem reading C++ code and writing programs that are both interesting and useful. So, let's dive in and learn C++.

Chapter 1

Anatomy of C++

Introduction to programming languages

As you already know, the program is nothing but a set of instructions. These instructions are executed by the hardware, which is the physical computer machinery. Though modern computers are fast, they have their limitations. Computers can only understand a set of instructions given in their native language. For this, you should understand the concepts of machine language, assembly language, and high-level languages.

Machine language

Though computers are very advanced machines, they cannot understand languages like C++ directly. A computer only understands 0s and 1s. They are called bits. And they can only understand instructions given in the binary format. Every set of instructions that we give to sleep you are translated into a set of instructions that tell the processor to do a particular job. You should understand that different types of processors have different types of instruction sets. For example, the Pentium processors will only understand their instructions set. It is a similar case with Macintosh. In the very beginning, programmers had to write their instructions in the binary language. It was very time-consuming and challenging. Luckily, we don't have to go through all of that.

Assembly language

As the machine language is tough to deal with, a new language called the assembly language was invented. Here every instruction is given a short name, and the variables are replaced by names and not by binary digits, making it easy for a programmer to write code. You may ask how you can understand and assembly language. It cannot. The assembly language will be converted into machine language with the help of an assembler. You should remember that each CPU has its assembly language. So, the assembly language of a CPU cannot be run on a different CPU. Even assembly language has got its drawbacks. They require large sets of instructions, even for simple tasks.

High-level language

The high-level programming languages came into existence to solve those problems that the assembly and machine languages were causing. These can run on any computer. High-level languages come with A program called a compiler. The role of a compiler is to generate an executable file or a program that a CPU can directly understand. These programs are standalone programs. The modern compilers that are available today are very efficient and fast and converting the code into an executable format. Some of the programming languages use the interpreter. The job of an interpreter is to execute the code but without compiling it to the machine code. But here we won't learn about an interpreter. Any given programming language can be interpreted or compiled. Languages like C, C++, and PASCAL are compiled while scripting languages like JavaScript and Perl are interpreted.

Ask this question, and you will get a dozen different answers, but, put simply, C++ is a compiled, object-orientated computer-programming language. If you are new to programming, even that has probably left you somewhat confused, so let's break it down a bit more.

There are two types of programming language – one is interpreted, and the other is compiled. Interpreted languages are run on an interpreter – this reads the code and executes the commands inside one at a time. The CPU reads compiled languages on your computer instead of a program. Computers cannot read letters; they can only read binary numbers so, when you write your code, it has to be translated into binary first. This is called compiling.

The object-orientated part of the explanation just describes how the code is structured, but I will be going into more detail on that later on.

What does this all mean to me?

To be successful at learning C++, you need to use both a text editor and a compiler. If you are using a Windows PC to do this on, you can use Notepad, which is already installed, on your computer as your text editor and, as your compiler, which is going to convert your code into an executable format, you should use GNU C/C++.

Linux/Unix

A simple way to check whether GCC is installed on your Linux/Unix computer is to bring up the command line and type in:

$ g++ -v

If GCC is installed you will get the following message, or something very like it:

Using builtin specs

Target: i386-redhat-linux

Configured with: ../configure --prefix=/usr ....

Thread model: posix

gcc version 4.1.2 20080704 (Red Hat 4.1.2-46)

If GCC is not installed, you can follow the instructions on http://gcc.gnu.org/install/ to do so.

Mac OS X
The best way to get GCC for Mac OS X is to go to http://developer.apple.com/technologies/tools, download xCode, and follow the installation instructions.

Windows
To get GCC on your Windows PC, you must first download MinGW from http://www. mingw.org. Make sure you download the latest version of MinGW, as well as installing gcc-core, binutils, gcc-g++, and MinGW runtime – these are minimum requirements.

One more thing you could consider is an IDE – Integrated Developments Environment. This text editor features an integrated compiler and syntax highlighting. The best one to use is Code: Blocks.

Is there anything else I should know?
Yes. C++ is very rigid in its syntax, and everything is case sensitive, so be careful what you are typing. In C++, the word "Hello" means something different to "hello" but this is something you will learn more about later on in the book. For now, let's get straight on with the programming.

Before we go into too much detail, let's get you started in writing simple code. This is a typical example for all types of computer programming tutorials, so, without further ado, let's break it down. First of all, the code is written as such:

```
#include <iostream>
 using namespace std;

int main ( )
{
        count << "Hello, World!";
        return 0;
}
```

Line 1 is telling your computer that you want to link iostream library to your program. The library is a repository where little bits of code are stored, along with variables and operators on occasion. The iostream library has code in it that lets us move characters to a text stream, which then appears on the screen.

Line 2 tells the computer that we want to use the standard namespace – this is where your code will be stored, useful if you write two bits of code with the same name, Line 4 is the start of the code. Everything that goes inside the braces is what the compiler reads and translates – this line must go in every single program you write; otherwise, nothing is going to happen.

The next stage is the printing of the program, which, in this case, is "Hello, World!" This is where we use some of the code stored in iostream – a piece of code called cout. The << that comes after the code is an operator, and this one translates to "output" which means we are telling the computer to send the code to a specified stream. The printing "Hello, World!" is called a string, which is nothing more than a character sequence enclosed in double quotations. Notice that the line ends with a semicolon – this is telling the computer that the code is finished, and if it is not used, the program cannot be compiled.

Line 8 is always placed at the end of main, and it is to inform the computer that the block is completed.

Now that you have the source code for the program, it has to be compiled using your compiler. More detail later, first, I want to start going over what makes up your code. The next chapter details all that you will need to learn to become a successful C++ programmer.

Structure of the C++ program

As we have already discussed, a computer program is nothing but a set of instructions in a sequence that tell the CPU what to do.

Statements and expressions

In C++, the statement is nothing but the smallest and an independent unit in the program. It is also the most common form of instruction in a programming language. In C++, statements are a way to convey your instructions to the compilers to carry out a specific task. We use ';' to terminate a statement. In C++, there are many kinds of statements, and some of the most common types of statements are given below.

int x;

x = 5;

std::cout << x;

We will discuss the functions of the above statements in the later chapters.

Functions

Functions are nothing but statements in a sequence, which are executed in sequential order. There is a function called the main function, and it is a must in every C++ program. When any given C++ program is run, the execution of the program starts within the main function. Functions have very specific jobs to perform. And they can perform only those jobs. For you to become a good C++ programmer, you need to know how to use functions efficiently. In the next chapter, you'll learn more about functions.

Libraries and the C++ standard library

Libraries are nothing but a collection of code, which is pre-compiled. They can be used within different programs. If you wish to extend the capabilities of your program, you can add libraries.

The core C++ language is minimalistic and straightforward, but it also comes with a built-in library called the C++ standard library. The C++ standard library provides the user with additional functionalities.

Syntax and syntax errors

We all know that in any language, sentences are constructed following the grammatical rules of that particular language. Take the example of the English language where you normally end of sentences in a period. All the rules, which govern the construction of sentences in a language, is called syntax. Similarly, C++ also has syntax. Not following the syntax will simply leave your code invalid. It is the responsibility of the compiler to see that the basic syntax of the C++ language is followed. If you violate the basic syntax, the compiler will compile the code and will complain about the syntax violation. That issue is called a syntax error. The C++ compilers only compile the program if there are no syntax errors found. It will display all the errors that are found and suggest for you to make them valid so that it could execute the code without any errors.

Compiling your first program

There are two important things that you should know before you can go to your first program.

Your programs will be written in the .cpp files, which will be added to your project later. Projects are also called as workspaces or solutions. The code files and the IDE settings will be saved to your project.

You should start a new project by creating one as there are many kinds of projects. Before starting, you need to specify the type of project you wish to work on. What makes the C++ code?

A variable is something that stores a value. It's like a box, each box has a name and category on it, and the category is the type of item stored in it – the name is the specific variable. Each variable has a specific type, name, and size, and these govern exactly what can be stored inside of it.

Line 7 is called an assignment. This assigns a value to the variable, and the = is the operator – this is what does the assigning. The value after the = is called a binary operator.

Note that there are no quotation marks around the cout statement this time. This is because, rather than displaying the string, we are outputting the value. Compiling the program now would print "42" on the screen.

As well as having a type a variable can also have a prefix added to the declaration and these changes how the variable behaves. Some will change the size of the variable while others let you use or block you from using negative numbers, while others do a completely different job. Almost all of them will be talked about here.

Size Changers

Two specific prefixes change the byte size of the variable – short and long. The idea behind this is to allow the variable to store more vales and bigger numbers. How big depends on the architecture of the computer that you are using:

On a 32-bit computer int and long int are both 4 bytes
On a 64-bit computer int is 4 bytes and long int is 8 bytes

On both architectures, short int is 2 bytes

There is nothing that dictates the size of the modifier for those particular keywords, except:

Short must be equal to or smaller than a normal variable

The normal variable must, in turn, be equal to or smaller than a long.

The only variable that can take a prefix is int

Even more confusing, you can omit int and just use long or short, for example:

short int s = 0;

int i = 0;

long int l = 0;

short s2 = 0;

long l2 = 0;

Sign Changers

Two other prefixes can restrict the values that are stored by a type – signed and unsigned. A signed variable can store negative and positive values, while an unsigned variable can only take positives.

Other Prefixes

There are some other prefixes that you can use in C++, not so common, and most of which we are not going to use and will not cover in this book. There are two very useful ones, though – const and static. The former is constant, never changing their value, and the latter keeps the value of the variable the same but only in between function calls; that's a topic for later on.

At the Core of The Language: Understanding C++

Computers run virtually everything around us today; at the core of computer or your preferred cellphone brand, are programs. For our learning process, I assume you are aware of what a computer program is and structures behind it. At the core of all programs is a computing language. This question then comes up. What exactly is C++?

C++ (pronunciation see plus plus) is at its core a general all-purpose programming language. What makes the language different is the fact that it integrates crucial object-oriented coupled with generic programming in addition to providing low-level memory management.

The language and its design have a bias towards systems programming, for example, embedded systems, and operating system kernels just to point out a few.

The language is a favorite of many programmers due to its performance, flexibility, and efficiency. The language has effective uses in many contexts such as servers, e.g., Web search SQL and e-commerce, desktop applications, performance-critical applications such as space probe and telephone switches, and more than anything else, entertainment software, which is where your favorite video game falls.

The language is termed as a compiled language with its implementations available on many platforms across the globe and in use in many multinationals such as Intel, FSF, Microsoft, and LLVM just to point out a few.

If you search the ISO (International Organization for Standardization), you will learn that C++ is standardized. ISO approved and published the current version of C++ in September of 2011 as ISO/IEC 14882:2011, which is informally known as C++11. C++ first was standardized in 1998 as ISO/IEC 14882:1198, then amended to C++03, and then again in 2003 as ISO/IEC 14882:2003. The above information though useful holds no importance to you.

What is more important is the current standard C++11, which supersedes all the others because of the integration of new features and a bigger standard library.

Everything related to computers, and in fact, everything else in the world has an origin. C++ is the brainchild of Bjarne Stroustrup at bell labs as early as 1979 (C). Every great innovation has a cause or purpose. Bjarne wanted a more flexible and efficient language such as C but also a language that provided higher-level features of organizing programs.

Here is a kicker; remember when I said that learning C++ would prepare you to learn other languages? Here is why. C++ has influenced many languages, including Java C#, and all later versions of C developed after 1998.

Before closing this first chapter, I should perhaps mention that C is the precursor to C++, and therefore, working with C++ will demand some knowledge of the latter.

Getting Started-Working with C++ For the First Time

While studying and learning C++ is exciting, there are some prerequisites before we embark on writing code. Before you can undertake any programming, you need an Integrated Development Environment (IDE). An IDE is a compiler that translates your code into a bunch of ones and zeroes that are the language or code your machine can comprehend.

If you do not already have a compiler installed, you can download a bunch of free and paid compilers.

Installing an IDE

An IDE forms a very central part of your programming. Therefore, there is some importance in us looking at some of the more fundamental aspects of an IDE, especially installation. As I have mentioned, you can use a bunch of IDE's. Most developers struggle with the question of which one, which IDE best suits me. Here is the thing, though; you can install multiple IDE on your system, so there is no one correct or wrong IDE. The most common and integrated compilers are Code::Blocks and Microsoft's Visual C++ 2005 Express Edition. Therefore, I can recommend you install either one of them, but if you have a compiler that you deem friendlier, better, or superior to these two, do not feel restricted by my choice; indulge yourself.

If you are programming on Windows, i.e., a Windows machine, chances are, the best option for you is Microsoft's Visual C++ 2010 Express edition that is downloadable from Microsoft's website. Perhaps it is also well to point out that the file you download from the website is simply a downloader; the actual IDE download commences when you run the downloader.

However, if you are working in an environment that has limited internet connectivity, and would like the download file for later use, with a little help from Google or your favorite search engine, you can find an offline installer.

P.s. I do not recommend downloading files from third parties

It is also important to note that most of the functions of C and C++ we shall look at are contained in the documentation file that comes with the installation of MSDN express. However, if you do not install MSDN on your drive, Visual C++ will use an online version available here. Depending on your internet bandwidth, the files may take some time to download, and once the download and installer are done, Windows will prompt for a reboot, so reboot the system.

You will probably notice a lag in your computer response time, a sort of "hang"; you should not be alarmed, or force shutdown since the lag is because your system is installing all the resources required to run the environment. Also, once your system boots up and opens the Windows desktop, you may find it necessary to rerun the installer similarly to the installation bit we just completed.

However, this time, the installer will not download the files; it will simply install the program.

On the other hand, you may be developing on Windows but are writing programs for porting with the Linux kernel or vice versa; in this case, your best option is to use Code::Blocks, the open-source, cross-platform free IDE that will run on both Windows and Linux.

Nevertheless, there is a key point to note for Windows users. If you intend to write C++ code on Windows using Code::Blocks, you should make a point of downloading the MinGW bundled version. If Code::Blocks does not tickle your fancy, you can also use Bloodshed's Dev-C++, which is also cross-platform, i.e., runs on Windows and Linux.

So far, we have covered almost all the other platforms except Mac OSX. If you are an OSX user, you can use Xcode or Eclipse. C++ on Eclipse is not automatically set; it will require downloading and installing optional C++ components.

The IDE installation part of programming is probably the hardest part of any programming tutorial. Now that we have completed that part, you are ready to begin coding your first program.

Your First C++ Program

Welcome to the most exciting part, perhaps the part that made you pick up this book, writing programs using C++. Like most computer language tutorials, our first focus will be to create a hello world program.

While the "Hello world" code may sound like a cliché, in our program creation, it is the best illustration of "spinal code" of virtually any and every program you shall create way after I am through teaching you my bit. Regardless of the complexity or simplicity of your program or code, it must have a few basic lines of code.

```
#include<iostream>
using namespace std;
```

The above code is what we refer to as a pre-processor directive. If you look at the code, you will notice that there is an 'i' and 'o' 'iostream'; they stand for input and output, respectively, and are an absolute requirement in any program you create using the C++. On the other hand, 'namespace std' informs the compiler that you intend to use the standard library. If you fail to use the code line to specify this, you will limit yourself and not be able to use cin, cout, or endl, which we shall look at in a little while.

```
int main ()
{
```

On the other hand, the code above indicates where our main program begins, which is where most of the coding happens. If you are wondering, the int means integer. An integer is what will pass back to the program.

It is also important to note that you should not overlook the parenthesis (); they are important even if they are empty. In the same breath, you should also not overlook the curly brace {, because it is necessary. Now that we have understood that, using the console out, let us print something to the screen.

```
cout<<"Awesome! My first program in C++ "<<endl;
return 0;
}
```

I do not know if you are familiar with the C language, but the cout in the code above is the printf statement. The code (cout) prints to the screen anything, text, or otherwise, that is within the quotation's marks. On the other hand, endl indicates the end of the line (it is similar to pressing the enter button while working on a word document file). The semicolon is also required, so do not forget it. In the code above, return 0 acts as the integer that returns to the int main. Not to sound like a broken record, do not forget to end in with the curly bracket because they signify the end of the main.

In the above code, here is how our main program code would appear.

```
#include <iostream>
using namespace std;

int main()
{
cout<<"Awesome! My first program in C++"<<endl;
return 0;
}
```

This may come as a surprise to you but, if you have followed everything we have done so far, you have just created your first program.

SURPRISE! The code we just used and created is the basic structure of all programs; think of it like learning the alphabet in kindergarten. You should make every effort to understand and memorize it. Secondly, you should remember in which order to use cout and endl. Do not forget to declare using namespace std; otherwise, the compiler will return an error.

However, there is a workaround. If you do not use namespace to declare, then you must use **std::** to declare each cout, cin, and endl.

Here is an example of what I mean by this. For clarity, we shall highlight the difference in the program in blue.

```cpp
#include <iostream>

int main()


std::cout<<"Awesome! My first program in C++"<<std::endl;
return 0;
}
```

If you are not very conversant with programming in general or C++, you will realize that cout, cin, and endl will come up a lot in your coding. Opting to use the method I have just described will be tedious. Therefore, you should opt to instruct the compiler by using the namespace std to make your work faster.

Chapter 2

Declaring constants

C++ Constants

Constants are fixed values that programs may not be allowed to alter, and they are referred to as literals. A constant can belong to any of the available basic data types. Note that are just regular variables with the difference being that the values of constants cannot be changed after definition.

To define a constant using the **#define preprocessor**, we use the syntax given below:

#define identifier value

The identifier is the name of the constant while the value denotes the value assigned to the constant. The following program describes how this can be done:

#include <iostream> **using namespace std**;

#define WIDTH 7

#define LENGTH 11.

int main() {

int rectangle_area;

rectangle_area = LENGTH * WIDTH; cout <<"The area of the rectangle is "<<rectangle_ area;
return 0; }

In the above example, we have defined two constants, namely WIDTH, and LENGTH. We have assigned values of 7 and 11 to these, respectively. We have also defined the variable rectangle_area and assigned it the value of the product of the two constants. We have then printed out the value of this variable.

When executed, the code should return the following as the output:

The area of the rectangle is 77

Using the const Keyword

We can also define a constant by use of the const keyword. To do this, we have to use the syntax given below:

const data_type variable = value;

Note that we have to define the data type of the constant. The value of the constant this time has been assigned using the assignment $(=)$ operator. Let us give an example demonstrating this:.

```cpp
#include <iostream> using namespace std;

int main() {

const int LENGTH = 7; const int WIDTH = 11; int rectangle_area;

 rectangle_area = LENGTH * WIDTH; cout <<"The area of the rectangle is "<< rectangle_
area; return 0; }
```

We have just created the same example, but this time, the constants have been defined using the const keyword.

When executed, the code should return the following result:

The area of the rectangle is 77

Note that programmatically, it is always good to name constants in the upper case.

Working With C++ Data Types

Now that we have created your very first program, there is something else of equal importance, if not greater, than spending every waking hour writing code; documentation.

Every program needs documentation, if not to help other programmers understand your program, to help you understand your program, years after writing it. That may sound like revealing your magic "code writing skill" but in the programming world, you are never a success until other programmers pay you accolades. When using the C++ language, you can add documentation in the form of notes to your program by using two slashes "//"the compiler will ignore anything you write between these two slashes on the same line.

Throughout your coding life and work, I would recommend you to document your work as often as possible. Additionally, you will also notice that most of the notes you write will have a different color from the code. If your compiler does not do this automatically, you should do it manually to avoid confusion.

Here is another fun fact you are probably not aware of; almost every program uses variables. Too "mathematical" for you? A variable in programming is the same as a variable in math, a letter used to hold a value. In programming, you use variables to hold different data types that you must declare before you run the program.

Therefore, to fix this, you must assign x value in the following manner:

x=12;

If we use this example in our program, each time we use the variable x, it will be similar to using the number 12 unless we specify otherwise. With this, when you want to print something to the screen, here is how you do it.

Note: in this case, we are printing x to the screen.

cout<<x;

If you have prior experience with the C language, it will not pass you that this is different. For one, there is no printf, and secondly, there is no place holder. This should not be cause for alarm. In the code above, the 'c' in cout is a placeholder for "console" and therefore, cout means console out. Let us assume a scenario whereby you do not want to assign a variable to your program but would like the program to assign a variable value while it is running. While this may sound very mathematical and complicated, you can easily achieve this by using cin, which, as you may have guessed, stands for the console in.

int x;
cin>>x; //Ask the user to input a value for x

As a programmer, you have to be very keen. Look at the code above and tell me if you notice anything different from what we have learned so far. Did you notice anything? The arrows in the above code are pointing in the opposite direction from when you use cout. In the above, we did not assign a value to the integer called x. This is because the program will prompt the user for a number value that will then be stored as the value for variable x. Here is how our program should now look like.

#include <iostream>

using namespace std;

int main ()
{

```
int x
cout<<"Please enter an integer"<<endl;
cin>>x;//the user will enter a value that will be stored in 'x'
cout<<"Your number is ";
cout<<x;//the program will print the value of 'x' to the screen
return 0;
}
```

The program above first declares an integer, integer 'X', then it asks you to enter a value that once entered, displays on the screen. In an instance where you or someone else wants to manipulate the variable either through multiplication or through division, you, the programmer, would have to declare some more variables and coin some form of expression. Let us add some code to the program above.

```
#include <iostream>

using namespace std;

int main ()
{
int x,y,z
cout<<"Please enter an integer"<<endl;
cin>>x;
cout<<"Please enter an integer"<<endl;
cin>>y;
z=x/y;//the value of 'z' equals 'x' divided by 'y'
cout<<"Your number is ";
cout<<z;
return 0;
}
```

In the above, the program declares three integers and equals variable 'Z' to the division of 'X' and 'Y'. When the program user assigns a value to X and Y, the program then displays the division held in variable 'Z'. While the above code may work ok, there are flaws bound to arise from Z being equal to the division of X and y. In the above instance, if the user assigns 4 as X and 2 as Y, that would not present a problem because 4 is divisible by 2. However, what would happen if the values were 6 and 4? Leaving the program code in its current state would prompt a 0 answer mainly because so far and as of right now, X, Y, and Z only hold integer numbers without decimals. In the above example of the user assigning 6 and 4, it is evident that they are not divisible, and subdivision will place a decimal. So, how do we fix this? The answer to this is relatively simple; rather than declaring Z, which is an integer that cannot hold values with decimals, we can declare it as a double. I would be tempted to say that double data types are superior to integers in the sense that double data types are capable of holding decimal numbers. Here is how our program would look like.

```cpp
#include <iostream>

using namespace std;

int main ()
{
int x,y;
double z;
cout<<"Please enter an integer"<<endl;
cin>>x;
cout<<"Please enter an integer"<<endl;
cin>>y;
z=x/y;
cout<<"Your number is ";
cout<<z;
return 0;
}
```

While the program code looks so much better so far, there is also something not entirely correct with it, and if you run the program, you will still not get the right answer. Can you guess why? Because of something called truncation. This might sound complicated but is, in fact, not. In the above program code, X and Y are integers. As we have seen, you cannot get the correct answer if the two integers result in a decimal.

Simply put, this is the meaning of truncation. To fix this, one of the variables has to be double type. Doing this prompts the compiler to recognize this and convert the other integer into a double albeit temporarily. Alternatively, you can simply declare each variable as a double; this is something at your discretion. Here is how the full program code would look.

```cpp
#include <iostream>

using namespace std;

int main ()
{
int x;
double y,z;
cin>>x;
cout<<"Please enter an integer"<<endl;
cin>>y;
z=x/y;
cout<<"Your number is ";
cout<<z;
return 0;
}
```

With everything we have seen so far in our C++ learning experience, you are well on your way to becoming a master coder. Nevertheless, practice is key.

Types of constants in programming

Integer Constants

First thing first, integers are stored in binary formation. You'll code integers as you use them in your daily routine; for example, you will code eight simply as 8.

The following table will show you different integers, their values in programming and their data types

Value in programming	Number	Data Type
98	+98	int
-865	-865	int
-68495L	-68495	long int
984325LU	984325	unsigned long int

Character Constants

Whenever, you'll find an integer, closed between two single apostrophes, this would be character constant. Moreover, there is a chance that you'll find a backslash "\" between those apostrophes.

For most machines, ASCll character set is used, i.e.

ASCII Characters	Symbolic Display
Null character	"\o"
newline	'\n'
horizontal tab	'\t'
alert (bell)	'\a'
backspace	'\b'
form feed	'\f'

vertical tab	'\v'
single-quote	'\"
backslash	'\\'
carriage return	'\r'

Float Constants

Float constants are stored as two parts in memory as float constants are numbers having decimal parts. The first part, they obtain in memory is significant, and the second is the exponent.

Float constant's default type is "double". You must write code to specify your desired data type, i.e., "float" or "long double". We may remember that "f" or "F" is used to represent float, and "l" or "L" is used to represent long double.

In the following table, some of the examples of float, double and long double are shown:

Value in Programming	Number	Data Type
.0	0.00	double
0.	0.00	double
3.0	3.0	double
5.6534	5.6534	double
-3.0f	-3.0	float
5.6534785674L	5.6534785674	long double

Boolean Constants

These constants are predefined keywords, and they cannot be defined or declared by the programmer. It has two predefined constants, "True" and "False". In programming, we represent this kind of constant as "bool".

Programming Constants

In this part, we are going to understand different programming constants and ways to write and define constants in a C++ program. Usually, there are three types of programming constants.

Defined Constants

A way to define a constant in a C++ program is to use a precompiler statement "define". Like every other precompiler directive, it starts with a "#". For example, a traditional precompiler directive for "define" would be: #define TABLE_SIZE 150.

Define directives are usually placed at the beginning of the program so that anyone reading your program can find them easily.

Memory Constants

Another way to code constants is by using a memory constant. These constants use a C++ type qualifier to remember that the specified data cannot be changed.

C++ programming provides us with an ability to define named constants. We just have to add type qualifier in our code, before constant. For example: **Code**.

```
#include <iostream>

using namespace std;

#define val 50

#define floatVal 9.7

#define charVal 'K'

int main()

{

  cout << "Integer Constant in our code: " << val << "\n"; cout << "Floating point Constant in our code: " << floatVal << "\n"; cout << "Character Constant in our code: "<< charVal << "\n"; return 0;

}
```

Output:

In the case of this code, a console screen will pop up with the output:

Integer Constant in our code: 50

Floating-point Constant in our code: 9.7

Character Constant in our code: K

Literal Constants

A literal constant is a constant which is unnamed and used to specify your desired data. As we know, a constant cannot be changed, so we just have to code its data value in a statement.

A literal constant is the most common form of constant. Here is a table to show a different kind of literal constants.

Values	Type
'C'	Character Literal
7	Numeric Literal 7
C + 8	Another Numeric Literal (8)
5.6534	Float Literal
Hello	String Literal

Chapter 3

Functions

You may remember from math class at some point where you had to deal with functions, like $f(x) = 2x + 5$. $f(0)$ would have been 5 $(2(0) = 5)$, $f(1)$ would have been 7 $(2(1) + 5)$, $f(2)$ would have been 9 $(2(2) + 5)$, and so on.

Functions in C++ work similarly.

Functions operate and then often return a value. They don't always have to return a value. However - functions that don't return a value are void functions.
First, take a look at this chunk of code. It doesn't have to make sense right now; we're going to go through it. Create a new project and erase the contents of main.cpp, and type this in.

```cpp
#include <iostream>
using namespace std;

int getArea(int l, int w);

int main()

{

int length, width;

cout << "Enter the length, and then enter the width.\n";

cin >> length >> width;

cout << "The area is: " << getArea(length, width);

return 0;

}
```

```
int getArea(int l, int w) {

 int area = l * w;

 return area;

}
```

So let's break this down line by line.

```
#include <iostream>
```
This includes the essential components for input and output.

```
using namespace std;
```

This denotes that we're using the standard input/output namespace.

```
int getArea(int l, int w);
```

This is where we declare our first function. C++ is procedurally compiled, so you can't just throw functions around willy-nilly. You have to declare them before you write them later, or they have to write entirely before your main function. For the sake of clarity, I prefer the initial declaration and then writing the function after my main function, but it's a personal choice. Regardless, we're creating a function here called "getArea". The int before the name denotes that it's going to return an integer value. Likewise, a float getArea(...) would return a float value, a char getChararacter(...) would return a character, and so on.

Within the declaration, we've given two variables, called arguments. Much like how in f(x) equations, x was the thing that the equation modified, the argument variables are what our C++ reads in and utilizes.

```
int main()
```

```
{
```

This is the start of our main function. In case you haven't figured it out, every program must have a main function. It's the entry point for your code, and the compiler will actively seek it out.
```
int length, width;
```

We declare two variables, length, and width;

```
 cout << "Enter the length, and then enter the width.\n";
```

cin >> length >> width;

We ask the user to input the length and width, and then accept their input.

cout << "The area is: " << getArea(length, width);

This is where a bit of further explanation is needed. The output stream puts out a value we give it, right? Since functions simply return a value, we can put them straight in the output stream.

Also, since this function returns an integer value, you could create a new integer and then assign its value as the value of the function, like this: int area = getArea(length, width);

You could then just output.

cout << "The area is: " << area;

This is a waste, though, because this variable doesn't need to be created for this program. If you do, however, need to store a variable such as the area of a rectangle, you could do exactly that.
return 0;

}
Simple, every main function must return 0.

int getArea (int l, int w) {

This mirrors the function declaration earlier and is where we start writing it.

int area = l * w;

 return area;

We create a new variable called area, which takes the two arguments from the function header and multiplies them to get its value. We then return that same integer.

We also could have simply written this:

return l * w;

Both are valid ways of returning this function and will give you an appropriate result.

That's a cursory introduction to functions. They're a vital way of structuring your program. Programs, where everything is only in one function, are tedious to read and challenging to maintain. Programs, where things are more split up, are easier to understand and manage by far.

Chapter 4

Polymorphism

Polymorphism means to exist in many forms. In programing, polymorphism occurs when we have many classes that are related to each other through inheritance.

In C++, polymorphism means that a call to a function will lead to the execution of a different function depending on the type of object that has invoked the function. Consider the example given below in which we have a base class derived or inherited by two other classes:

```
#include <iostream> using namespace std;

class Figure {

protected: int breadth, length;
public: Figure( int x = 0, int y = 0) {

breadth = x; length = y; }

int area() {

cout << "Area of parent class is :" <<endl; return 0; }

}; class Rectangle: public Figure {

public: Rectangle( int x = 0, int y = 0):Figure(x, y) { }

int area () {

cout << "Area of Rectangle class is :" <<endl; return (breadth * length); }

};
```

```
class Square: public Figure {

public: Square( int x = 0, int y = 0):Figure(x, y) { }

int area () {

cout << "Area of Square class is :" <<endl; return (breadth * length); }

};
```

```
// Main function
int main() {

Figure *figure; Rectangle rec(10,7); Square sq(5,5);

// store address of Rectangle figure = &rec;

// call rectangle area.

figure->area();

// store the address of Square figure = &sq;

// call aquare area.

 figure->area();

return 0; }
```

The code will return the following output:

```
Area of parent class is :
Area of parent class is :
```

The output is incorrect. The reason for this is that the call of area() function has been set only once by the compiler as the version that has been defined in the base class. |This is referred to as static resolution or static linkage of the function call. The function call is fixed before the execution of the program. Sometimes, this is referred to as early binding since our area has been set during the compilation of the program.

Let us make a modification to the code so that the area() function is declared within the Figure class. However, we will declare it with the virtual keyword as shown below:

```cpp
class Figure {

protected: int breadth, length;

public: Figure( int x = 0, int y = 0){

breadth = x; length = y; }

virtual int area() {

  cout << "Area of parent class is :" <<endl; return 0; }

};
```

This means you should now have the following code:

```cpp
#include <iostream> using namespace std;

class Figure {

protected: int breadth, length;

public: Figure( int x = 0, int y = 0){

 breadth = x; length = y; }
virtual int area() {

cout << "Area of parent class is :" <<endl; return 0; }

}; class Rectangle: public Figure {

public: Rectangle( int x = 0, int y = 0):Figure(x, y) { }

int area () {

cout << "Area of Rectangle class is :" <<endl; return (breadth * length); }

};

class Square: public Figure {

public: Square( int x = 0, int y = 0):Figure(x, y) { }

int area () {

cout << "Area of Square class is :" <<endl; return (breadth * length);
```

```
};

// Main function

int main() {

 Figure *figure; Rectangle rec(10,7); Square sq(5,5); // store address of Rectangle
figure = &rec;

// call rectangle area.

 figure->area();

// store the address of Square figure = &sq;

// call aquare area.

 figure->area();

return 0; }
```

The code should now return the following result:

```
Area of Rectangle class is :
Area of Square class is :
```

The compiler has considered the elements of the pointer rather than its type. The objects of rec and sq classes have been stored in the *figure; their respective definition of the area() function has been called.

This shows that each of the derived classes has a different implementation of the function named area(). This is known as polymorphism. You have more than one class with the same function name and the same parameters, but the implementation is different.

Notice that we used the virtual keyword to make the function virtual. When a virtual function is defined in the base class, and another version in the derived class, this will act as a signal to the compiler that a static linkage to the function is not needed. We only need a selection of the function to be called at any point in the program based on the type of object for which the function is being called. This operation is known as late binding or dynamic linkage.

Sometimes, you may need including a virtual function in the base class for it to be redefined in a derived class to suit the class objects, but you have no meaningful definition to give to the function in the base class.

In such a case, our virtual function area() in the base class can be changed to the following:

class Figure {

protected: *int* breadth, length;

public: Figure(*int* x = 0, *int* y = 0) {

 breadth = x; length = y; }

virtual int area() = 0; };

Notice the use of the = 0; in the function. This tells the C++ compiler that the function doesn't have a body. Such a function is known as a pure virtual function.

Object Destruction and Polymorphis

Object destruction is tricky, especially when it comes to the object being destroyed through an interface. You could have code like this, for example:

```
class Drawable

{

public:

virtual void draw () = 0;

};

class MyDrawable : public Drawable

{

public:

virtual void draw ();

MyDrawable ();

~MyDrawable ();

private:

int *mydata;
```

```
};

MyDrawable::MyDrawable ()

{

mydata = new int;

}

MyDrawable::~MyDrawable ()

{

delete mydata;

}

void deleteDrawable (Drawable *drawable)

{

delete drawable;

}

int main ()

{

deleteDrawable( new MyDrawable() );
}
```

What's going on inside deleteDrawable? Remember, when delete gets used, the destructor is called, so the line that reads

delete drawable;

makes a function call on the object. But how does the compiler know where the MyDrawable destructor is? The compiler doesn't know what the exact type of the drawable variable is, but it does know that it's a Drawable, something that has a draw() method. All it knows is how the MyDrawable destructor itself can found the destructor associated Drawable. As MyDrawable allocates memory in its constructor, to free the memory, the MyDrawable destructor must run.

Okay, so you could be thinking that this is what virtual functions are designed to fix. That's correct. What we should be doing is declaring the destructor virtual in Drawable; that way the compiler will know that it has to look for a destructor that has been overridden when delete has been called on a pointer to a Drawable: class Drawable.

{

public:

virtual void draw ();

virtual ~Drawable ();

};
class MyDrawable : public Drawable

{

public:

virtual void draw ();

MyDrawable ();

virtual ~MyDrawable ();

private:

int *mydata;

};

When we make the structure in the superclass virtual, and when delete frees up a Drawable interface, the overridden destructor gets called.

As a rule, when you make any superclass method virtual, the superclass destructor should be made virtual as well. Once one method has been made virtual, you are saying that the class can be passed around to methods that will take an interface. The methods can then do whatever they want, and that includes deleting the object, so making the destructor virtual makes sure that the object is cleaned up properly.

Chapter 5

Operator type and overloading

Operators in C+

C++ provides a rich set of operators that perform a number for different functions on constants and variables.

C++ has mainly following types of operators.

Arithmetic Operators as addition, multiplication, etc.

Relational Operators as less than, greater than, etc.

Logical Operators as AND, OR, etc.

Bitwise Operators

Assignment Operators
Arithmetic Operators

C++ mainly provides 7 arithmetic operators. We will discuss each operator with two variables x and y where x has value as 45 and y has value has 25.

Arithmetic Operator	Meaning	Example
+	Simple mathematical addition of operands	x+y gives 70
-	Simple mathematical subtraction of operands	x-y gives 20
*	Mathematical multiplication of operands	x*y gives 1125

/	Mathematical division of operands	x/y gives 1
%	It is a Modulus Operator which provides remainder after integer division	x%y gives 20
++	Named as Increment operator and increases the value of operand by 1	x++ gives 46
--	Named as Decrement operator and decreases the value of operand by 1	x - - gives 44

Relational Operators

C++ mainly provides 7 Relational operators. These operators provide a resultant value as TRUE or FALSE and generally used in condition checks. We will understand the meaning of each operator with two variables x and y where x has value as 45 and y has value has 25.

Relational Operator	Meaning	Example
==	Equality operator used to check whether two operands are equal or not. Will result as TRUE if they are equal otherwise false	(x == y) is FALSE.
!=	Inequality operator used to check whether two operands are unequal or not. Will result as TRUE if they are unequal otherwise false	(x != y) is TRUE.
>	Greater than operator and check if left operands is greater than right or not. If left is greater, returns TRUE otherwise FALSE	(x > y) is TRUE.
<	Less than operator and check if left operands is lesser than right or not. If left is lesser, returns TRUE oth-erwise FALSE	(x < y) is FALSE.
>=	Greater than or equal to operator and check if left operands is greater than or equal to right operand or not. If left is greater or equal , returns TRUE otherwise FALSE	(x >= y) is TRUE.
<=	Less than or equal to operator and check if left operands is lesser than or equal to right operand or not. If left is lesser or equal, returns TRUE otherwise FALSE	(x <= y) is FALSE

Logical Operators

C++ supports the following 3 logical operators, which we will explain using two variables x and y where x having value as 0 and y having value as 1.

Logical Operator	Meaning	Example
||	Logical OR Operator. Returns TRUE if at least one operand is non-zero	(x || y) returns TRUE
&&	Logical AND Operator. Returns TRUE if both operands are non-zero	(x && y) returns TRUE
!	Logical NOT Operator and reverse the logical value for its operand. If operand is zero makes that one as non-zero and operand is non-zero makes that as zero.	!(x && y) returns TRUE

Bitwise Operators

Bitwise operators perform their functionality bit by bit. Bitwise AND operator performs AND operator on every two corresponding bits of two operands and Bitwise OR performs OR operator on every two corresponding bits of two operands

x	y	x | y	x & y	x ^ y
1	1	1	1	0
0	0	0	0	0
1	0	1	0	1
0	1	1	0	1

Assume if x = 13; and y = 60;

x = 0000 1101

y = 0011 1100

x|y = 0011 1101

x&y = 0000 1100

Table showing bitwise operator with p= 60 and q = 13

Bitwise Operator	Meaning	Example
|	Bitwise OR Operator, gives 1 if any bit 1	(p | q) gives 0011 1101 which is 61
&	Bitwise AND, gives 1 if both bits are 1	(p & q) gives 0000 1100 which is 12
^	Bitwise XOR Operator, gives 1 on-ly when exactly one bit is 1	(p ^ q) gives 0011 0001 which is 49
~	Bitwise Ones Complement, change the logical value for bit.	(~p) gives 1100 0011 which repre-sents -61
>>	Bitwise Right Shift Operator which moves the left operand's value to-wards right by the bits specified which is a right operand	p >> 2 gives 0000 1111 which rep-resents 15
<<	Bitwise Left Shift Operator which moves the left operand's value to-wards left by the bits specified which is a right operand.	p << 2 gives 1111 0000 which rep-resents 240

Assignment Operators

Assignment Operator	Meaning	Example
=	Known as assignment operator which assigns the value of right hand side expression to left oper-and	p = q + r assigns value for q+r in-to p
-=	Involves first in subtraction then assignment	p -= q is similar to p = p – q
+=	Involves first in addition then as-signment	P+= q is same as p = p + q
/=	Firstly division is performed and after that assignment	p /= q is same as C = C / A
*=	Firstly multiplication is performed on the given operands and after that assignment	p *= q is same as p = p * q
%=	Firstly modulus is performed on the given operands and after that assignment	p %= q is same as p = p % q

>>=	Firstly Right Shift Operation is performed and after that assign-ment	p >>= 3 is same as p= p >> 3
<<=	Firstly Left Shift Operation is performed and after that assignment	p <<=3 is same as p = p<< 3
&=	Firstly Bitwise AND is performed on the given operands and after that assignment	p &= 3 is same as p = p & 3
^=	Firstly Bitwise Exclusive OR is performed on the given operands and after that assignment	p ^= 3 is same as p = p ^ 3
|=	Firstly Bitwise Inclusive OR is performed on the given operands and after that assignment	p |= 3 is same as p = p | 3

Operators Precedence and Associativity

Every operator has precedence and associativity associated with it. Precedence of operators is used in determining the sequence of operators for evaluating an expression in case expression has several operators. In an expression, the operators having higher precedence are evaluated first.

Associativity is the concept for determining the evaluation order of operators when there are multiple operators with the same precedence, then associative determines either to be evaluated from left to right or right to left.

Category	Operator	Associativity
Postfix Operator	[] () -> - - ++.	Left to right
Unary Operator	+ ! ~ - - ++ (type)* sizeof &	Right to left
Multiplicative **Operator**	* % /	Left to right
Additive **Operator**	- +	Left to right
Shift Operator	>> <<	Left to right
Relational **Operator**	< > <= >=	Left to right
Equality **Operator**	!= ==	Left to right
Bitwise AND **Operator**	&	Left to right
Bitwise XOR **Operator**	^	Left to right
Bitwise OR **Operator**	|	Left to right
Logical AND **Operator**	&&	Left to right
Logical OR **Operator**	||	Left to right
Conditional **Operator**	?:	Right to left

Assignment **Operator**	+= = -= /= *= %= <<= >>= &= |= ^=	Right to left
Comma **Operator**	,	Left to right

Overloading

In C++, we can specify more than one definition for a function or operator within the same scope. These are processes known as function overloading and operator overloading, respectively.

An overloaded declaration is done within the same scope as the previous declaration, but both definitions have different arguments and a different implementation/definition.

After calling an overloaded function or operator, the compiler will determine the most appropriate definition to use by comparing the types of arguments that you have used to call the function or operator with the types of parameters that have been specified in the definition. The process of determining the most appropriate definition to use is referred to as overload resolution.

Operators Overloading

C++ allows you to redefine or overload the majority of its in-built operators. This means that programmers can use operators with user-defined types.

Overloaded operators are simple functions with special names, that is, the operator keyword and then symbol of the operator that is under the definition. Just like a function definition, an overloaded operator will have a return type and a list of parameters. The definition of an overloaded operator is demonstrated below:

Rectangle operator+(**const** Rectangle&);

In the example given below, we are demonstrating the process of operator overloading by the use of a member function. We will pass an object as an argument, and the properties of the object will be accessed using the object. The object that will call the operator will be accessible by use of this operator as demonstrated below:

#include <iostream> using namespace std;

class Rectangle {

public: *double* getArea(*void*) {

return length * breadth; }

void setLength(*double* len) {

length = len; }

void setBreadth(*double* bre) {

breadth = bre; }

// Overload the + operator to add two Rectangle objects.

Rectangle operator+(const Rectangle& r) {

Rectangle rect; rect.length = this->length + r.length; rect.breadth = this->breadth + r.breadth; return rect; }

private: *double* **length**; // Length of a rectangle *double* **breadth**; // Breadth of a rectangle };

// Main function

int main() {

Rectangle Rectangle1; // Declare Rectangle1 of type Rectangle **Rectangle Rectangle2**; // Declare Rectangle2 of type Rectangle **Rectangle Rectangle3**; // Declare Rectangle3 of type Rectangle *double area* = 0.0; // Store the area of a Rectangle here

// Rectangle 1 specification **Rectangle1.setLength**(6.0); **Rectangle1. setBreadth**(7.0);

// Rectangle 2 specification **Rectangle2.setLength**(12.0); **Rectangle2. setBreadth**(13.0);
// area of Rectangle 1

area = Rectangle1.getArea(); cout << "Area of Rectangle1 : " << area <<endl;

// area of Rectangle 2

area = Rectangle2.getArea(); cout << "Area of Rectangle2 : " << area <<endl;

// **Adding two objects**: Rectangle3 = Rectangle1 + Rectangle2;

// area of rectangle 3

area = Rectangle3.getArea(); cout << "Area of Rectangle3 : " << area <<endl;

return 0; }

When executed, the code will return the following:

```
Area of Rectangle1 : 42
Area of Rectangle2 : 156
Area of Rectangle3 : 360
```

Consider the following section extracted from the above code:

Rectangle operator+(const Rectangle& r) {

 Rectangle rect; rect.length = this->length + r.length; rect.breadth = this->breadth + r.breadth; return rect; }

This is where the mechanism of operator overloading has been implemented. We have overloaded the + operator so that it adds the measurements of two rectangle objects. Here is another line extracted from the code:

Rectangle3 = Rectangle1 + Rectangle2;

In the above line, Rectangle1 will be added to Rectangle2. This means that the length of Rectangle1 will be added to the length of Rectangle2 to get the length of Rectangle3 while the breadth of Rectangle1 will be added to the breadth of Rectangle2 to get the breadth of Rectangle3. These two will then be multiplied to give the area of Rectangle3.

The meaning of + operator has been overloaded!

Chapter 6

Macros and template

Introduction to Templates

Templates are an important feature in C++ programming language, as it allows functions and classes to use generic types. They play an essential role in how functions and classes work by allowing them to define different data types without rewriting each other.

Using templates, you can write a generic code that can be used with any data type. All you need is to pass the data types as parameters. Templates promote code reusability and improve the flexibility of the program. You can create a simple class or a function and pass data types as parameters and implement the code to be used by any data type. Whenever you want to use the function, you make a call to the function and specify the return type.

For example, if you use **sort()** function to sort data in a warehouse, you can pass different data types as parameters to the function. You don't have to write and maintain multiple file codes to sort data. Based on the data type passed to the sorting algorithm, your data in the warehouse is sorted irrespective of that particular data type. Therefore, templates are used in situations where you need a code to be reusable with more than one data type.

Templates are of great importance when dealing with multiple inheritance and operator overloading. It is widely applied where code reusability is of prime importance.

Types of Templates

Templates are implemented in two ways:

- Using function templates

- Using class templates

A template can be defined as a macro. That is when you define an object of a specific type, the template definition of that type of class substitutes it with the appropriate data type. Templates are often referred to as parameterized class or functions since a specified data type will replace the defined parameter during execution time.

Class Templates

Class templates offer the specifications for creating a class based on the parameters. A class template accepts members with parameter type. That is, you can instantiate a class template by passing a given set of data type to its parameter list. Class templates are mostly used in implementing containers.

Syntax

Template <class identifier>

Class class-name

{

...

//class member specifications

...

};

Example:

Template <class M>
Class vector
{
        M*v,//type M vector
        int size, sum;

        public:
        vector (int n)
        {
        v=new M [size = n];
        for(int j=0; j<size; j++) v[j]= 0;
        }

        vector (M*a)
        {
        for(int j=0; j<size; j++)
        v[j]= a[j];
        }

        M operator* (vector & y)
        {

```
    M sum=0;
    for(int j=0; j<size; j++)
    sum+=->v[j]*y-v[j];
    return sum;
    }
};
```

A class template definition is similar to normal class definition except that in templates, you add a prefix template **<class M>** where M is the type. The template prefix tells the compiler that a class template is declared, which uses M as the type name in the declaration. In this case, the class vector is a parameterized class that uses type M as its arguments. Type M can be replaced by any data type or by using a user-defined data type.

If a class is derived from a class template, then it's called a **template class**. The objects of the template class are defined as follows: Classname<type> objectname (arglist);

Creating a derived class from class template is known as **instantiation process**. Before creating a template class, you have to debug the class template before converting it to a template class. The compiler checks for errors in a template class after instantiation has taken place.

Example: class template

template <Class TT>

Class Rectangle

{

TT width;

TT height;

public:

void setvalues(TT num1,TT num2)

TT area()

{
TT A;

A=width*height;

return A.

```
}

};

void Rectangle <TT> ::setvalues (TT num1,TT num2)

{

width=num1;

height=num2;

}

int main()

{

Rectangle obj1;

Rectangle <int> obj1(5,6);

Rectangle obj2;

Rectangle <float> obj2(5.6,4);
cout<< obj1.setvalues()

cout<<obj2.setvalues()

return 0;

}

//output

obj1=30

obj2=22.4
```

The above program creates a class of type TT. The <TT> in the (void Rectangle <TT> ::setvalues (TT num1,TT num2)) statement specifies that the function parameter is also a class template parameter and should always be included when calling a class.

Class Templates with Multiple Parameters

You can also have more than one generic data type in a class. You can declare the generic type class with a comma-separated list inside the template specification.

Syntax

Template <Class xy, Class xyz, ...>

Class class-name
{

//function body;

};

Example: class with two generic types

template<class f1,class f2>

class numbers

{

f1 j; f2 k;

public:

numbers (f1 x, f2 y)

{ j=x; k=y;

}

void print()

{

cout<<j<<"and"<<k<<"\n";

}

};

int main()

{

Numbers <float, int> numbers1 (2.53, 253);

Numbers <int, char> numbers2 (50,'Z');

numbers1.print();

numbers2.print();

return 0;

};

// output

1.53 and 253

50 and Z

Function Templates

Function templates work like a normal function except that the normal function works with only a single data type, while templates accommodate multiple data types. With templates, you can overload a normal function to work with different data types.

This makes function templates more useful since you only have to write a single program that works on all data types.

Templates are always expanded during compile time.

Just like a class template, you can create a function template with different argument types.

Syntax

Template <class type>

Return-type function-name (arguments)

{

Function body;

};

When defining function templates, you must include the template type in both the function body and parameter list when necessary.

Example1: Function to swap values

Template <Class T1>

```
Void swap (T1&num1, T1&num2)
{T1 val= num1; num1=num2; num2=val;};
```

Calling a template function works the same way as the normal function call.

Example 2: Implementation of function template

```
template <class test>

test max (test x, test y);

{

 test results;

 results=x>y? x:y;

 return results;

};

int main()

{

 int a=5, b=6, c;

 double l=4, m=6, n;

 c= max <int> (a,b);
 n=max <double> (l,m);

 cout<< c<<endl;

 cout<<n<<endl;

 return 0;

}
```

In this example, the test is the template parameter. The function max is called twice with different argument types (int and double). When the compiler instantiates, it calls the function each time by its type.

The output object produced (after instantiation of the template with specific type) will be of the same type with the parameters x and y.

The above program will sort values based on which is higher. If using an array of numbers, the sorting algorithm will be applied to sort the numbers from the smallest to highest.

Function Template with Multiple Parameters
Just like in class templates, you can have more than one generic data type separated by commas.

template<class T1, **class** T2,....>
returntype functionname(arguments of types T1,T2,...)
{
....
....
....
}

Example: Temple class with multiple parameters

template<class Temp1,class Temp2>

void display(Temp1 j, Temp2 k)

{

cout<<j<<" "<<k<<"\n";

}

int main()

{

j=display1(2019, "EDGE");

K=display2(18.54, "1854);

return 0;

}
// output

2019 EDGE

18.54 1854

Overloading Template Functions

You can overload a template function using its template function or using the ordinary function from its name. Overloading can be done through:

Calling an ordinary function that matches the template function.

Calling a template function that is built with the exact function.

Use normal overloading function on an ordinary function and make a function call to the one that matches the template function.

If there is no match found, an error message is generated by the system.

Example: Overloaded template using an explicit function

```
template <class M>

 void display(M n)

{

cout<<"Display template function:" << n<< "\n";

}

void display ( int n)

{

cout<<"Explicit template display: "<< n<<"\n";

}

int main()

{

 display (80); display (15.20);

 return 0;

}
```

//output

Explicit template display: 80 Display template function: 15.20

The function call display (80) calls the ordinary version of a display () function and not its template version.

Member Function Templates

When creating class templates, all member functions can be defined outside the class since the member functions in a template class are parameterized using type argument. Therefore, the function template should define the member functions.

Member functions (whether inline or non-inline) declared inside a class template are implicitly a function template. If a template class is declared, it inherits all the template functions defined in a class template.

Member function templates are defined in three ways:

Explicit definition in a file scope for each return-type used to instantiate a template class.

During file scope within the template parameters.

Inclined within the class.

A member function template can instantiate functions not explicitly generated. If a class has both a member function and an explicit function, then the explicit definition is given more priority.

Syntax

Template<class T>
returntype classname<T> :: functionname(arglist)
{
....
....
....
}

Example: Class vector with a member function template

Template<class T>
class vector
{ T*v;

```
int size; public: vector(int m); vector (T*a);
T operator*(vector & y);
}
//member function templates template<<classT>
vector<T> :: vector (int m);
{
v=new T[size=m]; for(int i=0; i<size : i++) v[i]=0;
}


template<class T>
vector <T>::vector(t*a)
{
for(int i=0; i<size ; i++)
v[i]=a [i];
}
template< class T >
T vector < T > :: operator*(vector & y)
{
T sum=0;
for (int i=0; i<size ; i++)
sum += this -> v [i]+y.v[i];
return sum;
}
```

Non-type Template Arguments

Templates can have single or multiple type arguments. You can also use a non-type argument template in addition to the type T argument. You can create a template argument using strings, constants, built-in types, and function names.

```
Template<class T, int size>Class array
{
T a [size];                    //automatic array initialization
//..........
//..........
};
```

The above template passes the size of an array as an argument. The compiler will only know the size of the array during the execution time. The arguments are specified during the creation of template class.

Template Classes

While template classes tend to be limited to library writers who want classes such as map and vector, everyday programmers can also benefit from being able to make their code more generic. You shouldn't use a template just because you can; instead, you should be looking for opportunities to get rid of classes that only differ by the type.

Yes, you are likely to find yourself writing more template methods than classes, but you still need to have some idea of how to use them, especially if you have a data structure of your own that you want to implement.

Declaring a template class isn't very different from a template function. Let's say that we want to build a small class that will wrap an array:

template <typename T> class ArrayWrapper

{

private:

T *pmem;

};

As with the template function, we begin with the declaration that a template is being introduced. We use the template keyword, and then the template parameters are added. We only have one parameter here, T.

Type T can be used whenever we want the type that would be specified by a user, just like with the template functions. When a function is defined for a template class, the template syntax also has to be used. So let's add a constructor called ArrayWrapper to our class:
template <typename T> class ArrayWrapper

{

public:

ArrayWrapper (int size);

private:

T *pmem;

};

// so that the constructor can be defined outside the class, we start by

// indicating that the function is a template

template <typename T>

ArrayWrapper<T>::ArrayWrapper (int size)

: pmem(new T[size])

{ }

We start with the basic template introduction and redeclare the parameter for the template. The difference is, the class name now has the ArrayWrapper template in it, which tells everyone that this belongs to a template class and isn't a template function on a standard class called ArrayWrapper.

In this implementation, the template parameter can be used to stand in for the provided type, just as with the template functions. However, the function caller will never need to provide the parameter—it gets taken from the first template type declaration. For example, instead of writing vec.size<int>()

or

vec<int>.size();

to get the size of a vector of integers, all you need to write is

vec.size().

Templates and Header Files

Up to now, the templates we have looked at have been directly written into .cpp files. What if we wanted to place our template declaration into the header file? Could we? The problem here is that code that makes use of template classes or template functions needs to be able to access the whole template definition for every single function call to the template as well as to every member function that is called on template classes.

This is not the same way that a standard function works; these only require the caller to know about the declaration. If, for example, you placed the Calc class inside its header file, you would also need to add the full constructor definition along with the add() method instead of putting them all into one .cpp file as you would normally. If you didn't do this, you would not be able to use Calc.

This is a rather unfortunate thing about templates, and it's all about how templates have been compiled. Most of the time, when the compiler parses them the first time, it pretty much ignores templates. It's only when a template is used that has a concrete type attached that the compiler generates the code for that type. To do that, the template has to be available to the compiler so the code can be generated. A result of this is that all template code has to be included in all of the files that will use that template. And, when a file that has a template is compiled, you may not learn of any syntax errors in that template until the template is used for the first time.

The easiest thing to do, when creating template classes, is to place all template definitions into the header file. It's also helpful if you use an extension other than .h, just to indicate that the file is a template—.hxx, for example.

Analyzing Template Error Messages

If there is one significant downside to using templates, it's that many compilers will throw out error messages that are not easy to understand when a template is misused, whether you write it or not. You could end up with pages of error messages just for one mistake.

Template error messages are not easy to read simply because the template parameters are expanded to their fullest, even those that you don't normally use, such as the default parameters.

There is a similar constraint on the second parameter for the vector template— this one requires a type that has support for more functionality than the humble basic integer gives us. The errors are all complaining about the multitude of ways that int just isn't a valid type for the parameter.

Finding the code line where the error is will always be the first step to working out where it all went wrong. More often than not, and even more so as you gain experience and confidence, a simple look at your code will tell you what the error is. If it isn't that obvious, you just keep going through the instantiation list until the proper error message appears: "error: int is not a class, struct or union type." The compiler expected a structure or a class, not any of the built-in types such as int. A vector should hold any type, so the error lies in the parameter given to the vector.

You should make sure you know how a vector is declared and that it only needs one template parameter.

Now that the problem has been found, we can fix it and then recompile the code. Sometimes you will be able to work out and fix a few errors at the same time, but where templates are concerned, the first error is usually the root of the problem for all others. Fix things one at a time, and you will find that any other errors fix themselves.

In our final example above, all those error messages resulted from one simple mistake: giving a second template parameter of an int.

Chapter 7

Classes

Introduction to Classes

At the heart of all object-oriented programming lies the notion of classes, objects that you create, and utilize throughout your code. This helps with modularity, with ease of use, with efficiency, and with higher-level programming that is far more logical and coherent.

In the early iterations of C, there was a primitive sort of class called a struct. Structs still exist in C++ but are mainly deprecated and shirked in favor of using classes instead. Nevertheless, structs are important to cover. C++ structs are also different from C structs. C structs didn't have much of the functionality which C++ structs do.

Before we jump into that, let's talk briefly about the notion of access modifiers.
We've talked about things like int, string, bool, and float called types. We created what could be considered somewhat of a type using enumerators. However, you can create an entire type that is made up of smaller pieces of data and innate functions. This is called an object.

Access modifiers describe what can change what within your code. There are three different access modifiers.

Public access means that the object and/or its internal data and functions can be accessed and modified by any other code in the program.

Protected means that the object and/or its internal data and functions can be access and modified by only its derivatives. (This will make sense when we get into inheritance and polymorphism.)

Private means that only the object itself can access and modify its data.

This is important for purposes of security, clarity, and code safety.

Structs and classes are both ways to create new objects. The primary difference between structs is that structs are public by default, and classes are private by default. Other than that, the differences are very negligible.

However, in the tech industry, structs have a fair bit of a negative connotation. Developers tend to see them as unprotected objects with limited functionality, while they tend to see classes as very functional objects with child classes that are well made and well structured. As such, it's generally better to create classes unless your object has very little in the way of functionality and simply contains very little data and innate function.

Look at this struct and declaration.

```
struct animal {

enum diet { herbivore, omnivore, carnivore };

int legs;

string name;

diet naturalDiet;

};

int main() {

animal dog;

dog.legs = 4;

dog.name = "Dog";

dog.naturalDiet = dog.carnivore;

}
```
This is the simplest way to declare a new object. You should not declare them within an existent function.

Let's go ahead and replace that struct with a class because we're going to be using classes going forward as they're generally a safer and better option than structs are.

Create a new project in CodeBlocks called "AnimalSimulator". Not the most creative title, but it'll work for what we've got to do. Redact the contents of main.cpp and import iostream and create your main method.

Above the main method, let's declare a class called Animal. You would do that very similar to how you'd declare a struct. For the sake of illustration, make it look like this:

```
class animal {

 string name;

};
```

Then within your main method, declare an instance and set its instance of name to the name of your favorite animal. Afterward, try to build.
You should have gotten an error that said "error: string animal::name is private".
Perfect. This is supposed to happen because now we have to fix this. This is where that whole notion of access description comes in.

Modify your class so that it looks like this:
```
class animal {

 public:

 string name;

}
```

Then try to build. It should work fine this time. That's because we made the string "name" public, which means other methods/functions outside of the class itself can access it.

This is generally considered bad practice though, so we're going to rewrite the class like so:

```
class animal {

 private:

 string name;

}
```

The best-practice way to modify values within a class is to use get/set methods. Here's the way the class would look if you implemented get/set methods.

```
class animal {

 private:

 string name;

 public:
```

```
string getName() {

return this->name;

}

void setName(string name) {

this->name = name;

}

}
```

Now, in your main method, after declaring whatever animal it is, instead of directly modifying its name, you should instead use the get/set method like so (assuming your instance animal is called "dog"):
dog.setName("dog");

Then you can test this by printing out the name in your main method:

cout << "The name of my favorite animal is: " << dog.getName() << "\n";
The way these works is by returning or setting the value of the variable via a method from within the class. "this->" is called the this pointer, and it refers to the variable of a given instance of a class. Every object has access to its variables and can modify them directly via the 'this pointer'.

Anyway, your code should work stunningly. But what if you don't want to go through get/set for every instance of every class? Well, you use what's called an initializer function.

Modify your class so it looks like this:

```
class animal {

private:

string name;

public:

animal(string name) {

this->name = name;

}
```

```
string getName() {

return this->name;

}

void setName(string name) {
this->name = name;

}

}
```

Now, in your main function, take out the chunk of code that says animal x followed by the x.setName("name") function. When you create an initializer function, you can set certain variables from the get-go.

For example, since your initializer function takes the argument of name, you can declare that when you declare the variable and circumvent the whole setName operation. Look at this code for an example:

```
animal dog("dog");

animal elephant("elephant");

animal bird("bird");
```

These are all separate instances of the class animal, and their names have been set without the use of a set function thanks to the function initializer.

This can take as many arguments as you'd like it to. This makes it incredibly easy to create new objects and pretty streamlined of a process too.

Now that we've spoken for a moment about declaring objects and things of that nature let's talk more about the specifics of what you can do with them. The object animal here, represents, of course, animals. We can give the entire class a set of methods that they can perform.

Let's think for a second about what every animal does. Every animal sleeps, eats, and drinks, right? So it wouldn't be very outlandish to include these within our class so that every member object of the class animal can perform these methods.

Let's say we had two specific kinds of food: meat and plants, both of which also represented by their respective objects.

We could create two different functions for this:

```
void eat(plant p) {
```

```
// code here

}

void eat(meat m) {

// code here

}
```

Even though these share a name, you can call either depending upon the type of object which you put include in the function call, and both will perform their respective code in response to the argument which you included. This is called function overloading. It's an essential technique in object-oriented programming that will help you to create functional and clear sets of code that are easy for people to use and understand. In the next chapter, we're going to start exploring some of the deeper things that you can do with classes, including the inherent qualities which make them both incredibly useful and incredibly practical in object-oriented programming.

Because it's unwieldy to create a large number of types while we're learning about classes in the first place, let's just leave "eat" as a void function that doesn't take arguments. Your code should look like this:

```
class animal {

private:

string name;

public:

animal(string name) {

this->name = name;

}

string getName() {

return this->name;
}

void setName(string name) {
this->name = name;
```

```
}

void eat() {

// eat food

}

}
```

In the next chapter, we're going to cover far more in-depth concepts regarding classes.

Objects and Classes

Classes are the special feature of C++, which casts C++ into Object-Oriented programming. Remember, C++ is not a pure object-oriented language because, in a pure object-oriented, we can perform no functionality without classes, but in C++, it is possible.

Class

It is a user-defined data type having data members and member functions that can only be accessed after an instance is created for that class. In general terms, a class is a blueprint that represents the states and behaviors for class's instances known as objects.

Data members are defined in class definition as variables and member functions as functions.

For example, a Class of humans, all humans can walk, run, eat, and they all have their specific color, weight, age. Here, walk, eat, and run are behaviors for humans and color, age, weight is their characteristics. There are several different human beings in this class, all having different names, but all of them have these characteristics and behavior.

So, the class is a blueprint that declares characteristics as data members and behaviors as member functions, and all the instances known as objects share all these characteristics and behavior.

Important points about classes

A Class name is conventionally started with an uppercase letter.

Class Human

A-Class has data members as variables and member functions as simple functions, and the access scope of these variables and data members is dependent on the access specifiers as Private, Public, or Protected, which we will discuss later.

We can define the member function of a class inside the definition of that class or outside the definition of class.

Class in C++ is similar to structures in C with the only difference that by default, access control for classes is Private while the structure has public.

C++ provides all important features of object-oriented programming as Encapsulation, Abstraction, and Inheritance, etc. with classes.

Each object of a class has its separate copy of data members, and we can create as many numbers of objects for a class as needed.

Objects

Class is just a blueprint. Just with defining a class, no memory is allocated to it. Memory is allocated only after objects are created for that class. These Objects are instances having the data variables declared in that class and the member functions of that classwork on these instances.

Objects are initialized with special Constructors – special methods which we will study later. Destructors are other special functions that destroy the object when it goes out of scope.

class Mobiles {

int Price;

void Calling (){}

Void Messaging (){}

};

void main(){

Mobiles m1; // an object created for class mobiles }

Constructors

Constructors are special functions similar to class member functions and having an important task of object initialization. As an object is created, Compiler makes a call to the Constructor. The constructor initializes the created object by initializing its members after the storage is provided to that particular object. There is at least one constructor for a class. If there is no explicitly defined constructor in a class, a by default constructor with no parameter comes into existence.

class Test

{

Char c;

public:

Test(); // A Constructor

};

class Test

{

int a;

public:

Test(); //declaration for constructor
Test::Test() // defining Constructor

{

a=1;
}

};

Destructors

Destructors are the special class functions having a special responsibility of destroying the object as that object goes out of its scope. Compiler automatically calls the constructor as an object goes out of the scope.

Destructor has the same syntax as that of constructor with a single difference that tilde sign symbol as ~ is used or destructor declaration. Also a destructor has no argument.

class Test

{

public:

~Test(); // Destructor for class Test

};

Example for demonstration of calling of constructors and destructors

class Test {

```
Test()

}

cout << "A Constructor has been called"; }

~Test()

{

cout << "A Destructor has been called"; }

};

int main()

{

Test test1; // Constructor is called

int a=18;

if(a)

{

Test test2; // again Constructor is Called }// obj2 is out of scope and Destructor is Called
for that obj2

} // Destructor is called for the object obj1
```

The Life Cycle of a Class

When creating classes, you want them to be as easy as possible to use. There are a couple of basic operations that any class will likely need to provide support for:

- It needs to initialize itself

- It needs to clean up memory and/or other resources

- It needs to copy itself

All of these are very important for the creation of good data types. We'll use the string to demonstrate this. Strings must be able to initialize themselves, even if they're empty. They should need to rely on external code for that. Once the string is declared, it's immediately available for use. When you're finished with the string, it must be able to clean up because all strings allocate memory. When the string class is used, there is no need for another method to be called for that; the string does it automatically.

Lastly, it must be able to copy from one variable to another, the same way that integers can be copied between variables. Put together, all of this functionality should be made a part of all classes so that they can easily be used.

We'll take these three features, one at a time, and look at how easy C++ makes all of this.

Object Construction

You might have spotted that we didn't have any code for initializing the board in our ChessBoard interface, which was the public section of the code. We can fix that now.

When a class variable is declared, the variable needs to be able to be initialized:

ChessBoard board;

When an object is declared, the code that runs it is called the constructor, and this should set the object up so that it needs no more initialization. Constructors can take arguments too—you saw this with the vector declaration of a particular size: vector<int> v(10);

The vector constructor is called with a value of 10; the new vector is initialized by the constructor so that it can hold 10 integers immediately.

Creating a constructor is nothing more than declaring a function with the same name as the class, with no arguments and no return value. You don't even give it a void value; no type is provided for the return value: enum ChessPiece { EMPTY_SQUARE, WHITE_ PAWN /* and others */ };

enum PlayerColor { PC_WHITE, PC_BLACK };

class ChessBoard

{

public:

ChessBoard (); // <-- no return value at all!

PlayerColor getMove ();

ChessPiece getPiece (int x, int y);

void makeMove (int from_x, int from_y, int to_x, int to_y);

private:

```
ChessPiece _board[ 8 ][ 8 ];

PlayerColor whosemove;

};

ChessBoard::ChessBoard () // <-- no return value

{

whosemove = PC_WHITE;

// empty the entire board to start with and then add in the pieces

for ( int i = 0; i < 8; i++ )

{
for (int j = 0; j < 8; j++ )

{

board[ i ][ j ] = EMPTYSQUARE;

}

}

// other code needed for board initialization

}
```

I won't keep showing you the method declarations, but I will continue to show you the class declaration, so that you can see how it all fits together.

Now, note that the constructor above is in the public part of the class. If we didn't make the ChessBoard constructor public, we couldn't create any object instances. Why not? Because, whenever an object is created, the constructor has to be called; if we make it private, it can't be called from outside the class. Objects can only be initialized by calling the constructor and, if you make it private, you won't be able to declare the object.

The constructor gets called on the same line the object is created on:

```
ChessBoard board; // calls ChessBoard constructor
```

Or when memory is allocated:

```
ChessBoard *board = new board; // this calls the ChessBoard constructor as part of the
```

memory allocation

When multiple objects are declared:

ChessBoard a;
ChessBoard b;

Constructors are always run in the order of object declaration—a and then b. As with a normal function, constructors can take one or more arguments, and several constructors can be overloaded by the type of argument if there is a different way of initializing the object. For example, a second constructor could be created for ChessBoard to take the board size: Class ChessBoard

{

ChessBoard ();

ChessBoard (int board_size);

};

The function definition is the same as any class method:

ChessBoard::ChessBoard (int size)

{
// ... code
}

The argument is passed to the constructor like this:

ChessBoard board(8); // 8 is an argument to the ChessBoard constructor

When you use the new keyword, passing an argument looks like you're calling the constructor directly:

ChessBoard *p_board = new ChessBoard(8);

A note on the syntax: although parentheses are used for passing arguments, you can't use them to declare objects that have no-argument constructors.

You can't do this:

ChessBoard board();

The correct form is:

ChessBoard board;

However, you can use parentheses when the new keyword is used:

ChessBoard *board = new board();

This is one of the unfortunate little foibles of C++ parsing because the details are kept very obscure. Just don't use parentheses when you declare objects with a no-argument constructor.

So, what happens if a constructor isn't declared?

If a constructor isn't declared, C++ creates one. It won't take arguments or initialize ints, chars, or any other primitive type, but it will initialize every class field by calling the default constructor for each one.

Generally, you should create constructors just to make sure everything gets properly initialized. As soon as the call constructor is declared, C++ won't generate the default for you. The compiler assumes that you know exactly what you're doing and that you're going to create the constructor you need. In particular, if you create constructors that take arguments, the code no longer has the default constructor unless you declare one specifically.

This can have unexpected consequences. If the automatically generated constructor is used and then you add a non-default one that takes arguments, the code that depends on the automatic constructor won't compile. It's up to you to provide a default constructor because the compiler won't do it for you.

Initialization List and Const Fields

If the class fields are declared as consts, the file has to be initialized in the list:

class ConstHolder

{

public:

ConstHolder (int val);

private:

const int _val;

};
ConstHolder::ConstHolder ()

: _val(val)

{}

Const fields can't be initialized by assigning to them because the fields are set and can't be changed. The only place where the class has not been formed fully is in the initialization list, so immutable objects can safely be set. For the same reason, if a field is a reference, it has to be initialized in the list.

Chapter 8

Library

The Standard Template Library

It's good to be able to write your own data structures. However, as you might have picked up, it isn't all that common. But you didn't work through all the previous content for no reason. You've now learned quite a bit about building data structures as necessary, along with some of the more common structures that you might need when writing a data structure.

However, C++ has a cool feature, a huge library of code that can be reused. It's called the Standard Template Library (STL) and contains the most common data structures, including those built on the binary trees and linked lists. These structures let you specify what data type they will store at the time you create them so that they can be used for anything—structured data, strings, ints, and so on.

Because you have this flexibility, the STL will, in many cases, eliminate the need for you to build structures of your own. Using it can raise your code level in these ways:

You can start thinking of your code in terms of the structures required rather than having to think about building and implementing them yourself.

You have free and easy access to the best data structure implementations, with space use and performance optimized for most problems.

You no longer have to concern yourself with the allocation and deallocation of memory for your data structures.

However, as with everything, using the library comes with its trade-offs:

1. You need to learn the STL interfaces and how they should be used.

2. When you get compiler errors from using the STL, they are incredibly difficult to read and understand.

3. You won't find all data structures in the library.

Thoroughly discussing the STL would require an entire book, so I will only give you an overview of the most common data structures that you will use from the STL.

Vectors

Contained in the STL is an array replacement—the vector. This is much like an array but is resizable automatically; you no longer have to worry about allocating memory and moving the other elements around. However, the vector syntax is different from that of a standard array.

The array syntax is:

int an_array[10];

whereas the vector syntax is:

#include <vector>

using namespace std;

vector<int> a_vector(10);

The vector header file must be included along with the namespace std. This is because, like cout and cin, the vector is a part of the standard library.

Furthermore, when a vector is declared, you must provide the data type being stored in the vector. This is done using angled brackets<>:

Vector<int>

This makes use of a C++ feature known as templates. Vector code is written in such a way that any data type can be stored. All you have to do is tell the compiler what type a vector is storing. What this really means is that we have two types here: the data structure type, which dictates the way data is organized, and the data type held in the data structure. Using a template lets you combine different data structure types with different data types within the data structure.

Finally, when the vector size is provided, it must be placed in a set of parentheses, rather than brackets:

vector<int> a_vector(10);

This is the syntax used for the initialization of certain variable types. For this, the value of 10 is passed to the initialization, called the constructor, and that sets the vector with the size ten. As we go through the guide, you will learn about constructors and objects that have constructors.

Once the vector is created, individual elements can be accessed in the same way as an array:

```
for ( int i = 0; i < 10; i++ )

{

a_vector[ i ] = 0;

an_array[ i ] = 0;

}
```

Calling a Method on a Vector

A vector provides you with much more than the functionality for an array. You can do all sorts of things, such as adding elements beyond the vector end. The vector provides functions to help with this sort of thing, but the function syntax isn't the same as the syntax we used before.

A vector uses a C++ feature known as a method. This is a function that you declare with the data type. Calling methods requires new syntax, as in this example:

```
a_vector.size();
```

This is calling a method size on a_vector, and it returns that size. It's much like accessing a structure field but, instead, you're calling a method that goes with the structure. Although something is being done to a_vector by the method, a_vector doesn't need to be passed as an argument to the method. The syntax already knows that a_vector is to be passed as an implicit argument into the size method.

The syntax below

```
<variable>.<function call>( <args> );
```

can be thought of as calling a function that goes with the type for the variable. In other words, it's a bit like writing:

```
<function call>( <variable>, <args> );
```

In the example:

```
a_vector.size();
```

it would be like:

size(a_vector);

Over the next few sections, we will discuss more methods, including ways to declare and use them. For now, it's enough for you to understand that several methods can be called on a vector, using the right syntax. The special method syntax is the only way of making that type of function call. You couldn't, for example, write this: size(

a_vector).

Other Vector Features

A vector also makes it very easy to up the number of items held without needing to allocate memory. For example, adding extra items to the vector would be written like this:

a_vector.push_back(10);

This adds another item of 10 at the end of the vector. The vector will take care of the resizing. If you wanted to do this with an array, the memory would have to be allocated, the values copied over, and the new item added in. While a vector does do memory allocation and copying, it does it intelligently, in a manner in which it doesn't have to resize itself every time a new item is added.

However, although you can use push_back to add items to the end of the vector, using the brackets on their own wouldn't be the same. Brackets let you work only with data that has already been allocated, mainly, so that memory allocation isn't done without you being aware.

So, a code like this:

vector<int> a_vector(10);

a_vector[10] = 10; // the last valid element is 9

wouldn't work and would likely result in the program crashing. Not to mention, it's dangerous. Writing it like this:

vector<int> a_vector(10);

a_vector.push_back(10); // add a new element to the vector

works to resize the vector.

Maps

We mentioned maps a little while ago using a value to look up another value. This is common in programming such as when you want to implement an address book for emails where addresses are looked up by name or a program where you look up an account using an account number or letting user's login to their games.

The STL gives us a map type that lets us specify the key type and value. An example would be a data structure that holds an email address book; this could be implemented as follows:

#include <map>

#include <string>

using namespace std;

map<string, string> name_to_email;

We have to tell the structure that there are two types: string, for the key, and another string for the value, an email address in this case.

One of these maps' helpful features is that when a map is used, the syntax can also be used as an array. If you want to add value, it's much like an array, except the key type is used instead of an integer:

name_to_email["Billy Bunter"] = "billybunter@thisemailaddress.com";

and getting value from a map is much the same:

cout << name_to_email["Billy Bunter"];

You get the simplicity that goes with an array, but with the ability to store whatever type you want. And what's even better is that, unlike the vector, the map size doesn't have to be set before the [] operator is used to add an element.

Removing items from maps is just as easy. Let's say that you fell out with Billy Bunter and want him removed from your address book. You can do that using the erase method:

name_to_email.erase("Billy Bunter");

And you can use the size() method to check what size a map is:

name_to_address.size();

And the empty() method to see if a map is empty:

if (name_to_address.empty())

{

cout << "The address book is empty. I bet you wish you hadn't deleted Billy.";

}

Do not confuse this with how you make a map empty. That's done using the clear() method:

name_to_address.clear();

Because of the consistency in the naming conventions in the STL, the same methods can be used on vectors.

Iterators

As well as data storage and the ability to access elements individually, you can also go through all the items in a data structure. With arrays or vectors, this is just a case of reading each element using the array length. But with maps, because they have both numeric and non-numeric keys, you can't always iterate through using a counter variable.

To get around this, the STL provides us with an iterator, which is a variable that lets you access the elements of a data structure sequentially, even if the data structure doesn't usually have a good way of doing that. We'll start by looking at using iterators with vectors and then move on to using one with the map elements. The idea is that the iterator will store the position in a structure so that you can use that position to access the element. Then you call a method on the iterator to move on to the next element.

Some unusual syntax is required for declaring an iterator. For a vector of integers, it would look like this:

vector<int>::iterator

What this says is that you have the vector and want an iterator that will work for the specific type, which is why we used the ::iterator. Because the iterator marks the position in the structure, the iterator is requested from the data structure: vector vec;

vector<int> vec;

vec.push_back(1);

vec.push_back(2);

vector<int>::iterator itr = vec.begin();

The begin method call will return an iterator that allows you to access the vector's first element.

Iterators can be considered similar to pointers—you speak of element locations in the structure or use it for getting the element. In our case, we read the vector's first element using this syntax:

```
cout << *itr; // print out the vector's first element
```

We use the * operator in the same way we do with a pointer; it makes sense when you consider that both store locations.

If you want the next element, the iterator is incremented:

```
itr++;
```

This lets the iterator know it needs to move on to the next element.

The prefix operator can also be used:

```
++itr;
```

You can see if you have reached the end by making a comparison with the iterator and the end iterator; to do this, call:

```
vec.end();
```

If you want code that will loop over a whole vector, it will look like this:

```
for ( vector<int>::iterator itr = vec.begin(); itr != vec.end(); ++itr )

{

cout << *itr << endl;
}
```

We can loop over a map using a similar approach, but remember that the map doesn't store single values; it stores key/value pairs. When you dereference an iterator, it has two fields—one for key and one for value:

```
int key = itr->first; // get the key from iterator
```

```
int value = itr->second; // get the value from iterator
```

Below is some code that will display a map's content in an easy-to-read format:

```
void displayMap (map<string, string> map_to_print)

{
```

```
for ( map<string, string>::iterator itr = map_to_print.begin(), end =

map_to_print.end();

itr != end;

++itr )

{

cout << itr->first << " --> " << itr->second << endl;

}

}
```

This code is very similar to what is used for iterating over a vector; the only difference is that the map data structure is used along with the first and second fields on the iterator.

Checking a Map for a Value

Sometimes you want to be able to see if a given key has been stored in a map. Let's say you're looking for someone in your address book. You use the find() method to see if the specified value is there and, if it is, retrieve it. An iterator is returned and will either have the object location with the specified key or will be an end iterator if the object wasn't found.

```
map<string, string>::iterator itr = name_to_email.find( "Billy Bunter" );

if ( itr != name_to_email.end() )

{

cout << "How it is to see Billy again. His email is: " << itr->second;

}
```

If you just want to access an element that isn't in the list, use the standard brackets:

```
name_to_email[ "John Doe" ];
```
The map will insert an empty element if the value isn't there already.

Taking Stock

I have only touched on the basics of the STL, but you now have enough information to use some of the foundational types in the library. The vector can be used to replace arrays altogether and, if you don't want to take the time to insert and modify, vectors can also be used in place of linked lists. With the vector type at your fingertips, there are very few reasons why you would want to use an array, and most of those reasons are advanced, such as when you work with the file I/O, which we will discuss at the end of the guide.

The single most useful data type is the map. Using maps makes it easy to write sophisticated programs without having to worry too much about data structure creation. Instead, your attention can be focused on solving problems. In some ways, the map can replace a basic binary tree. Most of the time, you'll want to go into binary tree implementation unless it's for certain performance requirements, or you specifically need a tree structure.
That's where the STL's true power lies: around 80 percent of the time, it gives you the core structures you need, leaving you free to write the code that solves the problems. The rest of the time, you will need the knowledge to build and implement your own data structures.

Some programmers prefer using their code instead of ready-built code. Most of the time, you should NOT use your own data structures; the built-in ones are faster, better, and more complete. However, knowing how to build does give you much better insight into using them.

So, when might you want to use your own structures? Let's say you want a calculator that allows arithmetic expressions to be input by users and then evaluates the inputs with the correct order of operations. An example would be something like 4*9+8/3, evaluated in a way that the division and multiplication are done before the addition.

This kind of structure can easily be thought of in terms of a tree. You could express 4*9+8/3 like this:

+

* /

4 * 8 3

Each node is evaluated in one of two ways:

If the node is a number, the value is returned.

If the node is an operator, the values of the two subtrees are computed, and the operation is performed.

To build a tree like this will require a raw data structure; you can't just use a map. If you only have the STL, you will struggle with this. However, once you understand recursion and binary trees, it becomes a lot easier.

Chapter 9

STL

STL/C++ Standard Library: Containers, Algorithms, Iterators

A common misnomer is to refer to the C++ Standard Library as the STL. The STL, or Standard Template Library, was a standard developed sometime in the past. The C++ Standard Library is a set of templates, many of which were adopted from the STL. The STL is now deprecated, but some extremely useful templates remain.

The Standard Library offers a solution to this problem in the form of containers. Containers manage sets of data of the same type. They include vectors, sets, and lists, among others.

Vectors are much like arrays, except they handle their own storage and size.

Much like with strings, you need to import the vector library in order to use the template:

#include <vector>

Now you're able to access everything regarding vectors.

You declare a template like so:

template<type> variableName;

Let's say we wanted to go back to the earlier example of grades, creating a self-sizing array of grades. We'd declare it like this:

vector<int> grades;

Adding values to a template is simple. You had an element by using the concept of pushing and popping. You push a new value onto the vector, or you pop a value off.

Let's say the first grade you wanted to add was a 55 (poor guy.) We could do this by typing:

grades.push_back(55);

You've now added your first value to the vector.

What if you want to add a set of values? Well, luckily, in C++11, you can also insert a set of vectors in a similar manner to which you initialize a set of values in an array, using the vector.insert() function. This takes two arguments: the index at which you start inserting, and the values you'd like to insert. If you have multiple values in your vector, you can just use vector.end() to find the point of insertion.
grades.insert(grades.end(), { 96, 64, 75, 83 });

In earlier versions, you would need to create a temporary array to insert the data.

int[] tmp = { 96, 64, 75, 83 };

grades.insert(grades.end(), tmp, tmp + 4);

To go through every item in the list, you can use something called a for each loop in other languages. If we wanted to print out every item on the list, we would do the following:

for (int i : grades) {

cout << i << "\n";

}

What if we weren't using a primitive data type but instead an object? There's support for that as well, using something called iterators. By the usage of iterators, you can access methods of the object (such as .length() or .substr() for a string).

If we had a vector of strings, for example, called j and we wanted to print the length of every string therein:

for (string i : j) {

cout << i << " - string length: " << i.length() << "\n"; }

You can do this for any object you create, but we'll talk more explicitly about that when we actually start creating objects in the next chapter.

Another type of container, lists, functions very similarly to vectors. The specific differences between these two are beyond the grasp of a relative beginner. Still, the general rule concerning these two types of containers is that vector is generally the one that should be used unless you have to continually add or erase elements from anywhere other than the end of the container.

There's another type of container called an associative container, which is formatted with a key value and a mapped value. It's generally ordered according to the keys. The most prominent type of associative container is called a map. This is great when you need to associate a set of data with a certain trait. For a real-world example, a store's inventory system could be kept with a map of SKU codes (integers - the key) and item names (strings - the mapped data).

For this, you'd import <map>, and declare a map by:

map<int, string> Inventory;

Inventory[00400030] = "Tamagotchi, blue";

Inventory[00400031] = "Tamagotchi, white";

Inventory[00324359] = "Twilight, DVD";

Inventory[44539294] = "Dark Souls, Xbox 360";
If you wanted to recall a specific element later in your code, you could do something along the lines of:

cout << "Inventory[00400030] is: " << Inventory[00400030] << "\n";

Calling Inventory[00400030] would print out the mapped value, here being "Tamagotchi, blue".

There's another type of associative container called a set. Sets function very similar to maps, except that they don't allow duplicates. Maps allow duplicate values, but not duplicate keys.

Also included in the STL is a library called "algorithms". This library can be used to search, sort, and manipulate element ranges.

Included in these are functions such as equal(), which determines if two sets of elements are equal to each other. There's also transform(), which applies a given function to a given range.

Conclusion

We've come to the end of this book, but this is just the start of a long and fruitful journey for you, a life of programming. With the basics of C++ under your belt, it's time to start your real learning. Start writing those programs! Start implementing data structures and algorithms.

If you enjoyed getting started with C++, there is so much more to learn and do with this wonderful language. Be sure to continue your journey with the second book in the series, which looks at slightly more complex topics while still being beginner-friendly.

C++ programming language is a competitive general-purpose platform which borrows some features of an imperative programming paradigm and can run on any platform. It is referred to as an imperative programming language because it uses step by step processes to achieve its goals. The language uses the concept of object-oriented programming to design and implement complex programs.

The next step is to start writing out some of the different programs and codes that you want with the C++ language.

Even if you are just starting and you just want to spend your time practicing with some of the codes that are in this guidebook, you are still on the right path to seeing some great results with this language.

The more practice you can get along the way with your own coding, the easier it will become to write and create your own codes along the way.

The C++ language is a unique option to work with, one that will help us to create some really powerful and strong codes, and the functionality that is found with this language is unlike any other that we are able to work with.

All of these can be important in some of the codes that you want to write along the way, and when we are done with this guidebook, you should feel ready to handle these and add them to your own codes as well.

As we can see, there is so much that we are able to do when it comes to working with the C++ language.

It is one of the best coding languages out there, whether you are a beginner, or you are someone who has worked with programming and coding for a long time.

When you are ready to start your own coding journey, and you want to be able to create some of your own programs in no time.

C++ programming language utilizes the features of OOP paradigms to develop and execute a program. Some of these features include the use of objects, classes, data abstractions and encapsulation, inheritance, and polymorphism.

The program focuses on the use of data rather than procedures to solve real-world problems. The program tries to eliminate the shortcomings of other conventional programming languages by improving the data security of programs, promoting code reusability, and its ability to use inheritance feature to make an effective program.

Just like many other OOP languages, C++ supports various building blocks. In this tutorial, you have learned how to use various built-in data types when handling simple to complex programs. The data types are divided into primitive data types, derived data types, and abstract data types. You not only learned how to use the primitive or standard data types but also how to declare your own user-defined datatypes.

Enjoy your journey. If you don't have fun while you program, it isn't for you. Make it fun, make it exciting, and make it the reason you want to get up in the mornings.

Good luck with your journey.

C# PROGRAMMING

A complete guide to master C# on your own. Build coding knowledge creating real projects and applications. Transform your passion in a possible job career as a computer programmer.

Michail Kölling

Introduction

Welcome to C# programming and thank you so much for picking up this book!

Whether you are a seasoned programmer or a complete novice, this book is written to help you learn C# programming fast.

By the end of the book, you should have no problem writing your own C# programs. In fact, we will be coding a simple payroll software together as part of the project at the end of the book. Ready to start?

Most people are scared of learning a new coding language. They know that it would open a lot of doors for what they would be able to do with their computers, but they worry that coding itself is too hard for them to learn how to work with. If you do not take the proper time to learn a new programming language, the whole process of programming could be difficult. But when it comes to finding a good language that will help you write almost any code that you would like, then it is time to take a look at the C# programming language. This book will take you through some of the basics that come with using the C# coding language so that you can start using it yourself.

What is special about C#?

The first thing that you might want to look into when it comes to a coding language is to understand why C# is so special and why you would even want to learn how to use this particular programming language.

There are many different coding languages out there to choose from, and they all work differently, but you will find that there are a ton of benefits that come with using the C# program, and we will explore some of them inside this guidebook. Even though you are just a beginner, this is a great coding language to work with and will allow you to design so many programs of your own.

While there are many different options available if you want to get started with coding, none are as great to work with like C#. Some of the benefits of going with C# rather than some of the other programming languages include:

- It can utilize a big library

As a beginner, there are a lot of parts of the code that won't be easy for you to learn. You will learn them as you go, but the library that you can use with C# is a great resource that will be of great help to you. You can place these functions into the code without a lot of hassle being involved. You can even use them to make some changes to the code, so it works the way that you want.

• Automatically disposes of the functions

When you are working with some of the other programming languages, you will have to go through and remove the items that you own. This will take up your time and can be a hassle if you end up missing some of them. Using C# will do all of this work for you to make things faster and easier.

• Easy to learn

C# is widely considered as one of the easiest programming languages you can learn how to work with. While there are a few parts that are more complicated than some other coding languages, this is not a difficult one, and you'll start recognizing different parts of the code pretty quickly as you continue to use it.

• Compatible with Windows computers as well as others

This programming language was originally created to work on Windows computers and help you design a program for them. But it also works well with some other operating systems such as Mac, Linux, and more as long as you download .NET on it. Windows has some great products that are easy to use, especially for beginners, so you will surely get great results once you get started.

• Works with .NET which helps make it easy

This is a program that already comes with the Windows computers, but you can add it to some of the other systems to make C# accessible on these other computers as well.

• Similar to C and C++

This makes it really easy to work with this program and learn the basics before going on to these other programs. Even if you choose to stick with this programming language, you will find that it is powerful enough to do most of the coding that you want and without all the hassle you might experience with some of the other programs.

Ready to dip your toes into the world of C# programming? Let's get started.

Chapter 1

Anatomy of C#

An Introduction to C#

Learning how to code is going to provide you with a ton of benefits along the way. It is going to make it easier to create some of the programs and applications that you would like. It is going to be able to help you further your career with a lot of options that are simple to work with and can allow us to get the best out of these new skills and more money as well. And then there are times when learning how to work with C# is going to be vital because it will allow us to learn more about our computers and how they work.

There are a lot of great options when it is time to work with programming. Many languages have been developed to work on different projects, and sometimes they will work on different types of processes and applications as well. While many of these can be useful based on what you would like to accomplish with the language in the first place, we are going to take a look at how to work with the C# language and how great this one can be for our needs as well. Let's dive into the C# language and how to make this work for our programming needs as well.

The first thing that we need to take a look at here is the C# language. C# is going to be an elegant and object-oriented language that is going to be helpful because it allows programmers to go through and built up a variety of robust and secure applications, all of which are going to run with the .NET Framework. It is possible to work with C# on a variety of projects, including with Windows client applications, Web services, client-server applications, XML database applications, and so much more.

When we are working with the C#, we will find that visually it is going to provide us with an advanced code editor along with some user interface designers that are more convenient to use, a debugger that is integrated, and some other tools that will ensure that it is easier to develop some of our applications based on this language.

The neat thing about the C# language is that it is not only going to be highly expressive and able to help us out with a lot of the more complicated codes that we want to handle, but it is also going to be easy to learn and simple. The curly braces that are part of the syntax of C# are something that is going to look familiar, primarily if you have worked with Java, C++, and C in the past. Developers who are good with these languages will find that it does not take that long to learn C# because of the similarities.

C# is useful because it is going to be able to simplify some of the issues that happen with the C++ language, and it is going to provide us with some powerful features, including value types that can be null, delegates, enumerations, lambda expressions, and direct memory access. None of these are going to be featured available with languages like Java.

In addition to this, you will find that the C# language is going to be able to support some of the generic methods and types, which is going to help us provide increased type safety and performance. It comes with some iterators, which enable the implementers of collection classes to help define custom iteration behaviors that will be easy to use by the client code.

Because this language is going to fit into the category of object-oriented, it is going to be able to support a lot of topics and options that fit into this category, and that we will be able to explore in more detail later on, including polymorphism inheritances, and encapsulation. All methods and variables that we use are going to be encapsulated within these definitions of classes. And a class can inherit directly from one parent class, but it can be set up to implement any number of interfaces.

Methods in this language will be able to override accidental redefinition. When we work with C#, a struct is going to be similar to a lightweight class. This means that it is going to be a stack-allocated type that will be able to come on board and implement interfaces, but it is not going to be able to help us when supporting inheritances.

In addition to some of the basic principles that we just took a look at, you will find that C# is going to make it easier to develop some of the components of software through a few constructs, and these are going to include the following:

It can go through and encapsulate some of our method signatures through the use of delegates. These are going to enable some of the type-safe event notifications that we need.

Properties that are going to be there to work as the accessors for some private member variables.

Attributes, which are going to help provide declarative metadata about some of the different types when the program runs.

LINQ, which is going to stand for a Language Integrated Query. This is useful because it is going to provide us with some built-in query capabilities no matter which sources of data that we are going to work with.

There are a lot of benefits that we can see when it is time to work with the C# language and make it work for some of our needs. It is an object-oriented language that makes it easier to organize and keep things together, and when we can utilize the right IDE, and the .NET platform that we will talk about in a moment, we will be able to utilize it to make the robust programs that we want, without all the complexities of the missing features that happen with other similar languages.

The C# IDE

Before we can get into details about how we can code, and what all we can do with the C# language, we need to get a better idea of what an IDE is about, and why this is such an important part of any coding that we want to do. To start, an IDE is going to be an integrated Development Environment, which is an application we can use to help with application development. In general, this is going to be a GUI or graphical user interface that is designed to make it easier for any developer to build software applications. Many times, these are going to have more of the tools that you need.

Most of the common features, such as data structure browsing, version control, and even debugging, are going to be there to help the developer execute actions without needing to switch back and forth between the different applications that they are working with. This makes it easier to maximize the productivity because we can provide similar user interfaces for the components that are related, and it is going to reduce the amount of time that it takes to learn a new language. Also, depending on the kind of IDE that you choose to go with, it can sometimes just support one language, and other times it will support many languages.

The concept that is behind the IDE is something that evolved from some simple command-based software, which at the time was not as useful as the menu-driven software. Some of the modern IDE's are going to be used more in the context of our visual programming, while the applications in these are going to be created quickly and efficiently by moving the code nodes or the building blocks of programming that will generate the flowchart and structured diagrams. These can then be either compiled or interpreted based on what you hope to get out of the process.

It is important that we take the time to pick out a good IDE, and there are several factors that we need to consider as we work through this. For example, we need to spend time looking at the language support, operating system needs, and some of the costs. Sometimes the IDE that we want to work with will be free, but sometimes these are going to have limited features. It often depends on what you would like to design with that language, and what features are important to your coding needs.

There are several good IDE's out there that are available with the C# language. It is important to do some research and learn more about how these work, and which ones are going to have the features that you would like to get the best results. When you can do this, it is infinitely easier to get the codes written that you would like.

How to Work with C# On Linux and Mac Computers

While C# is considered a Windows language, we can go through and work with it on a Linux and Mac computer as well. We may need to go through a few extra steps, and sometimes a few of the functionalities that we are used to seeing with Windows will be gone, but there are still a lot of benefits that we will see with using this option on other operating systems.

For the Linux system, the MonoDevelop IDE, which is part of the Mono Project, should be just what you need to develop some C# coding on a Linux computer. The easiest way for you to install this is to work with the MonoDevelop package that was developed to work with Ubuntu. Sometimes it is recommended to work with the WinForms toolkit, but this one is not going to be as efficient and easy to work with.

We can also set this language up to work on a Mac computer. The first step is to download an IDE, and Visual Studio Code is usually the best one here because it does work well with Mac and still provides you with the functionality that you need while the simplicity of use is still there. Just visit the Visual Studio website, and then make sure to click on the button to download to Mac. This should download what you need in a zip file.

Once you have been able to get this setup, you can unzip the file and then drag it over to the Applications folder. You should be able to download it from there. The next step is to go through and download the C# extension. You can go into Visual Studio Code and open up the Extensions that you need to make this work.

Now, as you are going through this process, you are going to notice that there is a search bar at the top of the extensions view. This is where you are going to type in "C#". The one that you need is going to be by Microsoft, so make sure to click on this one. Click to install, and you are ready to go.

Remember though this process that the C# language is one that has been developed to work the best with a Windows system. So, if you are on a Windows system, you are more likely to find this language easy to use, and all of the features and functionalities that you are looking for in coding are more likely to be where you put them.

This does not mean that you are not able to get this to work on your Mac computer at all. It merely means that you need to take a few extra steps to get this setup, and it may not be as easy to accomplish some of the things that you would like. Taking some time to get familiar with the C# language on a Linux or Mac computer will be important to helping you get the best results in the process.

How to Get a C# Compiler

There are several compiler options for C# to make the learning easy and smooth for the beginners; in this book, we will use the C# 4.0 version that comes with Visual Studio 2010. Still, it is also possible to use a later or older version. Most of the examples should be able to be compiled and run without any problem.

In case we cannot get the professional version of Visual Studio 2019, a better option is the Community version formerly known as the Express version. This version is free and can be downloaded directly from the Internet; all you need to do is go through a small survey.

To download the C # Visual Studio compiler (Community Version) completely free, you can access the Microsoft portal *here*.

Once we have downloaded the compiler, we can proceed to carry out the installation; this task is very similar to installing any other Windows program, but do not forget to register it within 30 days.

The Development Environment

Once the installation is finished, we can start the program by selecting it from the Windows Start menu. You will see a window that shows the user interface of the application.

The interface is divided into two parts: on the left, we have the search bar named **Open recent,** where we can find links to our most recent projects or solutions by entering keywords. And on the right side of the home page, we will see the options of **Create a new project, open a local folder, Open a project or solution**, and access to code repositories titled *Clone or check out code.* We can also receive announcements and news about software development using C # in this same part of the interface, but as we move through different pages, we will have the editing zones. These editing areas will allow us to edit the program code, edit the user interface, icons, and other resources.

Editing the program code is a very simple activity that should not make us worry if we know how to use any type of text editors such as Microsoft Word or Windows Notepad, and then we can edit the program code. The other editors are also quite user-friendly, but we will not need them to perform the examples shown in this book.

On the right side, we have a window that is known as Solution Explorer, in this same area other windows will appear that give us information about the project we are developing. We will see the details shown by some of these windows a little later in this book.

At the bottom, we find another window; in this area, there are usually the sections that the compiler will use to communicate with us. For example, we will see the window that indicates the errors that our program has; at the top of the window, we will see the menus and the toolbars.

If, for any reason, we close the source code editor or it does not appear in our user interface, the easiest way to find it is through the Solution Explorer. Simply go to the document that represents your source code and double click on it, the window with the source code editor will appear.

How to Create Our First Application

To become more familiar with C# Visual Studio Express, it is best to create the first project and work on it. We will generate a small program that sends us a message in the console, and then we will add other elements so that we can explore the different windows of the user interface.

There are mainly two ways to create a new project in Visual Studio 2019. The first one is merely clicking on Create a New Project from the bottom right part of the main visual studio interface.

Then type console in the search box and choose the Console App (.NET Framework) option and click the Next button as shown below.

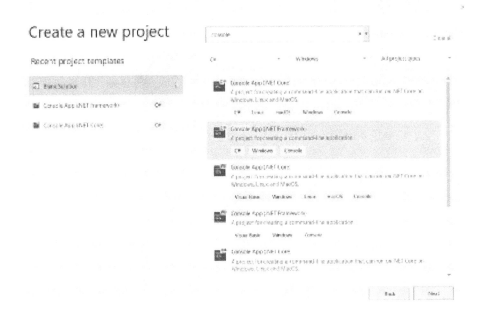

Then configure your new project with its Name and Location, save and hit the create button.

All set, the Visual Studio will instantly create a new project for you.

Alternatively, to create a project, we can select the **File** menu, and after that, we have to click on the option **New Project** as shown in the image below, this way we will see a dialog box that shows some related options.

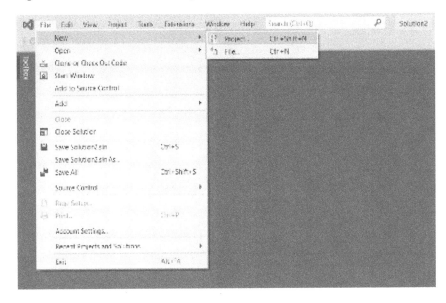

In the right part of the dialog box, the different types of projects that we can create are listed; for this example, we must select the one indicated by the console application and click the next button.

Note: If, for any reason, we close the source code editor or it does not appear in our user interface, the easiest way to find it is through the Solution Explorer. Simply go to the document that represents your source code and double click on it, the window with the source code editor will appear.

On the left side, we will write the name of our project, which in this case, will be MyProject. Each new project we will create will have its name; then, we will simply press the *Create* button.

Configure your new project

In a few seconds, C # Express creates the project for us. Visual Studio and the Community version make use of solutions and projects, a solution can have several projects, and for example, Office has different products such as Word, Excel, and PowerPoint. The office is a solution, and each product is a project. The project can be a stand-alone program or a library and can have one or more documents, and these documents can be the source code and additional resources.

We can see that our user interface has changed a bit, the windows already show us information, and we can also see that the skeleton for our program is shown in the editing area.

The Solution Explorer shows us the information about the solution in a logical way if we observe, it is like a small tree. At the root, we find the solution; each project we have in that solution will be a branch, each project, in turn, will also have its divisions. In our case, we see three elements; two of those elements are folders; in one, we keep the properties of the project, and in the other, the references (during this book, we will not use these folders). The fourth element is a document called Program.cs, this represents the document where we save the source code of our application. We see that the extension of the C# programs is .CS.

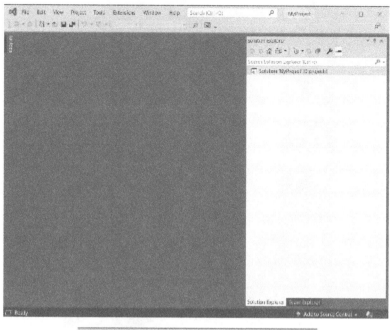

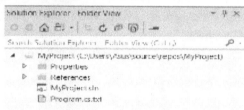

In the editing area, we can see that we have a skeleton so that, from there, we can create our program. To understand what we have, there is necessary to know a concept: namespace. The namespace is a logical grouping; for example, all the code that we can have related to mathematics can be grouped inside the namespace of Math. Another use that namespace has is to solve conflicts with names, for example, let's suppose that we have a massive project and several programmers working on it. Two or more programmers could have created a method that had the same name; this generates a conflict since the program could not know which version to use. The way to solve this is that each programmer has its namespace and refers to the corresponding namespace according to the version we want to use.

The .NET Framework provides us with various namespaces where we have thousands of classes and methods already created for our use. When we want to use the resources found in a namespace programmed by other programmers or by us, we must make use of a C # command known as using.

As we can see at the top of the code, we have several using references to the namespaces that our application needs; if we needed to add more namespaces, we would do it in this section.

Below is defining the proper namespace of our project; this is done as follows:

```
namespace MyProject
{

}
```

The namespace we are creating is called MyProject. As we can see, the namespace uses {} as delimiters; this is known as a code block, and everything that is placed between {} will belong to the namespace. This is where it will be necessary to write the code corresponding to our application.

Inside the code block, we find the declaration of a class, C# is an object-oriented language, and that is why it needs us to declare a class for our application. The class has its block of code, and in our application, it will be called Program. The concept of the class will be covered in Chapter 10 of this book.

All programs need a starting point, a place that indicates where the program execution starts, in C#, as in other languages, the starting point is the Main() function; this function also has its code block. Within this function, we will generally place the main code of our application, although it is possible to have more functions or methods and classes. The parts and characteristics of the functions are seen in Chapter 5 of this book.

Now it is time to create our first application. We are going to modify the function code, as shown below. When we are adding the statement inside Main(), we must notice that it happens immediately after the point is placed.

To Compile the Application

Once we finish writing our program, we can carry out the compilation, as we learned earlier; this will generate the assembly that will then be used by the runtime when executed.

To compile the application, we must select the Build menu and then Build Solution or simply pressing by the F6 button. The compiler will start working, and in the status bar, we will see that our solution has been compiled successfully.

To Run the Application

Once the compilation has been successful, we can run our program and see how it works. For this, we have two options: run with debugging and execute without debugging. In the Express version, only the execution with debugging appears, but we can use the execution without debugging with the keys CTRL+F5 or adding it using the tools menu.

The debugger is a program that helps us correct errors at runtime and also logic errors. Preferably we should use the execution without the debugger and make use of the execution with debugging only when we need it. Now we will run our application; for this, we press the CTRL + F5 keys.

When the program is executed, a window appears, we call it console, and it shows the execution of the program. In this way, we can read the message that we had placed in our example.

Since this is a starter book for programming with C#, so we will run all programs on the console. Once you understand the main concepts, you can learn how to program shapes, forms, and graphical interfaces in C#. This type of programming is not difficult, but it requires basic knowledge of object-oriented programming.

How to Detect Errors in a Program

Sometimes we may miswrite the program; when this happens, the application cannot be compiled or executed; if this happens, we must change what is wrong.

Let's write an error intentionally so that we can see how the compiler behaves.
In the program, we have changed '***Console***' to '***Consoli***' and reordered '***namespace***' '***HelloWorld***,' this will cause an error; now, we can try to compile again and see what happens.

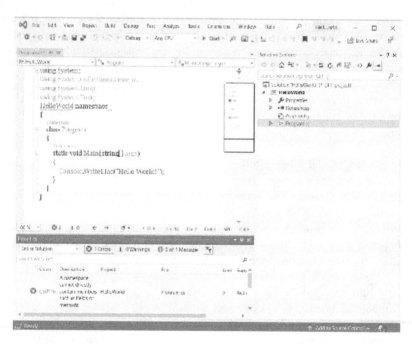

As we already know, the window that appears at the bottom of our user interface is used by the compiler to communicate; we see that a window appears that gives us a list of errors. In the next book, we will learn how to use it; for now, we simply need to know that it is always necessary to solve the first problem in the list and that we can go directly to the error by double-clicking on it.

The Class View

Now we are going to check the class view. In this view, we can get information about the solution we are creating, but unlike Solution Explorer, the information is arranged logically.

With this view, we can quickly find the namespaces of our solution and within them the classes they contain; if we wish, we can see the methods that are in each class. This view not only allows us to observe the logical information but also gives us the possibility to quickly navigate in our code.

In the Community version, there is no previously configured option, so it is necessary to add the command to the View menu.

To show the class view, we must go to the View menu and then select Class View or merely pressing **Ctrl + W, C** a window will appear in our user interface.

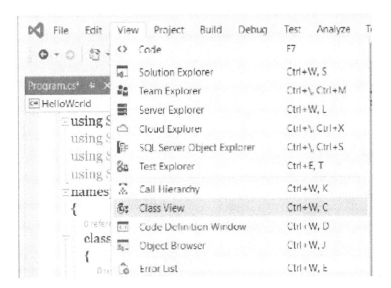

The class view window is divided into two sections; the upper section shows the logical and hierarchical relationship of the elements while the lower section shows the methods that make up a particular class.

At the root of the tree, we find the project; it will contain the necessary references and the namespaces of HelloWorld. If we had more namespaces, they would appear there, when opening the HelloWorld namespace, we find the classes that are unclaimed within it. In this case, we only have the Program class; if we select it, we will see that at the bottom, the elements that are declared inside are shown. In our example, we have the Main () method.

If, at this time, we double click on any of the methods, we will automatically go to the code where it is defined. Because our program is very small, we may not see the advantage of this, but in programs with thousands of lines of code, being able to navigate quickly is a great advantage.

Configuring Compiler Menus

To add the options we need in the menus, we must follow a series of very simple steps. First, go to the *Tools* menu and select the *Customize* option.
A dialog box appears, in which we must select Commands; in this section, we can choose the menu to which we want to add a command, for example, the View menu.

The current menu commands are listed, we click on the area where we want the new command to be inserted and press the Add Command button. With this, a new dialog box appears that shows all the possible commands that we can add classified.

In the categories we select View, and in the Class, View commands, this command is the one that allows us to have the class view. The Start Without Debugging command is in the Debug category.

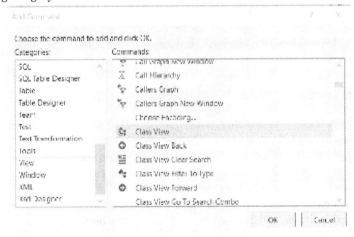

Up to this point, we have analyzed the most important basic concepts needed to understand the operation of .NET. From the next chapter, we will begin with our learning of programming and the C# language.

Main functions of C#

C# is a new object-oriented programming language, which enables programmers to write various applications based on Microsoft .NET platform quickly. Microsoft .NET provides a series of tools and services to maximize the development and utilization of computing and communication fields. It is precise because of the excellent object-oriented design of C# that it is an ideal choice for building various components-whether it is a high-level business object or a system-level application.

The functions of C# are mainly manifested in the following aspects:

- Designing Windows applications.
- Customize the Windows control library.
- Design console application.
- Design smart device applications.
- Design ASP.NET Web application.
- Design ASP.NET Web Service.
- Design ASP.NET Mobile Web Application.
- Customize the Web control library.

ASP.NET is the control and markup developed based on C#. In the field of intermediate language, C# is the most affinity language, which has the main characteristics of C language and Java language, powerful function library, and convenient template, and is one of the ideal languages at present.

Main features of C#

C# language almost combines the advantages of current high-level languages and has the following main features.

Concise grammar

C# language, like Java language, uses unified operators, eliminates complex expressions and pseudo-keywords in C++ language, and makes it described in the simplest and most common form.

Excellent object-oriented design

C# language is designed according to the idea of object-oriented, so it has all the characteristics that object-oriented should have, namely encapsulation, inheritance, and polymorphism.

C# language only allows single inheritance, that is, a class does not have multiple base classes, thus avoiding the confusion of type definition. In C# language, each type is an object, so there are no concepts such as global function, global variable, and global constant. All constants, variables, attributes, methods, indexes, events, etc. must be encapsulated in classes, which makes the code more readable and reduces the possibility of naming conflicts.

Close integration with the Web

In C#, complex Web programming and other network programming are more like operating local objects, thus simplifying large-scale and in-depth distributed development. Components built-in C# language can serve the Web conveniently and can be called by any language running on any operating system through the Internet.

Complete security and error handling

Language security and error handling ability is an important basis to measure whether a language is excellent or not.C# language can eliminate many common mistakes in software development and provide complete safety performance, including type safety. By default, the codes downloaded from the Internet and Intranet are not allowed to access any local files, and resources.C# language does not allow uninitialized variables and provides functions such as convenient check and overflow check. The garbage collection mechanism in memory management greatly reduces the burden of memory management for developers.

Version processing technology

C# language has built-in version control functions, such as handling function overloads and excuses, and feature support, etc., to ensure convenient development and upgrade of complex software.

Flexibility and compatibility

In the managed state, C# language can't use a pointer but uses Delegate to simulate the function of a pointer. If you need to use pointers in classes or methods of classes, you only need to declare these contents unsafe. Also, although the C# language does not support multiple inheritances of classes, it can be realized by inheriting interfaces.

Compatibility means that C# language allows interoperation with API with C/C++ language style that needs to pass pointer type parameters and allows interoperation between C# language components and other language components.

Better correspondence between business process and software implementation

If an enterprise's business plan is to be put into practice, a close correspondence must be established between the abstract business process and the actual software implementation. It is difficult to do this in most languages.

C# language allows type-defined, extended metadata. These metadata can be applied to any object. Project builders can define domain-specific attributes and apply them to any language element, such as classes and interfaces.

In a word, C# is a modern object-oriented language, which enables programmers to create solutions based on Microsoft .NET platform quickly and conveniently. This framework enables C# components to be easily transformed into XML network services so that applications of any platform can call it through the Internet.C# enhances the efficiency of developers. At the same time, it is committed to eliminating errors in programming that may lead to severe results. C# enables C/C++ programmers to develop the network quickly while maintaining the strength and flexibility that developers need.

With this, we have completed a brief introduction to the importance and applications of C# with varied examples. In the next chapter of this book, we will talk about the C# development environment that is essential for developing a well-versed C# desktop window application. Follow along to know more about it.

Chapter 2

Data Type

Data Types

In the C programming language, data types allude to a framework utilized for pronouncing variables or functions of distinctive data types. The type of a variable decides the amount of space it will take and how the bit pattern saved in it is utilized. The fundamental classification used for data types is given below.

- Basic Types: They are number-crunching sorts and comprises of the two following types: (a) integer sorts and (b) floating-point sorts.

- Enumerated sorts: They are again number sorts and are utilized to characterize variables that must be allocated discrete number values all through the system.

- Void type: The keyword void demonstrates that no value can be assigned.

- Derived sorts: They incorporate (a) Array, (b) Pointer, (c) Union, (d) Structure and (e) Function.

The array and structure data types are also referred to as aggregate types. The type of function defines the kind of value the function will return upon termination. We will discuss the essential data types in the accompanying segments.

Integer Types

Here is a list of data types that follow under this category. Also, the storage space occupied by them and their range is also specified for your reference.

- char
o Allocated Memory: 1 byte o Range: -128 to 127 or 0 to 255

- signed char o Allocated Memory: 1 byte o Range: -128 to 127

- unsigned char o Allocated Memory: 1 byte o Range: 0 to 255

- int

o Allocated Memory: 2 or 4 bytes o Range: -32,768 to 32,767 or -2,147,483,648 to 2,147,483,647

- short

o Allocated Memory: 2 bytes o Range: -32,768 to 32,767
- unsigned short o Allocated Memory: 2 bytes o Range: 0 to 65,535

- unsigned int o Allocated Memory: 2 or 4 bytes o Range: 0 to 65,535 or 0 to 4,294,967,295

- long

o Allocated Memory: 4 bytes o Range: -2,147,483,648 to 2,147,483,647

- unsigned long o Allocated Memory: 4 bytes

Range: 0 to 4,294,967,295

To get the precise size of a variable or data type, you can utilize the sizeof operator. The declarations sizeof(<data type>) yields the size of the data type or variable in bytes. Given below is an example, which illustrates the concept, discussed below: #include <limits.h> #include <stdio.h> int main() {

printf("Data type char (size in bytes): %d \n", sizeof(char)); return 0;
}
Upon compilation and execution of this code, you must get the following output: Data type char (size in bytes): 1

Floating Point Data Types
Here is a list of data types that follow under this category. Also, the storage space occupied by them, their range, and precision value are specified for your reference.
- float
o Allocated Memory: 4 byte o Range: 1.2e-38 to 3.4e+38

o Precision: 6 decimal places • double
o Allocated Memory: 8 byte o Range: 2.3e-308 to 1.7e+308

o Precision: 15 decimal places • long double o Allocated Memory: 10 byte o Range: 3.4e-4932 to 1.1e+4932

o Precision: 19 decimal places The header file named float.h characterizes macros that permit you to utilize these data type values. The following code will allow you to find the exact amount of allocated memory in bytes on your system for the concerned data type.

```
#include <float.h> #include <stdio.h> int main(){

printf("Allocated Memory for float : %d \n", sizeof(float)); printf("Precision: %d\n",
FLT_DIG ); printf("Max Range Value: %E\n", FLT_MAX ); printf("Min Range Value:
%E\n", FLT_MIN ); return 0.

}
```

Upon compilation and execution of this code, you must get the following output: Allocated Memory for float: 4

Precision: 6

Max Range Value: 3.402823E+38

Max Range Value: 1.175494E-38

The void Type

The void data type points out that no value is accessible. It is utilized as a part of three sorts of circumstances:

• Void returned by a function. You must have commonly noticed the use of the data type void as the return type of function. If not, you will see extensive use of the same as you move forward in your experience with C. The void data type signifies that the function will not return anything. Example of such an implementation is: void print(int)

• Function Arguments as void There are different functions in C, which don't acknowledge any parameter. A function with no parameter can acknowledge as a void. Example of such an implementation is: int print(void)

• Pointers to void A pointer of sort void * signifies the location of a variable. For instance, consider the following declaration: void *malloc(size_t size); This function returns a pointer to void. In other words, this function can return a pointer to a location of any type.

You may not be able to comprehend the use and meaning of the void data type in entirety right now. However, as you move forward, you will find it easier to relate to and use this data type in your code..

Chapter 3

Operators Variable

Variables

A variable is simply a name that is assigned to a storage area. Our programs are capable of manipulating such a storage area. Each C# variable is associated with a type that determines the amount of space allocated to that variable in the memory. This also determines the kind of operations that can be applied to the variable. For example, you cannot multiply string variables.

In C#, the following syntax should be used in the variable declaration:

<data_type> <variable_list>;

The data_type in the above syntax must be a valid data type in C# like int, String, float, etc. The variable_list can be many variable names separated using commas.

Below are examples of valid variable declarations:

int a, b, c; char c, d; float x, salary; double y;

A variable can be initialized during its declaration.

For example: int x = 40;

Variable Initialization

Variable initialization refers to the process of assigning a value to a variable. In C#, this is done using an equal sign then followed by constant expression. Here is the general syntax for initialization: variable_name = value; As we had stated earlier, variables can be initialized during their declaration. Here are more examples:

int x = 1, y = 6; /* initializing x and y. */
byte f = 22; /* initializes f. */
double pi = 3.14159; /* declaring an approximation of pi. */
char a = 'a'; /* the variable a has a value of 'a'. */

Variable initialization should be done correctly; otherwise, the program may give unexpected results.

For example: using System; namespace VariableDeclaration {
class MyProgram {
static void Main(string[] args) {
short x; int y ; double z; /* actual initialization of variables */
x = 5; y = 10; z = x + y; Console.WriteLine("x = {0}, y = {1}, z = {2}", x, y, z);
Console.ReadLine(); }
}
}
The code returns the following:

$$x = 5, y = 10, z = 15$$

Getting User Input

The Console class of the System namespace has a method named **ReadLine()** that allows us to get input from the user. The user's input is read and stored in a variable. The following example demonstrates how to use this method: using System; namespace UserInputApp {
class MyProgram {
static void Main(string[] args) {
string firstName = **"Nicholas"**; string lastName = **"Samuel";**

Console.WriteLine(**"Your name is: "** + firstName + " " + lastName);

  Console.WriteLine("Please enter a different first name:"); firstName = Console.
ReadLine();

Console.WriteLine(**"Your new name is: "** + firstName + " " + lastName);

Console.ReadLine(); }
}
}

When prompted to enter a new value for the first name, do so and hit the enter key. You will realize that your name has changed.

Operators

Operators are symbols that instruct the compiler to perform a certain logical or mathematical manipulation. C# has a wide variety of operators. Let us discuss them.

Arithmetic Operators

These are used for performing various mathematical operations. They can be used as shown in the following example.

```
using System; namespace AithmeticOperatorsApp {
class MyProgram {

static void Main(string[] args) {

int x = 31; int y = 10; int z; z = x + y; Console.WriteLine("1: - z equals to {0}", z); z = x - y;
Console.WriteLine("2: - z equals to {0}", z);

z = x * y; Console.WriteLine("3: - z equals to {0}", z); z = x / y; Console.WriteLine("4: - z
equals to {0}", z); z = x % y; Console.WriteLine("5: - z equals to {0}", z); z = x++; Console.
WriteLine("6: - z equals to {0}", z); z = x--; Console.WriteLine("7: - z equals to {0}", z);
Console.ReadLine(); }
}
}
```

Most of the above operators are well known except for a few of them. The ++ is the increment operator, and it increases the value of the variable by 1 for each iteration. The − is the increments operator, and it decrements the value of the variable by 1 after each iteration. The % is known as the modulus operator, and it returns the remainder after division.

The code returns the output shown below:

```
1: - z equals to 41
2: - z equals to 21
3: - z equals to 310
4: - z equals to 3
5: - z equals to 1
6: - z equals to 31
7: - z equals to 32
```

Logical Operators

C# also has a number of logical operators. Let us discuss them briefly:
Logical AND (&&)- the condition is true if both operands are nonzero.

Logical OR (||)- the condition is true if any of the operands is nonzero.

Logical NOT (!)- the operator reverses the logical state of an operand. If the condition is true, this operator will make it false.

The following example demonstrates how to use the above operators: *using* System;
namespace LogicalOperatorsApp {
class MyProgram {
static void Main(string[] args) {
bool x = *true;* bool y = *true; if* (x && y) {

```
Console.WriteLine("1: The condition is True"); }
if (x || y) {
Console.WriteLine("2; Thecondition is True"); }
/* let us change the values of x and y */
x = false; y = true; if (x && y) {
Console.WriteLine("3: The condition is True"); } else {
Console.WriteLine("3: The condition is not True"); }
if (!(x && y)) {
Console.WriteLine("4: The condition is True"); }
Console.ReadLine(); }
}
}
```

The code returns the following output:

```
1: The condition is True
2; Thecondition is True
3: The condition is not True
4: The condition is True
```

Assignment Operators

C# assignment operators can be used as demonstrated in the following example:

```
class MyProgram {
static void Main(string[] args) {
int x = 31; int z; z = x; Console.WriteLine("1: = The value of z is = {0}", z);
z += x; Console.WriteLine("2: += The value of z is = {0}", z);
z -= x; Console.WriteLine("3: -= The value of z is = {0}", z); z *= x; Console.WriteLine("4:
*= The value of z is = {0}", z);
z /= x; Console.WriteLine("5: /= The value of z is = {0}", z); z = 100; z %= x; Console.
WriteLine("6: %= The value of z is = {0}", z); z <<= 2; Console.WriteLine("7: <<= The
value of z is = {0}", z); z >>= 2; Console.WriteLine("8: >>= The value of z is = {0}", z); z &=
2; Console.WriteLine("9: &= The value of z is = {0}", z); z ^= 2; Console.WriteLine("10:
^= The value of z is = {0}", z); z |= 2; Console.WriteLine("11: |= The value of z is = {0}", z);
Console.ReadLine(); }
}
}
```

The code returns the following result:

```
 1: =  The value of z is = 31
 2: += The value of z is = 62
 3: -= The value of z is = 31
 4: *= The value of z is = 961
 5: /= The value of z is = 31
 6: %=  The value of z is = 7
 7: <<=  The value of z is = 28
 8: >>=  The value of z is = 7
 9: &=  The value of z is = 2
10: ^= The value of z is = 0
11: |=  The value of z is = 2
```

Chapter 4

String and list

List

The List<T> is the collection class that is most frequently used in all collection classes. It is a type whose main characteristic is the element accessibility by index. As mentioned before, List class comes under the System. Collections.Generic namespace. The List is a class that provides a lot of methods for the list and element manipulation. Some of them are searching, sorting, etc. It is used for creating a collection of many different types. It could be a collection of integers, strings, and many more. For the reference types, the List allows null value as an element. It is also possible to insert duplicate values inside any List collection. This class can use both the ordering and equality comparer. Arrays are similar to the lists, but the lists can resize dynamically, but arrays cannot.

String

String data type in C# is a type that represents text and works with text variables. It is an array of characters. Declaring a string data type is done by string keyword. When a string keyword is being used, it means that it is referring to the 'System.String' class (classes will be explained later in the book). There are many extension methods which could be used over some string variable. Some of the most popular are Concat - which is concatenating two strings, Contains - which determines whether the string contains the given string from the parameter as passed value, Equals - which determines whether two strings have the same value, etc. The default string data type is an empty string.

Chapter 5

Syntax

Loop structure statement

In real life, we often repeat the same thing many times. For example, when you scrape your eyes in the fourth round of eye exercises, you will repeat the action of scraping your eyes. When playing table tennis, you will repeat the swing and so on. In C#, there is a statement that can execute the same code block repeatedly, which is called a circular statement. Loop statements are divided into three types: while loop statement, do... while loop statement and for loop statement.

While loop statement

The while loop statement is somewhat similar to the conditional judgment statement mentioned in the above section, which determines whether to execute the execution statement in {} according to the conditional judgment. The difference is that the while statement will repeatedly judge the conditions. As long as the conditions are true, the statements in {} will be executed until the conditions are not true and the while loop ends.

The syntax structure of the while loop statement is as follows:

While (cyclic condition)
{
execute statement
...
}

In the above syntax structure, the execution statement in {} is called the loop body, and whether the loop body is executed depends on the loop condition. When the loop condition is true, the loop body will execute. When the loop body finishes executing, it will continue to judge the loop condition. If the condition is still true, it will continue to execute, and the whole loop process will not end until the loop condition is false.

Next, a case is used to print natural numbers from 1 to 4, as shown in Example below.

Example Program11.cs
```
public class Program11
{
public static void // This is where you need to enter the logic
{
int firstsample = 1;//define the variable 'firstsample' with the initial value of 1
while (firstsample <= 4)

// cycle condition
{
Console.Enteroptions("firstsample = " + firstsample);
//If the condition holds, print the value of Firstsample.
firstsample++;
//firstsample for self-increment
}
Console.ReadKey();
}
}
```
The running results are shown on the computer screen.

For example, the initial value of x is 1, and if the loop condition x <= 4 is met, the loop will be repeatedly executed, and the value of x will be printed, and x will increase automatically. Therefore, the values of x in the printed results are 1, 2, 3, and 4, respectively. It is worth noting that the code in line 9 of the example is used to change the value of variable x in each loop to achieve the purpose of changing the loop condition finally. Without this line of code, the whole loop will go into an infinite loop and never end.

Do-while loop statement

The function of do-while loop statement is similar to that of while loop statement. The difference between them is that while the statement needs to judge the loop condition first and then decide whether to execute the code in {} according to the result of the loop condition. In contrast, the do-while loop statement needs to execute the code in {} once before judging the loop condition.

Its syntax structure is as follows:
```
do
{
execute statement
...
} while (cyclic condition);
```

In the above syntax structure, the execution statement in {} after the keyword do is a loop body. The do-while loop statement puts the loop condition behind the loop body. This means that the loop will execute unconditionally once, and then decide whether to continue execution according to the loop conditions.

Next, use the do-while loop statement to rewrite Example, as shown in the below Example.

Example Program12.cs:

```
public class Classicprogram
{
public static void // This is where we usually enter the options
{
int secondinstance = 1;
//define the variable 'secondinstance' with the initial value of 1
do
{
Console.Getresults(" firstinstance= " + secondinstance);
//print the value of 'firstinstance'
secondinstance++;
//increase the value of 'firstinstance' by itself
}
while (firstinstance <= 4);
//cycle conditions
Console.Scanprogram();
}
}
```

The running results will be shown on the computer screen.

Examples above have the same running results, which shows that a do-while loop and while loop can achieve the same function. However, there are differences between these two statements in the process of a program running. If the loop condition does not hold at the beginning of the loop statement, the loop body of the while loop will not be executed once, but the loop body of the do-while loop will still be executed once. If the cycle condition x<=4 in the example is changed to x < 1, the example 2-12 will print x=1, while the example 2-11 will print nothing.

for loop statement

The while loop and the do-while loop was explained in the previous section. In program development, another kind of loop statement is often used, that is, for loop statement, which is usually used when the number of loops is known, and its syntax format is as follows.

```
For (initialization expression; Circulation conditions; Operation expression)
{
execute statement
...
}
```

In the above syntax structure, the () after the for keyword includes three parts: initialization expression, loop condition, and operation expression, with "; "between the separation, the execution statement in {} is a loop body.

Next, the initialization expression, loop condition, operation expression, and loop body are represented by 1, respectively, and the execution flow of the for loop is analyzed in detail by serial number.

```
for(1; 2;3)
{
4
}
```

Next, sum natural numbers 1~4 through a case, as shown in Example below.
Example Program13.cs:

```
public class Classicprogram
{
public static void // This is where we usually enter the options
{
int secondinstance = 1;
//define the variable 'secondinstance' with the initial value of 1
do
{
Console.Getresults(" firstinstance= " + secondinstance);
//print the value of 'firstinstance'
secondinstance++;
//increase the value of 'firstinstance' by itself
}
while (firstinstance <= 4);
//cycle conditions
 for (int first = 1; first <= 4;The value of first++)
//first will change from 1 to 4
{
sum += first;
//realize the accumulation of sum and i.
}
```

In example, the initial value of variable I is 1, and if the judgment condition i<=4 is true, the loop sum+= I will be executed. After the execution is finished, the operation expression i++, i will be executed, and the value of I will become 2. Then continue to judge the condition, and start the next loop until i=5 and the condition i<=4 is false, end the loop, execute the code after the for loop, and print "sum=10".

Chapter 6

Classes

Classes and Objects

In C# programming language, every component is associated with classes and objects, and these represent the basic concepts of object-oriented programming. A class is something like a prototype from which the user creates objects. A class represents a single, unique unit with all of its members, attributes, and functionality.

The objects are real-life, in-memory entities. When instantiated, they allocate some memory space and have reference to it. Every object created must be of a class type.

Class

Classes represent the unique programming components inside any object-oriented software. The **class** is defined with its access modifier, class keyword, and a unique name. Inside some class, there could be multiple members such as fields, properties, and methods. The default access modifier of a class is *internal*. This means that if the access modifier is not specified, then that particular class would be treated as *internal*. An example of a class is written below:

```
public class TShirt
{
    private string color;
    public string Color
    {
        get { return color; }
        set { color = value; }
    }

    public TShirt(string color)
    {
        this.color = color;
    }

    public string About()
    {
        return "This t-shirt is " + Color + " color.";
    }
}
```

This class contains its access modifier – public, which contains the keyword class; it has a unique name, *TShirt*. Inside this class, there are multiple members defined. There is one private field *color*, one public property *Color*, one constructor defined (with one parameter), and one public method *About*.

Apart from the usual classes, there is one special type of class - the *abstract class*. An abstract class is a special type of class in which an object cannot be instantiated. Abstract classes are mostly used to define a base class in the hierarchy, and it is also known as an incomplete class. The abstract classes typically represent a base class. It is designed to have derived classes implementing the abstract definitions. In the abstract classes, there could as well be *abstract methods* or non-abstract methods. The abstract methods, as well as every class member that is marked as abstract, must be implemented in the derived class. The classes that are marked with the abstract keyword have the purpose of providing the prototype for the derived classes. An abstract class can have a constructor implemented. An example is provided below:

```
class Program
{
    static void Main(string[] args)
    {
        Animal animal;
        animal = new Elephant();
        animal.LegsNumber();
        animal = new Pigeon();
        animal.LegsNumber();
    }
}

public abstract class Animal
{
    public abstract void LegsNumber();
}
public class Elephant : Animal
{
    public override void LegsNumber()
    {
        Console.WriteLine("Elephant has four legs.");
    }
}
public class Pigeon : Animal
{
    public override void LegsNumber()
    {
        Console.WriteLine("Pigeon has two legs.");
    }
}
```

In the provided example, we can see one abstract class with the name Animal. In this class, there is only one member, and that is an abstract void method LegsNumber(). When the method is marked as abstract, it means that every class derived from that class, as in this case, an Animal class, must have an override implementation of that method. Below the abstract class, there are two more classes, which are the 'normal' classes. Both classes have the override implementation of a LegsNumber() method from the Animal class. That is because both the Elephant and Pigeon classes inherit from the Animal class. Inheritance will be explained in detail in a later chapter, but for now, the ':' symbol next to the Elephant and Pigeon class means that they inherit from the Animal class. In this case, this means that they must have their implementation of the abstract method from the base class. In the Main method of a Program class, there is a declaration of an Animal type variable named *animal.*

Note that there is no instantiation of the Animal class because that is not possible, and the reason is that the Animal class is an abstract class - so it cannot be instantiated. In the next line, the program is instantiating an object of Elephant class into the Animal type variable. This is allowed because Animal is the base class of the Elephant class. After it, there is a call to the LegsNumber method from the animal variable. Furthermore, since the animal is instantiated to be an Elephant type, this call executes the LegsNumber method from the Elephant class. The next thing is the instantiation of the Pigeon object and assigning it to the same animal variable. It ends up with calling the LegsNumber method again from the animal object. This time implementation of the LegsNumber from the Pigeon class is used. The console output will look like this:

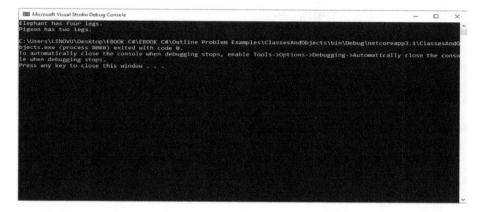

Object

Objects in C# represent the real entities in the system, with all of their class type characteristics and features. They are located somewhere in memory and have reference pointer to it. Whenever the keyword new is used, an object in memory is created. Objects must be of a class type. Every class which is created in C# programming language is derived from the System.Object class (inheritance will be explained in later chapters). This means that there is a built-in class Object in C #, and every object of any type is derived from that class. Every object created, besides its own functionalities, also has the methods that are available from their parent class Object. These methods are: Equals, ToString, Finalize, and GetHashCode. This could be checked in the example:

```
using System;

namespace ClassesAndObjects
{
    0 references
    class Program
    {
        0 references
        static void Main(string[] args)
        {
            var tshirt = new TShirt("blue");
            tshirt.|
        }                ⊙  About          string TShirt.About()
    }                    🔧 Color
                         ⊙  Equals
    2 references         ⊙  GetHashCode
    public class TS      ⊙  GetType
    {                    ⊙  ToString
        private str
        1 reference
    public stri  🔧  ⊙
        {
            get { return color; }
            set { color = value; }
```

This example is using the class TShirt, which was shown in the previous example in Class subchapter. In the Main method, an object of the TShirt class type is instantiated. This object is referenced by the tshirt variable. In the second line, you can see the available methods and properties that could be executed over the tshirt object. Besides Color property and the About method that are part of the TShirt class, there are also four methods from the parent class Object (Equals, GetHashCode, GetType, ToString).

Interface

Another important component in object-oriented programming is an interface. An interface represents multiple declarations of some functionalities. A class can implement one or more interfaces, but it can only inherit from one class or abstract class. This reveals another C# programming language characteristic - it does not support multiple inheritance. Classes that implement some interface must provide a full definition of all interface members. In the interface usage, there is no manipulation with access modifiers as all the interface members are considered to be public. This is because interface existence is all about its functionality to be implemented by other classes. If some class must implement interface members, it means that the interface members must be public to be implemented by other classes. The interface is an object-oriented component that has declarations, but it cannot have definitions - implementations. If you try to insert some implementations in the interface, the compile-time error will appear. The interface can contain properties and methods - everything that can have the implementation. It cannot have fields and a constructor - because it is not a class, and it cannot be instantiated. On implementation of the interface, the class must implement all of the interface members. As mentioned, multiple inheritance is not supported in C#, but it can be achieved with interface usage since a class can implement multiple interfaces. Example:

```
namespace ClassesAndObjects
{
    interface IPerson
    {
        bool IsRunning { get; set; }
        bool IsStanding { get; set; }
        bool IsSitting { get; set; }
    }
}
```

Here we have one interface defined. It has three boolean properties inside. A class that will implement this interface must have the definition of all these interface members.

```
namespace ClassesAndObjects
{
    class Person : IPerson
    {
        private string _firstName;
        private string _lastName;

        public Person(string firstName, string lastName)
        {
            _firstName = firstName;
            _lastName = lastName;
        }

        public bool IsRunning { get; set; }
        public bool IsStanding { get; set; }
        public bool IsSitting { get; set; }
    }
}
```

The program contains one class, which is a Person class. This class implements the IPerson interface that has been declared. This class has two private string fields, which are _firstName and _lastName. It also has a constructor where those field values are assigned. Besides that, this class has the definition of three members of the IPerson interface — the IsRunning, IsStanding, and IsSitting properties. The compiler is okay with this, as there are no errors. But, if we remove any of these three properties from a Person class, the compiler would report an error. For example:

```
IPerson.cs          Program.cs          Person.cs*  ✕

ClassesAndObjects                    ▼    ClassesAndObjects.Person            ▼    _firstName

 1     □namespace ClassesAndObjects
 2      {
            3 references
 3     □      class Person : IPerson
 4          {
 5              private string        •○ interface ClassesAndObjects.IPerson
 6              private string
 7                                    'Person' does not implement interface member 'IPerson.IsRunning'
            1 reference
 8     □      public Person(s        Show potential fixes (Alt+Enter or Ctrl+.)
 9          {
10              _firstName = firstName;
11              _lastName = lastName;
12          }
13
14          //public bool IsRunning { get; set; }
            1 reference
15          public bool IsStanding { get; set; }
            1 reference
16          public bool IsSitting { get; set; }
17      }
18     }
19
```

Here, we have commented on the IsRunning property that is inside the Person class. The compiler is reporting an error that the Person class does not implement that property, and the program could not build. After this, we will uncomment the property and return to the valid state of a program. Let us create a Program class with the Main method inside. There, we will create an instance of a Person class and run the program to check if everything is working well.

```
namespace ClassesAndObjects
{
    class Program
    {
        static void Main(string[] args)
        {
            Person person = new Person("Peter", "Parker");
        }
    }
}
```

Now, run the program:

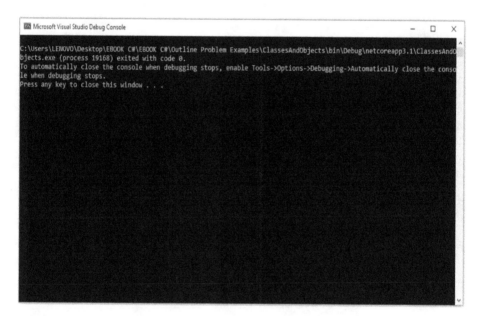

Everything went smoothly.

Chapter 7

LINQ, queries, operators – XAML

LINQ

Language integrated query, better known as LINQ, represents query syntax in C# programming language, and it is used for retrieval and filtering of the different sources of objects. LINQ produces a single querying interface for various kinds of objects and variables. This query syntax is integrated into C# programming language, as well as in Visual Basic. For better understanding, we will provide an example to explain it further. Therefore, you have SQL as a Structured Query Language. SQL is used to get and save some data into the database. It is a language designed to work closely with the database. In the same way as SQL, the LINQ is used to get and filter different data sources like collections, data sets, etc. There are many ways you can use LINQ; it is used to query object collections, ADO .Net data sets, XML Documents, Entity Framework data sets, SQL database direct, and other data sources by implementing the IQuerable interface. LINQ is like a bridge between some data and variables in the program. Every LINQ query returns objects as a result. It is good because it enables the use of an object-oriented approach to the data set. When using LINQ, you do not have to worry about converting the setups of data into objects. LINQ provides a way to query data wherever that data came from. It supports the compile-time syntax checking so that if you make a mistake while coding LINQ, the compiler will inform you immediately. LINQ allows you to query every collection such as List, Array, Enumerable *classes, etc.*

We are heading to the examples now:

```
class Program
{
    static void Main(string[] args)
    {
        List<Car> cars = new List<Car>()
        {
            new Car(100, true, false),
            new Car(200, false, true),
            new Car(300, true, true),
            new Car(400, false, false),
            new Car(500, false, true)
        };

        var carsThatAreAutomatic = cars.Where(s => s.IsAutomatic == true).ToList();
        carsThatAreAutomatic.ForEach(carThatIsAutomatic =>
        {
            Console.WriteLine($"The car with the trunk capacity of
{carThatIsAutomatic.TrunkCapacity} is automatic");
        });
    }

    class Car
    {
        public int TrunkCapacity { get; }
        public bool IsAutomatic { get; }
        public bool IsTurboCharged { get; }
        public Car(int _TruckCapacity, bool _IsAutomatic, bool _isTurboCharged)
        {
            TrunkCapacity = _TruckCapacity;
            IsAutomatic = _IsAutomatic;
            IsTurboCharged = _isTurboCharged;
        }
    }
}
```

In this example, we have one class named Car. In the Car class, there are three properties, which are the TrunkCapacity, IsAutomatic, and IsTurboCharged. Every property represents read-only property, and their initial state is set in the Car class constructor. The constructor takes three parameters and assigns their values to the properties mentioned above. In the Main method, we are creating a list of Car objects. The list of Car objects is populated in the declaration part, creating five Car objects with different values for the TrunkCapacity, IsAutomatic, and IsTurboCharged properties. After that, we would filter the list and take only cars that have automatic transmission. This will be done by using the LINQ query. We are creating an object named *carsThatAreAutomatic* and filtering the cars list with LINQ. Then we perform the *Where* LINQ extension method to get the objects that we need. How does it work? In the *Where* method, we are declaring an iterative variable that will be used for filtering conditions.

The variable in this example is s. So, what the filter does next is that for every s object in the cars list, it will grant us the object whose s.IsAutomatic property is equal to true. This will, in turn, create a filtered IEnumarble list. In order to make this a list of explicit type objects, we will do the simple ToList() method over the filtered IEnumerable list. This will create an object of List<Car> type and put it down to the carsThatAreAutomatic object. Now, we have the data that we need. In the end, we will iterate through the newly created collection of Car objects and print messages to the console output. For every object in the list, we will print "The car with the trunk capacity of {certain capacity} is automatic". We know this because we filtered the Cars and took only the ones who have automatic transmission. The output of this program looks like this:.

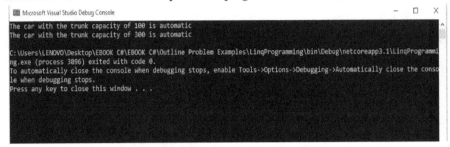

As yu can see, there are two cars with automatic transmission and their capacity is 100 and 300 respectively. You can check that in the creation of the Car list at the beginning, as only the first and the third car have true value for an IsAutomatic property passed in the object instantiation.

Another exampleis in the next page :

```
class Program
{
    static void Main(string[] args)
    {
        List<Person> people = new List<Person>()
        {
            new Person(1200, "Mark", "Pent"),
            new Person(3400, "Peter", "Parker"),
            new Person(2300, "Julian", "Stones"),
            new Person(5000, "Mike", "Deen"),
            new Person(3250, "Catrin", "Burns")
        };

        var seniors = people.Where(s => s.Salary > 3000).ToList();
        var seniorSalaries = seniors.Select(x => x.Salary).ToList();
        var seniorSalariesSum = 0;
        seniorSalaries.ForEach(seniorSalary => seniorSalariesSum += seniorSalary);
        Console.WriteLine($"The sum of all senior salaries is { seniorSalariesSum }");
    }

    class Person
    {
        public int Salary { get; }
        public string FirstName { get; }
        public string LastName { get; }
        public Person(int Salary, string FirstName, string LastName)
        {
            this.Salary = Salary;
            this.FirstName = FirstName;
            this.LastName = LastName;
        }
    }
}
```

In this example, we have a class named Person. This class has three properties, which are Salary, FirstName, and LastName. Each Person class represents one employee with its basic information. The object's properties are assigned in the constructor. In the Main method, there is a creation of a list with objects of the Person class type. We have added five Person object, each with different salary amount, first name, and last name. The manager wants to filter out everyone that has a salary greater than 3000, and these people will be marked as seniors. We will do that with the LINQ query. As in the previous example, we are filtering the people list with the *Where extension method*. In this method, we are declaring that we want only the Person objects that have a Salary greater than 3000. After the retrieval is done, the ToList() method takes the filtered IEnumerable list into the Person objects list. Now we have an object that is a list of Person class types, and it contains only the people who have a Salary greater than 3000. This variable is named *seniors*. Now the manager requests that he wants the total sum of the senior salaries. We will then do that by creating a list of senior salaries and then summing all of that values into one variable and end up printing it to the standard output. The creation of the *seniorSalaries* list will be done with the execution of the Select LINQ extension method. The Select method is used when there is a need for getting only certain property values from a collection of objects. In this case, we need the Salary property value from each of the objects inside the *seniors list*. The Select method does the next: for each x object from the *seniors list, take x.Salary* value. This creates a list of IEnumerable values. After the ToList() method execution, we succeeded in creating a List<int> object that contains elements that are senior salaries. Then we created a variable in which we will store the summation of all of the senior salaries - *seniorSalariesSum* variable. After this is done, we have one more statement that will finish the work. The *ForEach* method is done over the seniorSalaries list, which will gather and sum all salaries into one variable seniorSalariesSum. In the end, the program will print the result - seniorSalariesSum value to the standard output. The output of this program will look like this:

```
Microsoft Visual Studio Debug Console                              —    □    X

The sum of all senior salaries is 11650

C:\Users\LENOVO\Desktop\EBOOK C#\EBOOK C#\Outline Problem Examples\LinqProgramming\bin\Debug\netcoreapp3.1\LinqProgrammi
ng.exe (process 19176) exited with code 0.
To automatically close the console when debugging stops, enable Tools->Options->Debugging->Automatically close the conso
le when debugging stops.
Press any key to close this window . . .
```

This logic and solution to the problem could be much simplified, and the senior salary sum could be done in just one line of code. That line will look something like this:

```
var seniorSalariesSum = 0;
people.Where(s => s.Salary > 300).Select(x => x.Salary).ToList().ForEach(salary =>
seniorSalariesSum += salary);

Console.WriteLine($"The sum of all senior salaries is { seniorSalariesSum }");
```

After the Where method is being executed, the Select method would follow, after which the List will be created over which we could iterate with the ForEach extension method and do the sum calculation. This will produce the exact same result. This long statement is just split into a few smaller ones in the starting solution for better understanding. Let us close this LINQ chapter with one more example:

```csharp
class Program
{
    static void Main(string[] args)
    {
        List<Person> people = new List<Person>()
        {
            new Person(1200,  new PersonalInformation("Mark", "Pent",  123)),
            new Person(3400,  new PersonalInformation("Peter", "Parker",  155)),
            new Person(2300,  new PersonalInformation("Julian", "Stones",  133)),
            new Person(5000,  new PersonalInformation("Mike", "Deen",  143)),
            new Person(3250,  new PersonalInformation("Catrin", "Burns",  205))
        };

        var seniorsLT150 = people.Where(x => x.Salary > 3000)
                                 .Select(x => x.PersonalInformation)
                                 .Where(x => x.PersonalID < 150)
                                 .Select(x => x.FirstName).ToList();

        seniorsLT150.ForEach(seniorFirstName =>
            Console.WriteLine($"Senior name is { seniorFirstName }")
        );
    }
}

class Person
{
    public int Salary { get; }
    public PersonalInformation PersonalInformation{ get; }
    public Person(int salary, PersonalInformation personalInformation)
    {
        Salary = salary;
        PersonalInformation = personalInformation;
    }
}

class PersonalInformation
{
    public string FirstName { get; }
    public string LastName { get; }
    public int PersonalID { get; }
    public PersonalInformation(string firstName, string lastName, int personalID)
    {
        FirstName = firstName;
        LastName = lastName;
        PersonalID = personalID;
    }
}
```

In this example, we have modified the Person class from the previous example. Now, the Person class contains the Salary property and PersonalInformation class type property, and both are assigned in the Person class constructor. The PersonalInformation class contains three read-only properties. These properties are FirstName, LastName, and PersonalID. FirstName and LastName are of a string data type, while the PersonalID is of an int data type. These three properties are assigned in the constructor when instantiating the object of PersonalInformation class. Now, let's jump into the Main method of the Program class. Here, we are again going to create a list of Person objects, and it is the same as in the previous example. Though, this time is going to be a bit different because of the Class modifications. We are creating five Person objects, each of them with Salary, and PersonalInformation object assigned.

For every Person, we create a PersonalInformation object to instantiate the Person object correctly. Each of the PersonalInformation objects has the first name, last name, and personal ID passed to its instantiation. This way, we created a bit more complex object that contains another class object inside. Ok, we are ready to go. The manager asks us to find every first name of an employee who is treated as a senior and has a personal ID of less than one hundred and fifty. From the previous example, we have acknowledged that the senior is the Person with a Salary greater than three thousand (3000). We are doing something similar to the previous example, but this time, the Person class has changed. It does not have the same structure as in the previous example. So, we must analyze the class structure first and then create a solution. The first step is that we must filter the Person objects from the people list that have a Salary greater than 3000. After that, we must take the PersonalInformation object from every Person object to find the first names of all the seniors. Then, when PersonalInformation objects are gathered, we must filter them and take only the ones with the PersonalID that are less than 150. When that task is done, we can finally select the FirstName property of all the seniors, make a list out of it, iterate through that list, and print the FirstName values. All of this is done in the little complex LINQ query from which we create a *seniorsLT150* list variable.

The first *Where* method creates an IEnumerable list of seniors. Then, the Select method takes PersonalInformation objects from seniors list and makes an IEnumerable list of the seniors PersonalInformation objects. The second *Where* method is working over the PersonalInformation objects from the previously created IEnumerable list, and there we will filter the PersonalInformation object that has PersonalID property less than 150. From there, we are doing the Select method, which gathers the FirstName property value for each of the seniors PersonalInformation objects that has PersonalID less than 150. In the end, we then execute the ToList() method over the final IEnumerable that we created, and the final product is the list of strings that contain the first name of every senior with a personal ID less than 150. When all of this is finally queried, we can run through the list and print those names to the console. The only senior who will meet these criteria is Mike Dean, and his first name will be printed to the standard output. The program console output is below:.

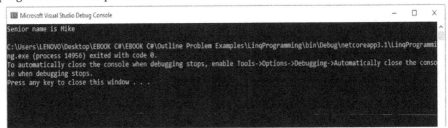

Chapter 8

Program to make decision

Decision Making

Not all problems are solved linearly, sometimes it is necessary to have to make a decision or execute specific actions when a condition is met, and others when it does not. Let us suppose that our problem is to maintain the temperature of a bucket of warm water. To do this, we can add hot or cold water. In this problem, we would need to decide what kind of water to add.

Similarly, there are many problems that we need to know a condition or make a decision on how to solve them. In C#, it is easy to achieve this since the language provides us with different tools to cope with it. We will have to use expressions, and these will be evaluated. In this case, we will use relational expressions, and logical expressions, which will be evaluated, and depending on the result of that evaluation, specific steps of the algorithm or others will be carried out. Let's start by knowing the expressions we need.

Making Choices and Decisions

While we are in the C# language, we need to take some time to work with the decision control statements or conditional statements. These are going to be the types of codes that can take the input from the user, compare it to the conditions that you set within the code, and then will make some important decisions on its own based on both of these.

There will be times when you write outcode, and you want to make sure that this program can handle some decisions on its own. You can choose to write it out so that there are specific conditions to find in the code ahead of time, and then the code can respond based on the input that the user has added into the computer.

The good news with this one is that there are a few options that you can choose from with these conditional statements. Each one is going to work in a slightly different manner based on what you are hoping to get out of the program as well, and how you would like it to respond to different inputs from the user. As we go through the different options, you will better be able to see how each one works and why it is such a great option for you to choose one of them along the way. Let's dive in and take a look at some of the main conditional statements available in the C# language, learn how each one is going to work, and explore some of the basics of coding with them as well.

A Look at the If Statement

The first kind of conditional statement that we want to take a look at here is known as our if statement. Out of all the conditional statements that we will look through, this one is going to be the most basic. It does miss out a bit on some of the functionality that we will see with these statements, but it does help us to learn more about conditional statements and can be useful in some situations as well, so it is important to learn.

When you handle this if statement, you will find that when it runs, the code will only provide us with a reply as long as the user gives us an input that matches with the conditions that are set in the code. When this does happen, then the code will be able to execute, and it will usually come up with some kind of message, depending on what the programmer puts into the code. Sometimes you will set it up to execute something else as well.

However, if the user comes through and puts in an input that does not match up with the conditions that we set up, then there will be nothing that shows up on the screen. This can cause some problems, which is why the if statement may not be used as much as some of the other options.

The good news out of all of this is that you will find, even as a beginner, that these if statements are easy to set up and work with. Let's take a look at the coding below to see how we can create one of these if statements in the C# language for our own needs: *If (x > 0)*

```
{
Console.Write("The value is positive.");
}
```

With the example that we listed above, certain things need to happen. If the value that the user put sin is higher than zero, then the program is set up to print off "The value is positive". However, if the expression turns out to be false, or the input is less than zero, then the program will ignore the whole statement that comes after Console. Write and will move on.

A Look at the If Else Statement

As we can tell pretty quickly when we work with the if statement, there will be many situations where these statements are not going to be able to help us get things done in the manner that we want. You do not want to set up some codes that are not strong enough to handle the work that you want. It is never a good idea to set up a code where the user can put in something, and then the program just ends or freezes up. And this is where we will take a look at a new conditional statement, known as the if-else statement.

The if-else statement is going to be a nice one to work with because it adds in a ton of power to the code that we are doing and writing, while still allowing us to add in more than one option and handle pretty much anything that the user will add to the program. Sometimes we will only add in one or two options, but sometimes we can use the if-else statement to handle a ton of options along the way as well.

To get to the point, we need to take a look at the syntax for the if-else statement so we get a better understanding of how this will work in the C# language. A good example of the syntax for this one will be below *If (the Boolean expression)*
{The statement/s you want to run if the result is true;
}
Else
{The statement/s you want to run if the result is false;
}
As you can already see with this one, there is going to be a lot more power that comes with the if-else statement. This is a basic option with the if-else statement, but you can add in some more lines to make it more powerful. With these, if-else statements, if the answer is false, your code will go on to the next part of the statement to see whether or not that one is true. If there are more than two options, it will keep going down the if-else statement until the answer turns out true, and then it will go and display the message that comes up.

Now that we have taken some time to talk about it, it is time to look at an example of how this will work so you can use it in your codes:
If (x > 0)
{
Console.Write("This value will be positive.");
}
Else
{
Console.Write("The value is less than or equal to zero.")
}
You are going to find that when we work with the example above, the else clause is going to be important, or at least hidden until the Boolean expression ends up being false. It is there when the process will need the else statement. But if we end up getting true value, then the first statement will be the one that will show up so we won't need the else statement at all.

What the Nested Conditional Statement is All About

Any time that we look through some of the new codes that come with C#, you should find that it is easier to work with two statements that we had above, or you can combine them to make a nested conditional statement for some of your codes as well. With a nested conditional statement, we are going to take one of the types of conditional statements above and place it inside of another one. The point of doing this is to add in some more complexity to the work that we want to see with coding and can really give us a chain of conditions when they are needed.

The main thing that we have to focus on when it comes to handling any nested conditional statement is that if there is some mistake that happens when you write out the statement, it is going to cause an error in the whole thing, and it can take some time to fix. This makes them a bit difficult to handle and work with along the way, so be careful.

The neat thing about them, though, and something that will make them pretty appealing is that they allow us to add in as many, or as few, levels as we would like. Even with this in mind, most professionals in this language will recommend that the nested statements stay around three levels or less so that they don't become too big of a mess along the way.

If you do end up going past the third level when working on these statements, then you may end up with something that is unruly and doesn't behave in the manner that you would like and may not even work. As a beginner, stick with the three levels and go up to more as you get better with the coding.

There are many codes that you are able to write that will rely on these conditional statements. They help you to make the code stronger and will ensure that we are able to handle some of the inputs that our users give to us, even if we are not able to guess ahead of time what answer the user is going to add to the program. These can base the input off any conditions that we set and will ensure that the program is going to behave in the manner that we would prefer. This makes it so much easier for us to see results and for us to make sure the program works the way that we want.

Chapter 9

Net

The .Net Framework

Programs that are written out in this kind of framework are going to be able to execute itself in the environment for the software rather than the hardware environment, known as the CLR or Common Language Runtime. The CLR is going to be an application virtual machine that will help to provide us with some different services, including security, exception handling, and memory management. Because of this, the codes that are written with this Framework is going to be known as managed code. Both the CLR and the FCL that we have talked about are going to make up the .NET framework that we are talking about.

First, the FCL is going to be important. It provides us with some of the user interface, database connectivity, data access, web application development, algorithms, network communication, and more. Programmers can produce some software when they combine the source code; they are working on with the .NET framework and some of the other available libraries.

This is a framework that is designed to work well with most new applications that we want to create on the Windows platform. In addition, Microsoft is going to produce an IDE that is specifically for the .NET software that is known as Visual Studio.

There are a lot of things that we can work with when it comes to the .NET Framework. Some methods have been developed to work not only on the Windows systems but also with some of the other operating systems, including Linux and Mac. And it can help us work with a variety of languages, especially with C#, while being portable, secure, high in performance, and good with managing the memory that we need while writing out certain codes.

In order to be able to program effectively with C#, one needs a little theoretical background knowledge, which concerns the so-called.NET Framework. That's why the. NET Framework is an integral part of this book. Before we get more involved with the. NET Framework, you should know that it is an integral part of .NET technology.

The task of a runtime environment is essentially to execute the code developed with the respective programming language. In the past, however, a separate runtime library (runtime library) usually had to be provided for each programming language - and in part also for each version - in order to be able to execute the corresponding programs. For example, C ++ the file MSVCRT.DLL and in Visual Basic 6, the file MSVBVM6o.DLL. The concepts of the supplied runtime environments were and are still fundamentally different today. Cross-language support provides key benefits of the.NET Framework:

Only one framework is needed.

Different (and very different) programming languages can be used, depending on the level of knowledge and personal preference.

There is exactly one runtime environment for all programming languages.

From these advantages, further derivations can be made:

The cross-lingual integratio.
The cross-language exception handling (Exception Handling refers to how a program should react when events occur that are generally not expected, such as errors..
Improved security (security can be controlled up to the method level.
Simplified versioning (several versions can exist side by side.

Because the.NET Framework provides a cross-language runtime environment, it ensures interaction and optimal collaboration between components of different programming languages.
You now know that the.NET Framework is part of .NET technology and what it has to do.
The.NET Framework again consists of three main components:
Common Language Runtime - the cross-language runtime environment
Class libraries (Learn more about classes and class libraries later)
ASP.NET - server-side applications for the World Wide Web

In this book, we will deal in detail with these three components. The common language runtime and class libraries will come up again and again throughout the book, as will ASP. NET in the context of web services. The two components - Common Language Runtime and Class Libraries - of the.NET Framework are also referred to as Base Framework.

Discover .NET
The .NET Framework is a solution to all the problems involved in the development of applications, providing great benefits not only to the developer but also to the development process. First of all, .NET allows us to work with existing code; we can use COM components, and even, in the situation where we need to use the Windows API. When the .NET program is ready, it is much easier to install on the client's computer than traditional applications since it has a strong integration between languages.

A C# programmer can easily understand the code of a Visual Basic .NET programmer, and both can program in the language they are most comfortable with. This is because all the languages that make use of .NET share the .NET libraries, so it does not matter in which language we program in, we can recognize it in any language. Next, we will know the different components of .NET: Common Language Runtime (CLR), Assembly, and Common Intermediate Language (CIL).

CLR

The first component of .NET that we will know is the Common Language Runtime, also called CLR. This is an execution program common to all languages. This program is in charge of reading the code generated by the compiler and starts its execution. It does not matter if the program was created with C#, Visual Basic .NET, or some other .NET language, the CLR reads it and executes it.

Assembly

When we have a program written in a .NET language, and we compile it, the assembly is generated. The assembly contains CIL in the compiled program and also the information about all the types that are used in the program.

CIL

The .NET programs are not compiled directly into compiler assembly code; instead, they are compiled into an intermediate language known as CIL. This language is read and executed by the runtime. The use of CIL and runtime is what gives .NET its great flexibility and its ability to be multiplatform.

The Framework of .NET has Common Language Specifications or CLS. These specifications are the guidelines that any language that you want to use .NET must meet to be able to work with the runtime. One advantage of this is that if our code complies with the CLS, we can have interoperability with other languages, for example, it is possible to create a library in C #, and a Visual Basic .NET programmer can use it without any problem.

One of the most important points of these guidelines is the CTS or Common Type System. In programming languages, when we want to save information, it is placed in a variable, the variable will have a type depending on the information to save, for example, the type can be to save an integer, the other to store a number with decimals and the other to save a phrase or word. The problem with this is that each language store information differently. Some languages store integers with 16-bit memory and other with 32-bit; even some languages, such as C and C++, do not have a type for storing strings or phrases. To solve this, the .NET Framework defines through CTS how the types will work in their environment. Any language that works with .NET must use the types as outlined in the CTS. Now that we know the basic concepts, and we can see how all this comes together.

How to Create a .NET Application

We can create a .NET application using a programming language. For this purpose, it will be C#; with this programming language, we can create the source code of the program (instructions that tell the program what to do).

When we have finished with our source code, then we have to use the compiler. The compiler takes the source code and creates an assembly for us. This assembly will have the equivalent of our code, but written in CIL, leading us to another advantage of .NET

- the compiler can optimize our code for the platform where we are going to use the program, that means the same program can be optimized for a mobile device, a normal PC or a server, without making any changes to it.

The .NET Framework can be run on many platforms, not just on Windows. This means that we can program on a particular platform, and if another platform has the runtime, our program will run without any problem. A .NET program developed in Windows can be executed in Linux, as long as it has the corresponding runtime.

When we want to invoke the program, then the runtime gets into the action, reads the assembly, and creates the entire environment for us. The runtime starts reading the CIL instructions from the assembly and compiles them as it reads them for the microprocessor of the computer on which the program is running; this is known as JIT or just-in-time compilation. In this way, the program advances in execution, and it is compiled; all this occurs transparently for the user.

The JIT compiler is also known as Jitter. It is part of the runtime and is very efficient if the program needs to re-run a code that has already been compiled, the Jitter instead of recompiling, runs what has already been compiled, thus improving performance and response times for the user.

For the programs that are running, the .NET Framework provides the services of memory management and garbage collection. In unmanaged languages such as C and C++, the programmer is responsible for memory management. In large programs, this can be a complicated task, which can lead to errors during program execution. Fortunately, managed languages like C#, have a model in which we, as programmers, no longer need to be responsible for memory usage. The garbage collector is in charge of removing all objects that are no longer needed when an object is no longer use the collector takes it and removes it. This frees up memory and resources.

The garbage collector works automatically for us and helps to eliminate all the memory and resource management that was necessary for Win32. In some special cases, like files, databases, or network connections are unmanaged resources. For these cases, we must explicitly indicate when they need to be destroyed.

## Chapter 10

Enum

An enum (which stands for enumerated type) is a special data type that allows programmers to provide meaningful names for a set of integral constants.

To declare an enum, we use the enum keyword followed by the name of the enum. The members of the enum are enclosed in a set of curly braces and separated by commas.

An example is shown below:

enum DaysOfWee.

{
Sun, Mon, Tues, Wed, Thurs, Fri, Sat
}

Note that we do not put a semi-colon at the end of the last member.

After declaring the DaysOfWeek enum, we can declare and initialize a DaysOfWeek variable like this:

DaysOfWeek myDays = DaysOfWeek.Mon;

The name of the variable is myDays. If we write

Console.WriteLine(myDays);

we'll get,

Mon

By default, each member in the enum is assigned an integer value, starting from zero. That is, in our example, Sun is assigned a value of 0, Mon is 1, Tues is 2, and so on.

As members of an enum are essentially integers, we can cast a DaysOfWeek variable into an int and vice versa. For instance,

Console.WriteLine((int)myDays).

gives us the integer 1 while

Console.WriteLine((DaysOfWeek)1);

gives us Mon.

If you want to assign a different set of integers to your enum members, you can do the following

enum DaysOfWeekTwo

{

Sun = 5, Mon = 10, Tues, Wed, Thurs, Fri, Sat
}

Now, Sun is assigned a value of 5, and Mon is assigned 10. As we did not assign values for Tues to Sat, consecutive numbers after 10 will be assigned to them. That is Tues = 11, Wed = 12, and so on.

Of course, if you use a byte data type, you cannot do something like
enum DaysOfWeekFour : byte

{
Sun = 300, Mon, Tues, Wed, Thurs, Fri, Sat
}

as the range for byte is from 0 to 255.

There are two main reasons for using enums. The first is to improve the readability of your code. The statement
myDays = DaysOfWeek.Mon;
is more self-explanatory than the statement
myDays = 1;

The second reason is to restrict the values that a variable can take. If we have a variable that stores the days of a week, we may accidentally assign the value 10 to it. This can be prevented when we use an enum as we can only assign the pre-defined members of the enum to the variable.

Struct

Now, let's look at the struct data type.

A struct is similar to a class in many aspects. Like classes, they contain elements like properties, constructors, methods and fields and allow you to group related members into a single package so that you can manipulate them as a group.

To declare a struct, you use the struct keyword. An example is:

```
1 struct MyStruct
2 {
3 //Fields
4 private int x, y;
5 private AnotherClass myClass;
6 private Days myDays;
7
8 //Constructor
9 public MyStruct(int a, int b, int c)
10 {
11 myClass = new AnotherClass();
12 myClass.number = a;
13 x = b;
14 y = c;
15 myDays = Days.Mon;
16 }
```

17
18 //Method
19 public void PrintStatement()
20 {
21 Console.WriteLine("x = {0}, y = {1}, myDays = {2}", x, y, myDays);
22 }
23 }
24
25 class AnotherClas.

26 {
27 public int number;
28 }
29
30 enum Days { Mon, Tues, Wed }

The struct is declared from lines 1 to 23. On line 4, we declared two private int fields for the struct. On line 5, we declared another private field called myClass. This field is an instance of the class AnotherClass. On line 6, we declared an enum variable myDays. The two fields (myClass and myDays) are specially included in this example to demonstrate how we can include a class instance and an enum variable as the fields of a struct. Structs (and classes) can contain enum variables and instances of other structs and classes as fields.

After declaring the fields, we declared the constructor for the struct (lines 9 to 16), followed by a method to print the values of x, y, and myDays. (lines 19 to 22).

After declaring the struct, we declared the class AnotherClass on lines 25 to 28 and the enum Days on line 30. In this example, we declared the class and enum outside the struct myStruct. However, we can declare the enum or class inside the struct itself. An enum, struct, or class can be nested inside another struct or class. We'll look at an example of an enum declared inside a class when we work through the project at the end of the book.

To use the struct above, we can add the following code to our Main() method:

MyStruct example = new MyStruct(2, 3, 5);

example.PrintStatement();

If we run the code, we'll get

x = 3, y = 5, myDays = Mon

There are two main differences between a struct and a class. Firstly, the struct data type does not support inheritance. Hence you cannot derive one struct from another. However, a struct can implement an interface. The way to do it is identical to how it is done with classes. Refer to Chapter 8 for more information.

The second difference between structs and classes is that structs are value types while classes are reference types.

For a complete list of differences between a struct and a class, check out the following page:

https://msdn.microsoft.com/en-us/library/saxz13w4.aspx

Chapter 11

Common mistake and how to avoid them

This guidebook has taken some time to look through all of the different parts of coding that we need to know to utilize the C# language to write some of our codes.

There are a lot of different aspects that we need to keep in mind when it comes to working on this language, but when we can put it all together, we will find that we can create some great codes and programs in the process.

Even though many of the modern coding languages that are out there have been designed to make programming easier for those who are beginners, there are still a number of challenges that are going to show up when you first get started.

One of the things that a beginner has to remember when they go through this process is that they do need to practice, and they need to learn from their mistakes and from some of the problems that show up in their coding.

Even taking a break is often enough to help you get going on this and can ensure that you won't burn out and have trouble with the process later on.

Some of the mistakes you should avoid includes:

Not Getting enough Practice

There are a ton of codes and suggestions and things to learn about in this guidebook, but if you don't actually open up the compiler with C# and try some of it out, you are never going to gain the skills and more that you need to make this work for you.

That is why the first rule that we need to follow here is to play around with the code and get as much practice as possible.

With any of the new subjects that we want to explore and learn about in any coding language, the sooner that we can get our hands dirty and start messing around with the code, the faster that we can learn some of the concepts that are there.

You can't go through and read the information without using it a bit, and then expect that you will remember that information and be able to utilize the code for your programs.

You have to mess with the code and see how it works.

Now, you will find that the best place for us to get started with this tip is just to open up our C# compiler and start to do some of the codings that we want right away.

Take some of the examples that are in this guidebook and just mess around with them a bit.

Even just typing them into the compiler to start with is a good step in the right direction and will ensure that we can get some practice.

You can then work and explore from there to get the right results.

Ignoring the Fundamentals

Even though it sometimes seems like the fundamentals are going to be too basic to work with, and you may feel like you should just race through them without a thought, it is still important to spend our time learning about how this work.

As easy as they are, they are really important to work with as well.

The better that we can work with these fundamentals, the easier it is for us to start mastering some of the more advanced stuff that is going to show up.

Those programmers who try to get into a programming language and then rush through the beginning parts and do not spend the proper time on some of the fundamentals are going to be the first ones who get stuck when they need to make the transition int some of the advanced material that will come later.

So, before you miss out on some of the first classes that we need here and skip through some of the basics that are important in all of this, make sure to learn more about the fundamentals and what we can do with it along the way.

Not Writing it Out

It is normal to want to get started with programming and to open up the compiler and start coding.

And while this is one of the methods to use, sometimes trying it out in a different manner, and writing it by hand rather than trying to type it in all of the time is going to be the trick that will help us to get this done.

Bringing out the pen and paper to write out our codes will help.

There are a ton of advances to the computers out there, and they're a lot of benefits to using it.

But sometimes the best way to learn something new is actually to write it out and work from there.

Whether you decide to use some scrap paper, a notebook, a whiteboard, or another option, taking the time to code out everything by hand is going to take more time to work with.

There is the requirement to use more caution, precision, and even intent behind all of the lines of code that you try to write out.

You also are not able to check out the code when writing it like you can on the computer, which forces you to pay more attention.

This method is going to take more time and be really consuming when it is time to get things done.

But it is going to be a great method that helps us to go through and become a better developer in the process.

And if you plan to use this through college or for a new job, being able to write out the codes that you are using and utilize this for your needs is going to be so important to the success that you are able to see as well.

The more time and practice that you are able to give to writing out some of your codes by hand, the better you will get at understanding the coding and all that you can do with it.

It forces the programmer to slow down and actually focus on what they want the codes to do.

And then you can use this as a way to catch your own mistakes and learn what works the best for you and what does not.

Not Asking for Help

When we first get started with writing out codes in this manner, it is possible that you have a ton of grand ideas of how things are going to work and how you will become the greatest code writer of all time.

You may believe that nothing is going to go wrong with this and that you can handle it all in no time at all.

And one of the biggest misconceptions that are going to show up with the work that we want to do here is that we assume we really don't need to start any kind of help with our coding at all.

While it would be awesome to get started with coding in any language, even C# on our own without any help, we have to face reality a bit and remember that we are going to learn in a faster and more efficient manner when we have the right kind of peer feedback and mentors to help us out with this.

What may seem like an impossible bug to work with or a topic that seems like it is unlearnable when you do it on your own, you will find that when someone with more experience steps in and can help out, things get a lot easier, and you can actually learn something new.

Whether it is online where you ask for help, or you are able to find someone who is able to come to you in person and offer advice, you should never be scared to ask someone for help.

All of the programmers who are more advanced right now were at one time in the same place as you are now.

And most developers are going to love that they actually get a chance to code again, and will be more than willing to help you out with some of the codings that you would like help with.

Of course, we need to be careful with this and not take it for advantage at all through the process.

The best rule to follow here is to never take more than 20 minutes getting someone to help you figure out something with your code.

And you should not ask for help without spending at least 20 minutes on it ahead of time, trying to learn how it works and what you are able to do with this as well.

Not Taking Breaks

There are going to be times when you are writing out some of the codes that you want to do in the C# language, and then you get stuck on something.

You spend some time on it, but that just seems to make the whole thing worse.

You keep working at it and working at it, effectively making the problem worse, or not being able to find the problem at all, and your frustration levels keep going up.

You want to be able to fix the problem and get on with your coding, but you just get angrier, and the codes get messier in the process.

When this happens, and this is something that can happen to everyone, we must take the time to take a break.

This is probably the last thing that we want to worry about when it comes to working with the C# language and some of our codes, but it is going to allow us to take a break from the problem and get some fresh air, or at least do something else for some time.

And often, after you take a break and then come back to it, you will find that the problem, which seemed impossible at the start, is actually really easy to fix.

No one wants to give up when they have put in so much time and effort to this process, but in the long run, it can cut down on the frustration and will ensure that you can fix up your code in no time.

Ignoring the C# Community

One of the neat things that we are going to find when it is time to do our coding in the C# language and more, is that there is a large community of different programmers and developers along the way who are able to help you out.

These communities are going to include a lot of programmers who have been in all stages of the process.

Some are beginners, some have been in the game for a bit, and some are more advanced.

This is great news for you because it allows us a chance to go through and learn a lot of things.

We can ask questions of those who are in the community.

We can find a lot of the codes that we need to help us work on a variety of programs and learn something new.

And we are able to talk to others about the programming language and meet some great people while asking a lot of questions along the way as well.

It is a good idea for you to go through and make sure that you are able to really find the community that works for you.

There are a ton of these communities found online, and we just need to make sure that we find the one that seems the best for us.

This is a great place to resort back to when there are some problems with your code or when you would like to be able to get something figured out that is not working out that well to start with for your code.

Failure to Utilize the Sample Codes Provided

While this guidebook took some time to show you a few samples of code to show how all of the different types of coding are supposed to work, it is not enough to build up your understanding just to look over the code.

To help develop a true understanding, and you need to take some time to run and tinker with the code to see what it can do.

The more times that you are able to spend working on the code, the better off you will be along the way.

With the addition of things like instructions and comments, the sample codes that you are going to work with are packaged in a manner that is digestible in an easy manner by the reader.

But you will find that sometimes, these are hard to replicate from scratch.

Reading is not going to be the same thing as understanding, and actually going through the process of writing out some of the code on your own, and then running it, is going to make sure that you can learn how to code much faster than before.

The more that we are able to spend writing and practicing some of the codes that we find, and then testing these codes out as well, and the more that we can tinker with these as well, the easier the coding language is going to be along the way.

This is a great way to make sure that we are able to learn what is going on, what will not work when we make changes and a lot more in the process.

Just reading the code may work in some cases, and it seems like it is the better option to work with, but it is not going to show us the best way to be efficient in order to actually create your own programs.

Working with the C# language is a great choice to make.

There are a lot of options that we are able to focus on, and it is a good option for most of the programs that we want to be able to create.

Even as someone who is brand new to the world of programming and is not used to doing any kind of coding, I will find that the C# language is a good option to work with.

When you are ready to get started with the process of learning a new coding language, you will find that avoiding these mistakes you will able to get started on the right foot.

Conclusion

If you have decided that the C# language is the right one for you to work with, then you are in good company.

There are many programmers throughout the world who are going to use this language, and now that you are done with this guidebook, you can join the ranks now as well.

There are so much knowledge and information inside of this guidebook that we are able to work with, and you will find that this is going to be one of the best options that we are able to utilize when it comes time to work with the C# language.

Contributing to C#'s ease of use is the reduction of some C++ features, and no longer macros, templates, and multiple inheritances. Especially for enterprise developers, the above features will only produce more trouble than benefits. New features that make programming easier are strict type safety, version control, garbage collect, and more. The goal of all these functions is to develop component-oriented software.

Your effort to learn C# is a big investment because C# is designed for the primary language of writing NGWS applications. You will find a lot of functions that you can achieve or laboriously implement in C++, which are just some basic functions in C#. For enterprise-level programming languages, new financial data types are popular. You use a new decimal data type that is dedicated to financial calculations. If you don't like this simple ready-made type, you can easily create a new data type based on the special needs of your application.

C# provides you with convenient functions such as garbage collection, type safety, version control, and so on. The only "cost" is that code operations are type-safe by default, and pointers are not allowed. It's all about type safety. However, if you need pointers, you can still use them with non-secure codes, and you cannot have column sets when calling non-secure codes.

C# is an easy programming language, making it good even to the beginners in programming. One only needs to setup the environment and start writing and running their C# code. You can use C# alone to develop a complete computer application.

As a beginner, you will accomplish amazing goals with this guidebook and gain valuable knowledge in learning how to work with the C# language. We have explored many different topics that come with this language, such as how to work with conditional statements, how to work with classes, and what the operators are all about, and so much more. This guidebook will help you to go through the C# language so that you can learn to write your own codes.

If you feel like you're ready to learn a new coding language and get started on programming, C# is a great one to go with. Make sure to check out this guidebook to learn all the basics that you need to know to create really useful codes in no time at all.

Good luck and happy programming.

RASPBERRY PI

A complete guide to start learning RaspberryPi on your own. Learn an easy way to setup and build your projects, avoid common mistakes, and develop solid skills in computer technology.

Michail Kölling

Introduction

We can find a lot of different programming languages to work with to write codes and a lot of tools and accessories that sneak in and help us get things done as well. With all this technology growing and changing all the time, sometimes, this is going to make beginners feel like they are too far behind and that they should just give up rather than trying. They worry that the work is going to be too hard for them to get it done. The neat thing here is that Raspberry Pi is going to be there to help to solve this problem. This is a small computer board, which is about the size of a credit card, that can hook up to the computer monitor or your TV.

To start, the Raspberry Pi device is going to be anything that we would expect our traditional desktop computer to do, such as processing different voices, looking online, creating tables, doing gaming, playing videos in HD, and more. Even more than this, we will find that this device also comes with the ability to interact with the world outside as well.

As you can see, there is quite a bit that we need to know when it is time to work with Raspberry Pi, and you will be able to utilize it for a lot of the different projects that are out there.

The following chapters will discuss the Raspberry Pi. The Raspberry Pi is increasingly popular. Why, though? What's all the fuss about? So many people are interested in this amazing little microcomputer and all of the things that it can do. This book will focus on all of the reasons that people are falling in love with the Raspberry Pi and its various capabilities. We'll also be learning how to program in Python and the plethora of different things that you can use the Raspberry Pi for.

We will look at some options that are out there for this device, and we will learn some coding that is necessary to get it started. It is such a simple device that we can work with, but it does make the difference when it comes to how well we can learn about and work with computers and even how we can work through the process of learning new coding and programming language.

If you take a look at the structure of the Raspberry Pi, the first thing you'll notice is how small it is. The size of a Raspberry Pi is similar to that of a typical credit card. This small form-factor of the Raspberry Pi is itself a characteristic feature of the device, although it may not look entirely like a final product straight out of the box.

When compared to the modern PC motherboards, the Raspberry Pi is a computer that has been made available to the general consumer in a tiny form-factor, low price tag, and functionality, which you would normally expect from a full-sized Personal Computer. Owing to such characteristics, the Raspberry Pi is suitable for a wide range of purposes. Browsing the internet, playing modest video games, interacting with popular social media channels, the perfect system to learn programming and coding, all the way to using the Raspberry Pi in innovative and creative projects building devices such as retro emulator in variety of forms and controlling and handling complex circuits. The Raspberry Pi does not have one specific use, in reality; it's the complete opposite; in the sense that the limitations of the Raspberry Pi are in actuality the limitations of one's imagination regarding the projects in which this device can be used.

Moreover, there's an entire Raspberry Pi community on the internet dedicated to helping out people in their queries regarding the device. Whether you bought your first Raspberry Pi and need help setting it up or if you're using a Raspberry Pi in a project, you will be surprised at how positively and quickly the community joins the discussion forums and give their suggestions and feedback to your questions.

The birth of Raspberry Pi was inspired by the notion that fully functioning computers in a compact size made available to the general consumer at a plausible price would hold enough power as to not only facilitate the educational industry but also making computer technology easy to implement and customize in various projects (educational projects, DIY projects or any experiment that can use the prowess of the Raspberry Pi); in short, the prospects are virtually unlimited). The Raspberry Pi Foundations was established in 2012, and after a limited production of units, the beta testing became a huge success and today, Raspberry Pi is the leading device which has taken a strong foothold in various human interactive environments including homes, offices, smart factories, data centers, interactive classrooms and other such places which can take advantage of the features of a small handheld computer.

When we think about computers, we usually find a monitor, a keyboard, a mouse, and a CPU. But the Raspberry Pi is a fully functional computer system that is embedded into a small single credit-card-sized board and costs less than most of the video games you'll find. With it, people will be able to do a variety of things such as building robots, learning how to code, and an assortment of other fascinating and strange projects.

Society needs programmers now more than ever before, and the release of the Raspberry Pi has echoed a brand-new love for computer technology and science.

The Raspberry Pi might not be a great choice for primary PC with its 512 MB to 1 GB of RAM and for storage purposes, an SD card, but it can even be used for several other reasons from giving power to robots made from home and developing retro video games to becoming home theater PCs and to online-connected weather stations.

If you're searching for motivation to begin your very own Raspberry Pi venture, at that point, you've gone to the perfect spot since we have arranged probably the best use cases around to give you a few thoughts.

Chapter 1

Basics of raspberry PI

What is Raspberry Pi?

Raspberry Pi is a low-cost single computer developed by Raspberry Pi Foundation, a charity based in UK. The Raspberry Pi can be connected to a monitor or television and can be operated using a USB mouse and keyboard. The dimension of the device is comparable to that of a credit card and requires low operating power. It comprises all the commonly available interfaces used in general purposes computers such as USB ports, audio ports, HDMI output port, ethernet ports, etc. In addition to these standard interfaces, some general-purpose input/output(GPIO) ports are also available in this device. These GPIO pins can be configured to act either as an input or as an output port, thereby making the device to function as a low power high performance embedded system. There are several versions of the Raspberry Pi available in the market, depending on the features provided. The Raspberry Pi Foundation developed the Raspberry Pi in England, and the first device was launched in early 2012. To this date, many versions of the Raspberry Pi have been released and have continuously improved with each version.

There are even industrial models and versions that have become smaller and smaller, such as the Raspberry Pi Zero. By the end of 2017, more than 17 million Raspberry Pi units had already been sold.

The goal of the Development

The goal of the Raspberry Pi Foundation is to introduce young people to hardware and software programming and to facilitate their entry into programming.

The Raspberry Pi is relatively inexpensive to buy, and therefore the entry barriers to development with the Raspberry Pi are very low. The unique thing about the Raspberry Pi is that this small credit card format hides a full-fledged computer.

In the meantime, numerous projects for everyday and professional life can be implemented very easily. The Raspberry Pi Foundation also plays an important role here. On the website raspberrypi.org, you can find numerous suggestions for very ambitious projects, which can be easily rebuilt.

The Raspberry Pi Foundation also carries out numerous school projects to introduce young students into programming. Since there are many different kinds of software and hardware-based on Raspberry Pi projects out there, I would like to showcase some of them in the next chapter.

So much can be said in advance, as there are now entire business models and commercial devices based on a Raspberry Pi. This already shows that the Raspberry Pi has become very widespread and is no longer just a learning device for young people.

Hardware Specifications

Your Raspberry Pi has the following hardware specifications:

BCM2837Bo Chip

Quad-core 64-bit ARM cortex A53 CPU

Clocked at 1.4GHz

Cypress 43455 chip for wireless and Bluetooth

400 MHz Video Core IV GPU

1 GB LPDDR22-900 SDRAM

802.11 ac Wireless LAN

Bluetooth 4.2 chip
Power

Micro-usb power in

2.5 Amp supply recommended

PoE Connector Added

Browsing the internet

You can connect you Raspberry Pi to the internet either by Ethernet cable or wireless connection. To connect to wi-fi, look at the top right side of the screen. You will see an icon with a red cross. Select the correct network from the drop-down menu. Provide the password for your wi-fi connection, and your Raspberry Pi is connected to the internet.

What is Raspberry Pi meant for?

A Raspberry Pi laptop can be used like any other Linux based system. The "hard disk drive" of this system is small – instead of a traditional hard disk, it uses a micro SD card. You can easily work on your office documents, run games, and play videos.

You can connect to the command line interface of the Raspberry Pi using Secure Socket Shell (SSH) from any computer. SSH is a network protocol that supplies administrators with a secure manner to access a remote computer. In such a scenario, you will not get a graphical interface from the connection. You WILL, however, be able to execute commands from the terminal application on another computer. The commands will execute through the SSH onto your Raspberry Pi.

If there is a requirement to access the raspberry pi remotely and you require a graphical interface as well, you can do so with the help of virtual network computing. This would be a slow affair but would allow you to connect visually to your Raspberry Pi if you needed to.

What is required along with the Raspberry Pi 3b+ model

For the Raspberry Pi to work fully as a desktop computer, you will require the following equipment to attach to the ports and connections listed earlier:

•*Power supply*: You would require a USB-A to micro-USB lead. A 5.1-volt micro USB supply powers it. The best choice would be to buy a 300-watt power supply from your local retailer. This would provide enough power to your Raspberry Pi to allow you to work on it with no further upgrades. Make sure that you do not overload the power supply. Take a close look at the specifications provided on the power supply to give you a fair idea of the power handling capacity of the system.

•*Keyboard and Mouse*: Raspberry Pi allows you to connect to any USB or wireless keyboard or mouse. The unit comes with 4 USB ports, down to two free USB ports after connecting the keyboard and mouse.

•*Monitor*: The original Raspberry Pi supported HDMI and RCA ports. Raspberry Pi 3 has HDMI and magic 3.5mm media ports. Every version of Raspberry Pi is HDMI compatible, meaning that you can easily connect it to your home HDMI–compatible TV.

•*Micro SD card*: If you want to use your own micro-SD card in your Raspberry Pi, you will have to get the NOOBS installer. NOOBS stands for "New Out Of the Box Software". This can be a relatively complicated process, so buying a prepared micro SD card is recommended. Prepared micro SD cards are not expensive and are likely to save you a lot of time, money, and headache. If you insist on preparing your own SD card, go to www.raspberrypi.org/downloads. While preparing your card, you can opt for a wide range of operating systems distributions, which can be a great advantage. If you are a new user to Linux; however, it is best to go for the NOOBS installer and use the standard Raspbian operating system it has to offer.

•*Case*: Your Raspberry Pi is only a motherboard. It does not have an enclosure. This is the reason it is priced so low. It is recommended that you purchase a case for the unit to protect it from wear and tear and prolong the duration of its life.

Booting from NOOBS

If you purchase a Raspberry Pi with a micro SD card containing NOOBS preinstalled, your setup will be much easier. After connecting to the monitor, it will show that the installer has been loaded. Click on "Install" and installation will be completed in a short time.

Raspberry Pi provides a Linux desktop that you can use like any other PC. It is easy to use and navigate if you are familiar with Windows environments.

Now that your Raspberry Pi is fully installed and configured, we can start exploring it in more detail. Get ready to dive in!

Accessories

Camera: back in 2013, the Raspberry Pi Foundation and its distributors were able to release the firmware update that would allow for a camera to be used with the Raspberry Pi. The camera is a flat cable that you can plug into the CSI connector. When you are looking at Raspbian, you are going to have to make sure that you enable the camera to run on the board through configuring the camera option. The Raspberry Pi camera can take up to a 1080p photo or shoot a 640 x 480p video. Three years later, the 8 megaPixels was released to the public.

Gertboard: the foundation made this accessory for educational purposes only so that the GPIO Pins were able to be expanded so that the interface could be controlled with a series of switches and sensors.

Infrared camera: this camera was going to be part of the camera module that would not contain the infrared filter, and it is known as the Pi NoIR.

Software

Operating system

As mentioned earlier, you are going to want to try and stick to the Raspbian operating system, which is an extension of Linux. There are other operating systems that you can use if you do not want to work with a Linux based operating system.

Driver APIs

The video-core iv for the graphics processor is going to be using a binary blob in which you will be able to prime into the graphics processing unit from an SD card and then only adding in the additional software when it has booted up. Most of the work that is done with the driver is going to be done with a closed source for the graphics processor and its related code. Any software use calls are going to run their code closed source, but there are specific applications that you can download to open the driver of origin that is inside of the kernel. The kernel's API is going to be designed for these closed libraries to make sure that the Pi is processing correctly, and the code is not being messed with, which could end up causing the Pi not to operate properly.

Firmware

All of the firmware that the Raspberry Pi uses is going to be closed sourced and use a binary blob that is freely redistributable. You are not going to find a lot of firmware that is going to be open source for the Pi.

Chapter 2

Setup

Setting Up Your Raspberry Pi

In this chapter, we're going to outline everything that you have to do to set up your Raspberry Pi. This will include everything that you need to get it up and running, so pay close attention. It is difficult at first, but it only gets easier from here! This guide assumes that you're working with a Raspberry Pi Model 3 B, the most recent model. However, if you're working with an older model, things will remain largely the same throughout the process.

First off, here's what you're going to need to set up your Pi so that it runs as a desktop computer:

- Monitor (obviously)
- Keyboard and mouse
- MicroSD card
- Operating system
- Choosing an Operating System

What operating system should you use on your Raspberry Pi? There are many different answers to this question. Many different companies have made versions of the operating systems that can run on the Raspberry Pi's software. Even Microsoft has released a version of Windows that can run on the hardware of the Raspberry Pi. So, bearing all of this in mind, what software specifically should you use on your Raspberry Pi?

Regardless of what operating system you want to use, NOOBS will offer support for it and is an excellent operating system installer. While I would recommend that you install Raspbian, ultimately, you have autonomy over whatever you decide to install on your Pi. Let's now talk about the setup process.

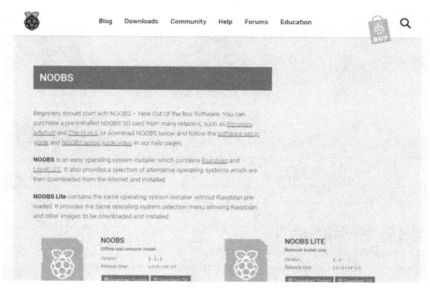

Installing NOOBS

These instructions will tell you how to set up Raspbian only. If you decide to install a different operating system, then this book will not be able to help you with that. However, as long as the installation is through NOOBS, the process should be the same for all operating systems. Therefore, you shouldn't have any problems installing them. With that said, let's install NOOBS first.

To set up your Raspberry Pi with an operating system, you will need to grab your SD card and insert it into your computer.

Search for SD Formatter 4.0. Download and install it. (Kindle formatting doesn't play nice with links, so I cannot link you, unfortunately.) It's released by an organization called the SD Association, so as long as you're getting it off their website, you should be in the clear.

Install the software and start up the SD Formatter program. Select your SD card's disk drive and then format it exactly as the default settings indicate.

Go to your download of the NOOBS installer. You can get it by searching for NOOBS and then heading to the link hosted by the Raspberry Pi organization.

Extract the files somewhere, such as your desktop. Copy the files that were extracted over to your SD card, and then you're set.

Take out the SD card and put it in your Raspberry Pi's SD card slot.

Plug-in everything: your monitor via the HDMI port, your keyboard, and your mouse. Ensure that your monitor is on the right setting.

If all goes well, you should be clear to finally plug your Raspberry Pi into the wall and get to some heavy development. If you're using a newer Pi model, it should have built-in WiFi. Older models, however, will require you to connect to the internet via Ethernet or to plug in a WiFi adapter that is compatible with the Raspberry Pi.

You'll know your Raspberry Pi is on when the indicator link on the Raspberry Pi is blinking. At this point, you'll know if everything is going well because the indicator light will be on, and you should have video displaying on your monitor.

Installing Raspbian

Now that we've installed NOOBS, we can proceed with installing Raspbian or your operating system of choice. Again, this book will only discuss Raspbian. Still, the process of installing the operating system is the same for all other operating systems that you can use for the Raspberry Pi.

On the main screen upon the operating system powering up, ensure that Raspbian is selected. This is the recommended operating system across most communities, especially for people who are new to Raspberry Pi.

Click Install next and then click Yes to confirm that it's going to overwrite your SD card.

Wait, and after a bit, your operating system will be installed. It's a straightforward process like I said.

Your Pi will reboot, and you'll be brought to the main screen for the Raspbian operating system.

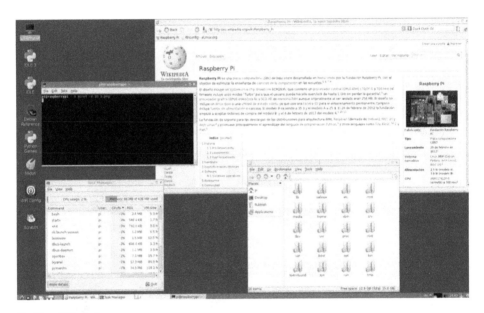

Getting Started

Now that you're on Raspbian's main screen, it's time to make the magic happen. This is where your adventures with the Raspberry Pi begin. Feel free to poke around a little bit and see what it has to offer. You can see right out the gate that there are quite a few programs built in that aim to help you learn to do various things, which betray the origin of Raspberry Pi as something intended to help underprivileged people learn about computer science and programming in general.

So now, you're confronted with your operating system. If you've never used a Linux operating system before, you more than likely have a few questions. Moreover, even if you have used a Linux operating system before, there's the chance that this is not anything like what you've used before if you've primarily stuck to KDE distributions. So let's answer some questions first.

What am I looking at? The answer to that question is simple: Raspbian. Raspbian is a distribution of the Linux operating system, which you've most likely heard of before. It's an offshoot of a popular Linux distribution called Debian. There are many other Linux distributions, one of which is Ubuntu. Raspbian has been designed to be a perfect match for the Raspberry Pi's hardware demands and its specific CPU architecture.

What is Linux?

Linux itself is an offshoot of another operating system from long, long ago called Unix. Unix was extraordinarily famous for various reasons that a book could be written about all on its own (and numerous have, and they are quite good).

Unix itself would inspire many operating systems that people use every day, including Linux (which in itself inspired the extremely popular Android mobile operating system) and macOS (from which the iOS mobile operating system was derived). In other words, if you have a phone or a non-Windows computer, you've already been using a computer inspired by Unix.

Because of its ubiquity in the '80s and the fact that operating systems such as Linux, Minix, and FreeBSD would fit extremely well into the hacker subculture's belief in freedom of information and free software (free as in speech and free as in beer, both), Unix would remain the king of the software development world for quite a long time. Quite a long time leads up to the current day, where you're sitting in front of an unfamiliar operating system wondering what to do.

How quaint

Let's look for a second at our operating system. First, the most important part of a Linux system is the Terminal. If you use an Apple computer, you've probably poked around in the Terminal a few times as well. The Terminal was one of the most heavily used features of Unix because it offered an extremely easy way to get packages, manage your system, and do much, much more. This remains true today. Understanding Linux systems means, to an extent, understanding how the Terminal works and all of the many different things that you can do with it. So, if you want to have an idea of how Linux works, poke your head around a guide aimed at teaching you how the Terminal works.

One of the prime pulls of Linux, too, is the fact that it's completely free, and this applies here no less. You can poke around your system's information and have complete control over the computer and its motherboard. This is why so many geeks like me love Raspbian: it's easy to use, but it offers all of the control and autonomy that Linux distributions do. You'll notice that Raspbian comes with quite a few different things packed in. Of note is a program geared at helping you with algebra related problems called Mathematica. You'll also notice that there is a version of Chromium included. This browser is much like Google Chrome. It is just the open-source version of Google Chrome. There's a difference between standard versions of Chromium and this version, though; this version is much lighter weight than other versions, and as a result, it runs much better on the Raspberry Pi's delicate architecture. You can open as many tabs as you want! (Don't open as many tabs as you want, it won't go well.)

The last thing of note is the fact that the operating system comes with a version of Minecraft, which is referred to as Minecraft Pi. This is a lot like Minecraft, except it's geared towards helping kids learn how to program. However, you might find it kind of fun if you poke around and try it. Besides, this is a long book, so it won't hurt to give yourself a bit of a break to play a game.

Linux is the best choice for tinkerers. There are many reasons. The first is that it keeps the overall cost of tinkering down since Linux's culture endorses the use of open-source and free software. This means that you can spend a lot less money obtaining software and a lot more time using your software. The fact that it's completely open is great as well because if you get to be good enough at programming, you can crack open the source code and modify it as you wish. There are no secrets, and you know exactly what you're getting into. Also, perhaps the biggest pull is the fact that there are so many open-source tools available to you as a Linux programmer. People have been working with Unix-based systems for almost 50 years now, not to mention that the free and open-source software movement has been around for more than 40. Believe me, if there is anything you want to do, there is almost certainly a program out there already that's been written to do exactly that. If there isn't, Linux makes it extremely easy for you to make it yourself.

Embedded Linux

Technically speaking, there is no such thing as Embedded Linux. When we talk of embedded Linux, we use it as an umbrella term to refer to an **embedded system that runs Linux**. An embedded system refers to a piece of computing hardware designed for a singular, specific application. In contrast, a Personal Computer has a multitude of purposes—browsing the Internet, playing video games, or writing eBooks about the Raspberry Pi. Lately, though, the line that separates general-purpose computing devices and embedded systems are blurring. The Raspberry Pi, this book's main topic, can be classified as both. It just depends on the purpose you bestow upon it.

To be clear, embedded systems are still different from general-purpose computers. They have distinct qualities that are theirs alone. These include the following:

- Their purpose is very specific, and they are often dedicated to this purpose.

- They are usually underpowered. They tend to lack the beefy power that personal computers usually have.

- They operate in a larger system, acting as a hub for other sensors and devices. This is in contrast with PC's, which usually act alone.

- Their roles are often quite significant, thus why they are assigned that specific task.

- They process things in real-time.

You can have an embedded Linux setup by going nuts on the Terminal in Raspbian. The setup is a complicated process, and it assumes you already know a thing or two about technical stuff. Feel free to research it yourself. We still have more things to learn about Pi.

Chapter 3

How to use Raspberry PI

You can run several types of software on the Raspberry Pi, especially in very operating systems – with which you can run your computer. Of all the available operating systems, the most popular one out of these is Raspbian, which is the Raspberry Pi Foundation's official operating system. Raspbian is based on Debian Linux and is made specifically for the Raspberry Pi that features an array of pre-installed add-ons that will help you get started.

Welcome Wizard

When you run Raspbian for the first time, you'll be introduced to the Welcome Wizard. This tool will enable you to configure the settings in Raspbian so that Raspberry Pi will behave just like or close to how you wanted to.

Note: if you want to close the Welcome Wizard, you only need to click the Cancel button at the bottom of the wizard. However. We would advise against this as there are certain features, including the wireless network that won't be able to work until the first set of questions that you get are answered.

After clicking the Next button, there will be a dropdown box for language, country, and time zone, which you need to click per your geographical location. There will also be a checkbox that will allow you to choose the appropriate keyboard layout; if, for instance, you're using a keyboard with a US-layout, then be sure to check the box that says US-layout. If English isn't your first language, but you prefer anyway over your country's native tongue, then click the 'Use English language' checkbox. Then click Next when you're done.

The next screen is about changing the password from the default one which is 'raspberry'– this is strictly for security reasons, and it's a good idea to create a new password just so hackers and bots aren't able to guess easily and have access to your account and so on. Enter your new password in the spaces provided. If you're using a complex password and wish to know what it looks like, then click the take right next to 'Hide characters' to show the password and write it down on a piece of stationary or additional notepad that only you have access to. Remember, you have to reenter the password to be on the safe side. You've done all that, you can click Next.

The next screen will have you set up your Wi-Fi network. You can choose from a range of networks that are already listed with your keyboard or mouse. Choose your desired network's name by clicking on it, before clicking Next. To ensure that your wireless network is secured, you'll need to insert its pre-shared key, which is also its password; this is usually written at the bottom of the router itself or written on a card along with the router. When you click Next, you'll be able to connect to the network. If you prefer not to choose a wireless network, you can click Skip.

Note: Only the Raspberry Pi 3, Pi 4, and Pi Zero W series have built-in wireless networking. If you are using any other model besides the ones mentioned above and one wireless networking capabilities, you'll need to invest in a USB Wi-Fi adapter.

In the next screen, you will have to install some updates for the Raspbian operating system as well as any other software on your Raspberry Pi board. Be advised that the Raspbian should be regularly updated to add new features, improve performance, but, more importantly, fix technical issues. You can click Next to install the updates or click Skip if you want to move on and install them later. Be advised that downloading and installing the updates could take several minutes, so please be patient. After the updates have been installed, a dialog box that says 'System is up-to-date' will appear, after which you only need to click the OK button.

Finally, the last screen of the Welcome Wizard is a simple process known commonly as rebooting, which is when you have to restart your Raspberry Pi so that certain changes can take effect. All you have to do is click on the Reboot button, and your Raspberry Pi system will restart, and this time, the Welcome Wizard will not appear. With that being said, time for action.

Using the Desktop

The Raspbian operating system that is installed in many Raspberry Pi models these days is commonly known as 'Raspbian with the Raspberry Pi Desktop,' which is the system's main graphical user interface. The desktop will be accompanied by a wallpaper in the background with some of the base programs – that you will be using – appearing on top of that wallpaper. You will find a taskbar at the top of your desktop that enables you to load any program you wish to open; tasks in the taskbar represent those programs.

The right side of the menu bar is where you will find the *system tray*. If there are any removable storage devices connected to the Raspberry Pi, like USB memory sticks, then you need to click on the eject symbol to eject and remove them safely. To the far right, you'll find the timer where you can bring up a digital calendar when you click on it.

Next to the timer is the speaker icon; click on the icon using the left mouse button to adjust the audio volume of your system, or you can click the right mouse button so that you can choose the output you want your system to use. Right next to that is the network icon; you'll know that you're connected to a wireless network when you see your network signal strength is displayed in a series of bars, but if you're connected to a wired network, only two arrows will be displayed. You can bring up a list of nearby networks by clicking on the network icon, whereas the Bluetooth icon right next to it will enable you to connect to any Bluetooth device nearby.

To the left of the menu bar, you will find the launcher, where all the programs installed on the Raspbian operating system can be run. Some of the programs will appear as shortcut icons, whereas others that are hidden away somewhere in the menu can be brought up by clicking the raspberry icon located to the far-right side.

Every program in the menu is split into categories and are explicitly named based on their purpose: for example, the Programming category has software that allows us to write programs – we will elaborate in the later chapters – or as the Games category enables you to play whatever games are listed. Please note that we haven't covered every program in this guide, so you're more than welcome to inspect them at your own volition.

Chromium

The first thing to do when you start using your Raspberry Pi board is to open the Chromium web browser: on the top left side of the menu, you need to click the raspberry icon. Move your mouse's cursor to the Internet category and then click the Chromium Web Browser to open it up.

Chromium is not hard to get used to, and those who have used Google's Chrome browser on other computers will find that it is quite similar in operation. Like any other web browser, chromium allows you to open and view websites, communicate with several people around the world using social media platforms, chat sites, and forms, as well as play games and watch videos.

For a better experience, we suggest maximizing the window of your chromium web browser: on the top right side of the chromium window title bar, you'll find three icons. You will need to click the middle, up-arrow icon, which will maximize the window to fill the entire screen. The button to the left of the *maximize* is *minimize* on the taskbar, which will hide the window when you click on it. And to the right of maximizing is the *close* function which, of course, closes the window.

Note: You must save your work before closing the window. Although most programs will give you the warning to save your work when you hit the close button, other programs don't have this facility.

The big white bar with a magnifying glass that sits at the top left-hand side of the Chromium window is the address bar. Click in the address bar, type www.raspberrypi. org, and then hit *ENTER* on your keyboard. The official Raspberry Pi website will open up. You can also perform other searches in the address bar by simply typing 'Raspbian,' 'Educational Computing,' or 'Raspberry Pi.'

When you load Chromium for the first time, several tabs will be shown at the top of the window. You wish to view another tab, click on it, and if you want to close a tab without necessarily closing the browser itself, then click the cross that you will find at a tab's right-hand edge. To open up a new tab, you can click the tab button that is to the extreme right side of one tab, or you can also hold the *CTRL* key down on your keyboard and then press the *T* key before you let go of *CTRL*.

If you want to close the browser, all you have to do is hit the close button at the top-right corner of the window.

File Manager

Any file that you save be it the programs that you write, videos you create, or the images that you download from online – will go right to your *home directory*. To view your home directory, click the raspberry icon once more to pull up the menu, point the mouse over to Accessories, and then click File Manager to load it.

With the file manager, you can browse a variety of folders (also called *directories*) and files that are already there in the Raspberry Pi's microSD card or on any removable storage device such as a USB flash drive that you can connect to the board's USB ports. When you open it for the first time, your home directly opens up automatically. Here, you'll find lines of folders, also called *subdirectories*, which – similar to the menu – are organized in categories. The main subdirectories that you will find include:

Documents: this is where most of the files that you create will be saved up, from poems to short stories and recipes, and more.

Desktop: When you first load Raspbian, this will be the folder that you will see; if you create and save the file in this folder, it will appear on your desktop, which makes it easy to find as well as load.

MagPi: this folder contains the electronic copy of the Raspberry Pi Foundation's official magazine, The MagPi.

Downloads: downloading any file online using the Chromium web browser will be saved in the Downloads folder automatically.

Pictures: This folder is maintained explicitly for pictures, which are technically known as *image files*.

Music: any piece of music you put or create on the Raspberry Pi board will be stored in this folder.

Videos: This folder is reserved for any video that you upload from an external storage device or download from the Chromium web browser.

Public: any file or folder that you store in this folder will be available to other Raspberry Pi users, despite having their own account.

You will notice that the File Manager window is divided into two panes: the left pane displays your Raspberry Pi's directories, whereas the right pane displays the files and subdirectories of the directory chosen in the left pane. If you insert a removable storage device into the USB port of the board, a dialog box will open up, asking you if you'd like to open it in the File Manager; by clicking the OK button, you'll be able to view the files and subdirectories in that device.

You can easily copy your files on a removable device on your Raspberry Pi's microSD card, or even transfer them from the microSD card to your removable device. When you've opened both the removable device and your home directory in separate File Manager windows, choose the file that you want to move from one window by clicking and holding the left mouse button and then sliding it to the other window before letting go of the mouse button. This process is called *dragging and dropping*.

Another method would be to click once on the file, select the Edit menu, select Copy, click the other window, choose the Edit menu, and then click Paste.

The Move option, which you can find from the Edit menu, is similar in execution, only that it deletes the file from its original home after being copied. A faster way would be to use keyboard shortcuts *CTRL+C* for copying or *CTRL+X* for cutting and pasting via

CTRL+V.

Note: to copy text, a file, or folder using keyboard shortcuts such as *CTRL+C*; you need first to hold down the key *CTRL*, and present along with the second key C before letting both of them go.

After you're done with that, click the close button on the top left corner of the window to close the File Manager. If there are other windows open, you need to close all of them. If there's a removable device connected to your Raspberry Pi board, you'll have to eject it by clicking the eject button at the top right corner of the screen before you unplug it.

Note: be sure to click the eject button before you unplug your external storage device. If you don't do this, the files in your storage device may become either corrupt or unusable.

LibreOffice Productivity Suite

If you want to write a document, an article, a poem, or anything else written, then the LibreOffice Writer is what you need. If you've used Microsoft Office or Google Docs, then you have a good idea of how to use LibreOffice's word processor.

One thing to note is that LibreOffice might not be installed on every Raspbian OS image by default. And if that's the case, then you can use the Recommended Software tool to install them.

Besides being able to write documents, this word processor also allows you to format them in a variety of creative ways: you can change the font color, size, insert images, tables, charts, add effects, and any other type of content you choose. Like other word processor programs, the LibreOffice Writer will inspect whatever you've written for mistakes, as well as highlight spelling and grammatical errors in red and green, respectively, as you type.

If you don't know what to write, then we suggest writing a passage on everything that you've learned about the Raspberry Pi board and the software installed in it so far. There are several icons at the top of the window that you can experiment with to see what they do: see if you can increase the font size, as well as change the color. If you're uncertain how to get this done, move your mouse cursor over each icon one at a time to see a 'tooltip' that lets you know what the icon is about and what it does. If you're satisfied with what you've written, click the File menu and then choose the Save option to save all of your work. Give your file and name, and then finally click the Save button.

Note: you should always have the decency of saving your work as you'll never know when you might encounter a power outage, short circuit, or any other mishap that would disrupt your work with the Raspberry Pi board.

The LibreOffice Writer is one of many programs that you will find in the LibreOffice productivity suite. Other Office programs included in this suite are:

• LibreOffice Calc: a spreadsheet used for creating charts and graphs and handling numbers.

• LibreOffice Base: a database used for storing, looking up quickly, and analyzing information.

• LibreOffice Impress: a tool used for creating presentation slides as well as running slideshows.

• LibreOffice Draw: an illustration program where you can create diagrams and pictures.

• LibreOffice Math: a tool for creating appropriately formatted mathematical formulae that can also be used in other documents.

LibreOffice is also made available for other computers as well as operating systems. You prefer using it on your Pi system; then you can visit libreoffice.org download the file and then install it on any operating system, be it Linux, Apple Mac OS, or Microsoft Windows. If you wish to know more about how you can use LibreOffice, click the Help menu. And if you have no more use for it, then you can close LibreOffice Writer by pointing and clicking the close button that is on the top right corner of the window.
Note: many programs have a help menu with which you can learn about a certain program and how you can use it. This can be handy if you are having trouble operating a program.

Recommended Software Tool

Although you already have access to a wide collection of preinstalled software with your Raspbian operating system, you can get more if you like. This is where the Recommended Software tool comes into play as it has some of the best lines of software that you can find. Be advised that the Recommended Software tool requires an Internet connection for you to operate. Once you're connected, click the raspberry menu icon, move the cursor to Preferences, and then click on Recommended Software. This will open up the tool and start downloading information about any software that's available.

Then a list of some of the compatible software packages will appear after a couple of seconds. Like the raspberry menu software, the ones here are also organized in several categories. Click on any category in the left pane to view software under that category, or you can click All Programs to view everything.

If you see any software with a tick right next to it, it means it's already installed on your operating system. And if there's no tick in the box, then use the left mouse button to click the checkbox so you can prepare it for installation. Mark, as many numbers of software you want to prepare for installation. But make sure that there's enough space in your microSD card for these programs; otherwise, you'll have to limit the installation.

Similarly, you can also uninstall software this way: you look for any software with a tick in its checkbox and then left mouse click on the box to remove the tick. But if you have changed your mind or have made a mistake, then you can go back in the previous section and put the tick back in the box again.

When you're all set, click the OK button to start installing or uninstalling the software that you have selected/unselected. After you've downloaded and installed or uninstalled any software in your selection, a message box appears; click the OK button to exit the Recommended Software tool.

The Add/Remove Software tool is another tool that can help you install or uninstall software. It is located in the same Preferences category in the Raspbian menu. There is a wide range of software that is available with this. However, none of them have been approved by the Raspberry Pi Foundation.

Raspberry Pi Configuration Tool

You'll find that it functions similar to the Welcome Wizard that you used in the beginning: you'll be able to change plenty of settings in the Raspbian operating system. First, click the raspberry icon and then move your mouse cursor to the Preferences category, and then select Raspberry Pi Configuration to be loaded.

This tool is divided into four tabs, each controlling a certain part of Raspbian. The first thing you will see when the tool is loaded for the first time is System: you can set up a hostname – this is the name that the Raspberry Pi board uses on your wired or wireless network – change your account password, as well as a bunch of other settings though most of these settings don't require any changing.

Note: this overview is to help you get acquainted with the tool and how to use it.

Move your mouse cursor to the Interfaces tab and click it with your left mouse button to pull up the next category. You'll see a big list of settings that have been disabled. You can only change the settings if you include new software into your Raspberry Pi, including the Raspberry Pi Camera Module, and only if the manufacturer of the hardware instructs you to. The only exceptions here include VNC, which enables a 'Virtual Network Computer' and allows you to see as well as control the Raspbian desktop from another computer on your network thanks to a VNC client; Remote GPIO, where you can use the Raspberry Pi's GPIO pins from another computer on your network; and SSH, where you enable a 'Secure Shell' and enables you to log into the Raspberry Pi using another computer on your network with an SSH client.

When you click on the Performance tab, the third category can be viewed. From here, you can configure the amount of memory that the Raspberry Pi's graphics processing unit (GPU) uses and, depending on some models, increase the performance of your board thanks to a process called *overclocking*. Though, it would be better to leave these settings as they are unless you need to change them.

Lastly, you get to view the final category by clicking the Localization tab. From here, you can set up your locale, in which you can control how the numbers are displayed, the language used in Raspbian, change the layout of your keyboard, change the time zone, and also set up your country for Wi-Fi capabilities. As of now, however, you need to exit the tool by clicking the Cancel button without making any further changes.

Warning: there are different rules for different countries about the kind of frequencies that are Wi-Fi radio can use. For instance, if you set the Wi-Fi country in the Raspberry Pi Configuration Tool to a country other than the one that you're in right now, it will confuse your device and have a struggle when connecting to your networks. What's worse, is that it can also be illegal under radio licensing laws. So, in other words, don't do it.

Shutting Down

After exploring the Raspbian desktop and having your way with it, it's time to learn how to shut your Raspberry Pi down safely. Like any other computer that people use, the

Raspberry Pi stores your files in *volatile memory* – which is a memory that gets emptied as soon as the system is powered off. For every document you make, it's important to save as you type – this is where your files will be transferred to a *non-volatile memory*, which is the microSD card – so that you can retrieve the files that you saved and resume working on them.

But the documents that you're working on aren't the only ones opened. The operating system Raspbian several files opened while running, and if for any reason, the power cable is pulled from the Raspberry Pi board as the files are still opened, it could lead to the entire operating system becoming corrupt. You'll have to install it all over again.

So, to prevent this from occurring, you need to instruct Raspbian to save all of your files and documents and prepare itself for when it's time to be powered off – a process known as *shutting down*.

Warning: remember not to pull the power cable out of the Raspberry Pi board until you shut it down first. If you don't do this, it will corrupt Raspbian, and you could end up losing any file that you created or downloaded.

To shut down, click the raspberry icon at the top left corner of the desktop and then select Shutdown. A dialog box with three options will show up: Shut down, Logout, and Reboot. Shut down is the option that you mostly use clicking this will instruct the operating system to shut all open files and software, shutting the entire system down. When you see the display turn black, with a couple of seconds until the green flashing light on the Pi disappears, that's when it's safe to turn the power supply off.

And if you want to turn the Raspberry Pi back on, all you have to do is disconnect and then reconnect the power cable, or you can toggle the power switch at the wall socket.

The remote process is similar to Shutdown, it will close every one of your files, but instead of shutting down, it will restart your Raspberry Pi – similar to if you had chosen the shutdown option, and then had to disconnect and reconnect the power cable. Certain changes you make with your Raspberry Pi require a restart to implement them – like installing certain core software updates – or if the software has crashed and has left your operating system in an unusable state.

And lastly, the Logout feature, which is quite useful if there is more than one account on your Raspberry Pi: it will close any program that you currently have running and will immediately bring up the login screen for which you can access another account using their designated username and password. And if by mistake you hit Logout, then you can get back in by simply typing 'pi' as your username and the password you chose in the Welcome Wizard.

Data and Variables

The first thing that we're going to look at is mathematical program operations and how you can perform them. To understand this, though, you need to understand a thing or two about data.

Python understands data in a relatively unique way, but there's a reason that it's relative; all programming languages understand data in this same kind of detached manner. Data is, for lack of a better term, any singular piece of information that is used to represent some given concept. Any individual piece of data is referred to as a value. **Values** can take on several different forms.

However, under it all, computers don't actually understand any of these different forms; instead, computers understand the raw idea of ones and zeroes, binary calculations that are happening far, far under the hood of the computer. On top of the binary code is one layer of abstraction, known as Assembly code, which operates upon the bits, or the different sets of binary code that represent individual values. On top of that is another layer of abstraction, known as the operating system. Then there's yet another layer of abstraction, the programming language in use. This works with the operating system to convert something that we can understand into assembly language, which the computer's processor then converts into a set of different calculations. All of this happens in the matter of micro or even nanoseconds.

The key point of all of this is that computers understand things in terms of ones and zeroes, and the way that we see a value means next to nothing to a computer. In order to solve this, programmers long ago decided that computers would categorize different values into different **types**. These types of data tell the computer how and in what manner to perform operations to the given values as they correspond to the ones and zeroes. This is a super complex architecture, so don't feel too bad if it doesn't immediately make a whole lot of sense.

Anyhow, in pursuit of properly understanding all of this, we must start to break down these data types a little bit and look at them with a more abstract eye than we currently are. So let's do that. The next thing that we're going to do is take a sincere look at the different kinds of data that you can use in Python.

Integer

The integer data type refers to any piece of data that corresponds to a whole number in our abstract understanding. Therefore, these would be numbers such as 7, 39, or -3.

Float

The float data type refers to any piece of data that corresponds to a decimal number in our abstract understanding, so things such as 3.141569 or 94.3332.

Double

Double stands for "double precision" number and refers to a very specific kind of decimal number. You don't need to understand this **too** in-depth at this point because of float and double act rather synonymously in Python. The reason for this distinction goes back to a time when computers had less RAM and less processing power than they do now, but for our purposes, you can largely ignore this.

Boolean

Boolean means true or false. This will make a lot more sense later on when we start to talk about programmatic logic and the way that logic actually plays a part in computer science.

Character

The character stands for any singular alphanumeric or symbolic character that can be printed out in a computer console. These could be things like A, 3, or $. This is a fickle understanding, though, because characters correlate to an ASCII value, which means that any given character also has a numeric integer value. For this reason, if you had the character "3" and the integer 3 and tried to see if they were the same, they wouldn't be. Bear this in mind as you program.

String

We'll talk about strings more in-depth later, but strings are essentially long chains of characters that are put together. Any set of character values is a string, whether it is 2 characters or 2000 characters long.

These are not all of the values available for you to use in Python. However, they are the ones that you are most likely to use almost immediately, so we've covered them here for that reason specifically. These values may be expressed in any given expression in Python. For example:

print(3 + 3)

would print 6

print("Hey there!\n")

printing a string to the console

print('C')

printing a character to the console

In other words, these form the very nucleus of everything that you're going to be doing in programming. Every piece of code you ever write will be working with values like these and manipulating them in one way or another. As you work with more and more code, you'll come to appreciate how truly often you make use of all of this and how every statement in a program is just the manipulation of data in one way or another. This is the nature of programming, for better or worse.

Sometimes, you're going to want to keep up with these data pieces so that you can recall them or change them at a later point. What can you do for this purpose? The answer is simple. You can use **variables**. Variables offer a method by which you can keep track of values over a long period as you work through a program.

Recall earlier how we talked about data types. Data types were especially useful and a bit more diverse than they are in Python because Python tries to go out of its way to make things easy for you; however, all of these values are stored in the computer's memory, and they're stored in boxes of pre-allocated size depending on how much space any given data type uses.

These individual boxes in the computer's memory can be referred to as variables. Picture it like the overhead view of a given city. You may have a bunch of lots that you can place houses in. You then will refer to any given lot by its address. The lot is like the variable itself, and the address is the **name** of the variable.

Therefore, you can actually store all of these values in variables where you decide the name to refer to it by. So, let's say that you had a variable called something like ***dogAge***. If your dog was 4 years old, then you may set this like so:

dogAge = 4
If your dog's name was Lucky, then you may set a string variable like so:

dogName = "Lucky"

Python makes it extremely easy to name and declare variables. Some other languages have a bunch more hurdles to the process, but Python most definitely does not. This can be both a blessing and a curse. In other languages, you may have to say the type of the variable when you declare it, but Python takes this burden off you.

Why would this be a bad thing? Well, simply put, it can be confusing for a newer programmer who doesn't have much experience working with different data types. You may end up forgetting and trying to make a comparison between two pieces of data that aren't of the same time, actually messing up your data in the meantime because the computer doesn't compare different pieces of data in the same way.

This is the reason that you actually want to learn what the individual data types are. It will help you realize, for example, that the string "34" and the integer 34 are not the same and should not be compared, and may explain to you why your comparisons may be off at one point or another if you're not careful about this.

Python Math

Of course, working with variables is much more useful if you're actually doing operations on the data in question—for example, if you're actively performing math operations or performing useful equations. In this section, we're going to be exploring the different ways in which you can work with data.

Bear in mind primarily that you can refer back to variables. For example, if you wanted to print a string that you saved in a variable, you could do it like so:

print(dogName)

Or, if you were ambitious and wanted to print out your dog's name and dog's age both, you could do it like so:

print("My dog's name is " + dogName + " and they are " + dogAge + " years old.")

But what if something changed? What if, for example, your dog aged by a year? What could you do?

Well, you'd want to take your dog's age and then add one to it. But how can you do this? Well, you can do this by actually assigning it a new value. You can reassign values to variables and manipulate the variables that they have much like you set them and initialized them in the first place. The process is similar for the most part. Let's say, for example, that we wanted to add 1 to the variable dogAge. We could do that like so:

dogAge = dogAge + 1

The variable dogAge would take the old value of dogAge, 4, ,and add 1 to it, and this would be set as the new value for the variable **dogAge**. Make sense? Therefore, if you printed the variable dogAge now, it would print out the number 5:

print(dogAge)

Python has numerous different operators that you can use to do the math. The Python mathematical operators are like so:

c + d

This is the addition operator. It is used to add one number to another.

c - d

This is the subtraction operator. It is used to subtract one number from another.

c * d

This is the multiplication operator. It is used to multiply one number by another.

c / d

This is the division operator. It is used to divide one number by another.

c % d

This is the modulo operator. It is used to find the remainder when you divide c by d. For example, 7 % 3 would yield 1 since 7 divided by 3 has a remainder of 1.

These are the primary different mathematical operators in Python that you need to know. Using this knowledge, you can carry out complex mathematical operations in Python and make some really cool things happen. But this is only the beginning!

Let's note for a second that the way that we reassigned a value earlier wasn't necessarily the best way to do it. That is to say that the statement "dogAge = dogAge + 1" can easily be shortened and made easier to both read and understand. There are a few different shorthand operators in Python for assignment. These are as such:

```
c += d
```

```
# This just means c = c + d.
c -= d
```

```
# This just means c = c - d.
```

```
c *= d
```

```
# This means c = c * d.
```

```
c /= d
```

```
# This means c = c / d.

c %= d

# This means c = c % d.
```

As you can see, these operators aren't terribly difficult to understand, but they can go a long way to simplify your code and making it easier to read as a whole.

Comments

Comments are essential for programming unless you want to get lost in your own code. It is especially important when working with a team. Comments are parts of code that, from the computer's perspective, do ***absolutely nothing***. Why is it important, then? Comments are important so that you can insert text in your code and not have it affect the program itself. You can use these to tell your fellow programmer not to touch a certain part of the code because it's currently a band-aid solution as you try to fix another part of the code. For our purposes, you can use this as a guide for yourself so you know what part of the code does what and how.

Formatting

If you've ever programmed in another language, then you'll have noticed by now that Python is quite different in many ways. Not the least of these ways is how Python handles formatting. Many popular languages are ambivalent in regards to whitespace; a semicolon separates statements, and you could put your whole program on the same line if you really wanted to. There are even competitions in languages like C and Java to obfuscate code and make it as pretty as possible at the expense of readability.

Python, on the other hand, cares a ***lot*** about whitespace. Whitespace in Python—that is, line breaks, spaces, and tabs—indicates to Python the hierarchy of the code. This is the main engine by which Python actually starts to understand your code, so you need to pay close attention to your whitespace. Make sure that you're indenting things just as I do and paying attention to how the indentations actually affect the flow of your code as well as how your code works altogether.

User Input and Casting

Here, we're going to spend a brief minute talking about taking in user input. There are going to be many times where you're going to need to retrieve information from the user. For example, you may be asking for the name of the file or some kind of data necessary to the program from the user. It may even be something as innocuous as a book title if you're writing something like a library or bookkeeping program. One way or another, programs thrive not off just existing but off interaction and their ability to interact with the user and make things happen.

Because of this, you must understand how user input in Python works. It's relatively simple.

All user input in Python—at least using the console—is handled through the ***input*** method. The input method allows you to take in information from the console. It will read everything up until the Enter button is pressed and return all of that information as a string.

The input method works like so:

input("Prompt text")

You can set the prompt text to whatever you want or leave it out entirely. All prompt text indicates is that the text that is fed to the input method, as an argument, will be displayed to the user in question.

You can set the input method as the value of a variable, and this will set whatever the user enters as the value of that variable. For example, if my text were like so:

food = input("What is the last thing you ate?")

and the user entered **nachos**, then the value of **food** would be **nachos**. Therefore, if we printed the variable **food**, it would print as nachos:

print(food)

would print as nachos

Sometimes, though, this isn't the end of the line. Let's say that you were writing a calculator program, and you needed to accept numbers that the user entered. Of course, the input method returns a **string**. You know from our discussions earlier about how data types work that strings are not the data type that we need at the moment; no, we need a float value or an integer value. So how can we convert whatever the user entered into one of those values?

You can do this by casting. **Casting** is simply the conversion of one data type to another data type. In Python, variables can hold any data type, so you can actually just set the casted data type as the new value for the old variable, but you don't really want to do this just for the sake of maintaining clean code and being, well, a good programmer. In fact, it's probably best that you avoid this particular plan at all costs and just make new variables because it's more readable and secure anyway. Use a single variable for your user input and then just set your other variables as the casted form of that. For example:

in = input("What is the number?")

number = #casted in

Casting values is easy. All that you do is put the type you're trying to cast them to in between parentheses right next to the value, like so:
number = (float)in

This would set the value of the **number** to be the value of **in** casted to a float. Python automatically handles these tricky type conversions for you, for the most part, so you don't have a whole lot to worry about there.

Chapter 4

Interfacing Hardware

Interfacing to the Raspberry PI Inputs/Outputs

In this chapter, you will learn about GPIOs and interfacing. It's crucial to learn about this subject because understanding the fundamental concepts can facilitate the formation of custom electronics circuits that are controlled and interfaced from within an embedded Linux.

The GPIO

Raspberry Pi features an expansion header with forty pins. These pins are numbered from 1 to 40.

[Source: http://geek-university.com/raspberry-pi/raspberry-pi-board/]

These GPIO pins are as follows:

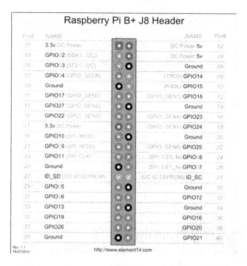

The expansion header contains different types of pins.

The light red pin is connected to the 5V rail of the Raspberry Pi. It's consistent at +5 V.

The dark red pin is connected to the 3.3V rail of the Raspberry Pi. It's consistent at +3.3 V.

The black pin is connected to the ground of the Raspberry Pi. It's consistent at 0 V.

The yellow pin is a new addition. It is seen on the Raspberry Pi Model B+. The I2C bus is dedicated to the expansion boards.

The rest of the pins are called General Purpose Input/Output (GPIO). This GPIO is a generic pin on the circuit. Its behavior, regardless of whether it is an output or an input, is controllable by the user at run time.

These GPIO pins are also connected to +3.3V rails. If you use them for input, they can read voltages. If you use them for output, they can be set to 0 V for low and +3.3 V for high.

Different Types of GPIO Pins

The green pins are generic GPIO pins that do not have any special purposes.

The blue pins may be used as I2C bus or GPIO.

The orange pins may be utilized for UART or as GPIO.

The purple pins may be used as SPI bus or as GPIO.

All in all, there are twenty-four GPIO ports. Even though you can use any GPIO pins, you should use the green ones first as much as possible.

Interfacing Electronics

Your Raspberry Pi would be useless if you weren't able to use it to interact and use other electronic devices, wouldn't it? Here, we'll discuss how to set up your Pi to work with other electronics. First, you'll need to have the proper equipment to make sure you won't destroy your circuit or even your Pi.

Digital Multimeter

You must have one of these before starting to tinker with circuitry. This device measures many things, such as voltage, current, resistance, etc. This ensures that you don't accidentally pump your circuit with more than it can handle.

Breadboard

A breadboard is a base for you to use when making prototypes for electronics. Before trying things out on your Raspberry Pi, try it on a breadboard first. Make sure to get the good ones!

Discrete Components

Diodes

A diode is a semiconductor component that simply allows one current to flow in one direction but not the other.

Light Emitting Diodes (LEDs)

An LED acts similarly to a diode, just that it emits light if the current flows in the correct direction. These come in many shapes, sizes, and colors. The length of the leg determines which leg is positive (cathode) and which is negative (anode).

Capacitors

A capacitor is a component that can be used to store electrical energy. It stores energy when there is a difference in voltage between its two plates. Once the voltage difference dissipates, it releases the stored energy.

Transistors

A transistor is a semiconductor component that can be used to amplify or switch electricity or electric signals.

Optocouplers

These are digital switching devices that allow you to isolate two electrical circuits from one another.

Buttons and Switches

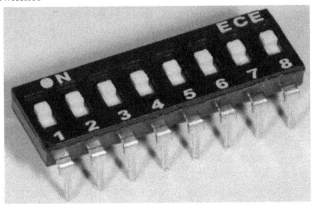

These are quite self-explanatory. These are the input devices that you interact with to make your circuit do something. Their basic function is to open or close a circuit. They come in different shapes and forms, depending on what you need.

Communication Protocols

For embedded systems to work harmoniously, there needs to be communication between them. This is how data is transferred between embedded systems. There are specific standards that are set in place to make sure there is consistency and coherence in their communication. These are communication protocols.

Some communication protocols exist, and the difference between them would be better understood if you learn these few concepts first:

Bit rate

The bit rate describes the number of bits that are sent per unit of time. This is usually described in bits/sec.

Baud rate

Whereas the bit rate describes the number of bits sent per unit of time, the baud rate describes the number of symbols sent per unit of time. These **symbols** can each be of any number of bits. This depends on the design. If ever the symbols are only 1 bit, the baud rate would be equal to the bit rate.

Parallel Communication

In parallel communication, multiple bits are sent at the same time.

Serial Communication

In serial communication, bits are sent one bit at a time.

Synchronous Serial Communication

This describes a serial communication protocol wherein data is sent at a steady, continuous stream at a constant rate. This requires that the internal clocks of the two embedded systems be synchronized at the same rate so that the receiver receives the signal at the same intervals that the transmitter used.

Asynchronous Serial Communication

This form of serial communication does not require synchronized internal clocks. In place of the synchronization signal, the data stream instead contains start and stop signals before and after the transmission, respectively. When the receiver receives the start signal, it prepares for a stream of data. Conversely, when it receives the stop signal, it resets to its previous state to receive a new stream.

Now that you've learned about the basic concepts of communication between embedded systems, we can now learn about the different communication protocols.

I2C

I2C is short for Inter-Integrated Circuit. It is asynchronous serial communication protocol that uses two wires: one for data (SDA), and one for the clock (SCL). It is a multi-master, multi-slave serial computer bus. Most of its uses are confined to attaching lower-speed peripheral integrated circuits to processors and microcontrollers. Because of how it works, I2C must validate the data passing through it by evaluating whether or not the data on the SDA line changes when the SCL is high. The data on the SDA line should only ever change when the SCL is low. Otherwise, the data is rendered invalid.

I2C supports a wide range of voltages.
I2C is half-duplex.

I2C can support serial 8-bit data transfers up to a speed of 100kbps. This is the standard clock speed of SCL. I2C is also capable of a higher bitrate: 400 kbps (fast mode) and 3.4 Mbps (high-speed mode).

I2C is mainly used for short-distance communication.

UART

UART is short for Universal Asynchronous Receiver Transmitter. In this protocol, one wire is used for transmitting, and another wire is used for receiving. UART uses a serial type of communication; therefore, bits travel in one wire.

UART supports communication through RS232.

Standard baud rates for UART include 110, 300, 600, 1200, 4800, and 9600.

UART can only support communication between two devices at any one time. This is because it is a point-to-point communication protocol.

SPI

SPI is short for the Serial Peripheral Interface. It is an asynchronous serial communication interface protocol used for short-distance communication. It can operate with one master and several slave devices.

SPI is a full-duplex type of communication protocol.
SPI protocol has no limit for message size, making it very flexible.

Real-Time Interfacing Using Arduino

In case you aren't familiar, an Arduino is a powerful microcontroller. You can use it in tandem with a Raspberry Pi, creating some impressive projects. Obviously, you'll need an Arduino for this to work. You'll need a lot of programming expertise and mastery of interfaces to make use of this and explaining that will make this book longer than it needs to be, so feel free to do some further research on this topic. However, I'll discuss a few key things.

You can interface with the Arduino using any of the communication protocols discussed above (I2C, UART, and SPI).

You can configure the Arduino as an I2C slave. This means you can connect several Arduinos to one Raspberry Pi.
A straightforward UART connection can only support one slave at a time.
If you require a fast, high-level interaction between your Arduino and Pi, configuring the Arduino as an SPI slave will be the way to go. This is because the Arduino's clock speed will only limit an SPI connection.

Input and Output

You probably have noticed that row of pins along the top edge of the Raspberry Pi board. These are the GPIO pins. GPIO is short for General Purpose Input/Output. Using the software, you can designate whether each of these pins is for input or output. You can do many things with this.

Two of these pins are 5V, and two more are 3.3V. There are also several ground pins, which you cannot configure. The rest are general-purpose 3V3 pins.

If you designate a pin to be an output pin, you can set it to high, at 3V3, or low, at 0V. Conversely, input pins can be read as high (3V3) or low (0V).

Chapter 5

Download the Operating System

Downloading and Installing Raspberry Pi

You are not going to be able to run Raspberry Pi without first downloading the operating system.

You can find the software you need at www.RaspberryPi.org.

Noobs

Noobs is a great program for Pi beginners. The word noobs stands for new out of the box software. If you want to, you can download a card that has noobs preinstalled on it from any retailer that sells Pi products. Or, you can go to the Raspberry Pi website and download it from there.

Noobs is easy to use an operating system that has Raspbian installed on it for you to choose and download an operating system off the internet for your computer.
Noobs Lite is using the same installer but without downloading Raspbian. Everything is a thing else is going to be the same.

Raspbian

This is the official operating system that was created by the foundation and can be installed with NOOB, or you can install it on its own.

Most Raspbian is going to come with the software you need to be preinstalled so that you can do more educational programming than you would be able to on NOOBS. Raspbian is also going to come with several different programming languages installed with it.

There is a PIXEL image that lies inside of a ZIP file on the Raspbian operating system where all your features are going to be archived, but the old tools that were used to unzip these files are not going to be supported on all platforms.

If your download for Raspbian is corrupted or is not opening correcting, you are going to want to attempt to use 7Zip or The Unarchiever before trying a reinstall.

Chapter 6

Projects

LibreELEC Media Center

LibreELEC is a multimedia center in which you can turn just about any TV into a smart TV. You can use it to download apps, access hard disks, and play movie files from the remote PC on the TV.

You can also receive internet radio broadcasts and stream them to your sound system. Additionally, there is a Spotify app for LibreELEC if you have an account. This is a project where Raspberry Pi can make itself useful in everyday life.

Homebridge

An exciting project in the area of Smart-Home is the project Homebridge (homebridge. io). This software-based project is relatively easy to implement. By using Homebridge, even non-Apple certified Smart-Home devices can be used with Apple's HomeKit and be controlled without any additional apps.

The whole thing can be implemented very easily with a Raspberry Pi. The practical thing about it is that the software is relatively easy to install and control. This means that you only have to add plugins from different manufacturers and then control them directly via Apple's HomeKit.

The picture below shows two virtual lamps that can be switched on and off directly. You can easily add such devices later in HomeKit with a simple QR code. Just scan the code with the photo app, and you can control the device from your iPhone, iPad, or even your Mac.

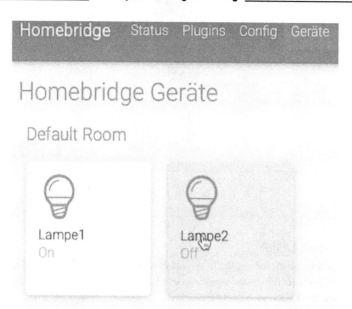

And the whole thing is very easy to install. This will be discussed later in this manual.

MagicMirror

Another interesting project from the area of Smart-Home is the project MagicMirror (magicmirror.builders). The software is relatively easy to install. You can use it to set up a display in the mirror, which you can hang in your house or apartment. In the mirror, you can display various information, such as time and weather. The mirror can also be connected to other Smart-Home devices. So, the project is a very nice gimmick, which can be easily realized with a little tinkering.

Pi-Hole Ad-Blocker

Another useful project we will look at in this book is the Pi-Hole project (pi-hole.net). Pi-Hole is a network-wide advertising blocker that can be installed on the Raspberry Pi. If you redirect the Internet settings on your router to Pi-Hole, all Internet traffic will be filtered through the Raspberry Pi. From this point on, the pi-hole server will ensure that, for example, most advertisements on each device are filtered out. We will take a closer look at this later in the book to see how it works in detail.

RetroPi Game-Console

This is a special operating system where old arcade and console games up to Playstation 1 can be emulated and played on the Raspberry Pi. This project is a nice opportunity to recreate in your free time or to spend time with your kids.

Chapter 7

Raspberry with Python and Linux

Raspberry pi with Linux Systems

When it comes to embedded systems, startup time is crucial. For example, when you switch on your TV, your goal is to start watching your favorite show within five seconds of pressing the power button.

So, how can you develop a program that can boot quickly and not need any other kind of user input to work? Well, you can use embedded systems programming, which is also referred to as bare-metal programming.

If you want to enable the boot loader of the Raspberry Pi and be able to run your desired program, you have to strip the Raspbian operating system of your micro SD card as well as load certain files onto it. This way, you can directly access the hardware and find out how you can turn a couple of LEDs on and off with the use of GPIO pins.

You want your Raspberry Pi to function as an embedded system. After the operating system has been stripped off, you can start programming your desired functionality with the use of an assembly. You will be accessing the hardware as instructed by the manufacturer.

So what are embedded systems exactly? They refer to computers that do not feature any operating systems. They are typically created for specific purposes.

In the past, for instance, all systems used embedded systems for computing because there were no operating systems yet. At present, these embedded systems remain available for specialized applications.

In addition, embedded programming is ideal for firmware due to its time benefits. Just think of your own Mac or PC. How much time does it take to boot up after you hit the power button?

The majority of the startup time is affected by the complexity of the operating system you have on your computer. Moreover, while you use your computer in the operating system environment, it's hardware does a lot of work to run several background processes.

Through embedded systems, you can be freed from performance restraints. They get rid of the operating system and directly run the program from a hard drive. This lets the device boot up within a short period as well as utilize the performance of your hardware well.

This may seem very appealing. You may even wonder why not all programs run this way.

Well, convenience is a key factor. The needs of the system should also be considered. This is the reason why a lot of computers did not become famous before Microsoft and Apple came into the market.

The development of a graphically driven interface lets users access computers with relative ease. The operating system, despite killing performance and loading very slowly, was useful and convenient. In fact, a lot of individuals, including the developers themselves, were amazed by its advantages.

Then again, this does not mean that computers were not useful before the invention of the operating system. Embedded systems were actually highly beneficial before the development of the operating system.

In addition, computers that use operating systems are usually multi-purpose devices. A lot of people have to do spreadsheets, word processing, mathematical computations, and internet browsing, among other activities. They need something that can allow them to do all of that with just one machine.

Such variety calls for a more complicated system that makes use of various hardware for various purposes. On the other hand, embedded systems tend to focus on dealing with just one piece of equipment with a narrower functionality scope.

How to Program Embedded Systems

Instead, you have to use something that computers can understand. You need to communicate using a language that would sound native to them.

You need to compile your assembly into your kernel that the Raspberry Pi will look into, rather than the usual Raspbian kernel. For this to happen, you have to strip off all data from the SD card of the Raspberry Pi. You need something to load the kernel into. See to it that you always keep a backup of your data.

Kernels typically act as bridges between the software and the hardware. The Raspbian kernel makes it easier for users to acquire data from their monitor or keyboard and then manipulate it.

However, in embedded systems, there is no need for you to communicate with most of the hardware. There's also no need for a GUI. You can make your way around without using it.

Embedded design is generally programmed for specific purposes. For example, you may want a couple of LEDs to blink. Hence, you need to have a system that is time-sensitive for booting since you have to take away anything that is not needed to make LEDs blink.

Linux Usage
Commands
- They refer to advanced and basic commands used in Linux

Tex editors
- These refer to a set of text editors used for the Raspberry Pi

Root
- The prefix "sudo" and the user "root"

Users

- Allows for setting up multiple users on the Raspberry Pi system

Scripting
- It refers to the combination of commands to perform complex actions

Crontab/Cron
- It sets up pre-scheduled tasks
.bash and .bashrc aliases
- They are your aliases and shell configuration

rc.local
- It refers to the initialization configuration

Additional Help for Beginners
The following are explanations of some of the basic uses of Linux, as well as the commands used to get around the Raspberry Pi.

The Linux File System
- This is where files are kept, the software is installed, and danger zones are seen, among others. It contains Home, Whole File System, and Backup.

Home
- This is where files are kept. It is the home folder

Whole File System
- It refers to the rest of the file system of Linux

Backup
- It backs up files as well as operating system images

Raspberry Pi and Python

Python language presents a high-level syntax; we say this because its form of writing is very close to human language. Also, Python supports object-orientation.

Fundamentally, python requires precise writing of code. Still, it also offers a friendly user interface where you are guided along the way of writing codes by the application itself (marking mistakes in code and offering useful suggestions).

This specific integrated development environment for python has two modes, a normal mode, and a Simple mode. The simple mode makes things even easier for beginners, and in this guide, we will be referring to the Simple model of this application.

This is the toolbar that you'll see while in the application's Simple Mode. Beneath each friendly icon on the toolbar, you'll see that they are labeled with the purpose for which they are used.

This is the application's script area. The purpose of this area is precisely similar to the Scratch application. We write down codes in this area, the numbering on the left side of this area indicates the line number. As you keep writing codes, it's automatically indexed. In the scenario where your code encounters an error, you will know which line of code the error is referring to and because every line is indexed, you can quickly navigate to the faulty line of code and fix it. This simple indexing can be useful and timesaving.

This is the Python Shell. This area provides information about the code which is currently being run by the application and, you can input individual lines of code and execute them by merely pressing the ENTER button.

This is specifically the variables area. This area shows you information (name and value) of all the variables that you created for a specific program.

Programming with Python: Making a Program

After you start up python, the first thing you will notice is that, unlike Scratch, there are no colorful blocks or sprites. This is because Python is more of a traditional programming language that relies on code being manually written down (without any typos or errors, of course!).

Open up python from the Raspberry Pi menu and wait for Thonny Python IDE to load up (Thonny will startup in the Simple Mode by default). Go over to the Python shell area and type in

Print("Good Morning!")

After typing in the following instruction, all you need to do is press the ENTER key, and you'll see the message "Good Morning" displayed below the instruction. We have just created our first program. It was as simple as that!

As soon as you hit ENTER, the code will execute. On the other hand, when you press ENTER after writing a line of code, instead of executing the lines of code, you just get a new blank line to write more code. To execute the codes in the scripts area, you need to do so by clicking the 'Run' icon in the toolbar (When you click the Run button, Thonny will prompt you to save your current program first, just type in a name for your program and click save). Notice that when you run a saved program from the scripts area, the message in the shell area is a bit different this time

>>> %Run 'Name you used to save the program.py.'

Good Morning!

You can also write the same line of code in the scripts area as well, but this time, we'll use a different and more popular phrase "Hello, World!" and while saving it, we will give it the name Hello, World!

(Here's the message you'll see in the shell area)

>>> %Run 'Hello World.py'

Hello, World!

The First line instructs the Interpreter to execute the program, which has just been saved, and the second line is the result or the output of running that program, in our case, displaying a message. We have successfully written our first program on Python and ran it in both interactive and script modes.

Using Loops and Code Indentation

Indentation is basically python's way of controlling the sequence in which the lines of code are executed. In Scratch programming, we would use the colorful blocks and place them above each other in the sequence, which we wanted, but in Python, we need to use indentation to tell the computer that this is the sequence in which the lines of code are to be run.

Open a new project by clicking on the 'New' icon in the toolbar. This will open a separate new window for you to work on. In the scripts area, type in the following lines of code;

```
print("Loop starting!")
```

```
for i in range (10):
```

In the above lines of code, the first line works exactly in the same way as demonstrated in the Print("Good Morning") example. However, the second line is rather interesting. This line initiates a definite loop sequence, with the defined limit being set by the range followed by the desired integer. The i is the loop counter which will count the number of times the program loops, in this case, it will count upwards till nine because the stop instruction is the number 10, as soon as the 9th loop is completed, the loop will exit. Also, look at the colon ":" at the end of the line. This tells the computer that the following lines of code are actually a part of the loop.

Moreover, in Scratch, we saw that the instruction which is to be added into the loop function could be placed on the loop block directly. But in Python, we indent the instruction code by using a colon (":"). An indentation is characterized by four blank spaces left at the beginning of the new line; the IDE application does this automatically as soon as you press ENTER after an indentation.

```
print("Loop starting!")
```

```
for i in range (10):
```

```
print("Loop number", i)
```

This indentation is what allows python to differentiate between instructions that are not included in the loop and instructions, which are to be included in the loop (this indented code is known as being nested).

All the lines following this indentation will automatically contain four blank spaces because Thonny assumes that the following lines of code will also be the part of the loop. This will keep happening until you have written all the instructions which are part of the loop. To close the indentation, simply make a new indented blank line and press BACKSPACE, this will return the line to normal. Now, close the indentation as described and write the following line of code.

print("Loop finished!")

The sequence of the lines of code should be something like this;

print("Loop starting!")

for i in range (10):

print("Loop number", i)

print("Loop finished!")

In this program, the first line and last line is outside of the loop because they are not indented. The second line is where the loop starts and contains the indentation, whereas the third line is part of the loop.

Let's save this program as "indentation" and run the program. In the shell area, we will see the following output;

```
Loop starting!
Loop number 0
Loop number 1
Loop number 2
Loop number 3
Loop number 4
Loop number 5
Loop number 6
Loop number 7
Loop number 8
Loop number 9
Loop finished!
```

The reason why Python counts from zero instead of one is that Python is designed as a zero-indexed language. This means that it considers 0 as the beginning integer rather than 1. You can change this behavior by specifying the range instruction to be a range (1, 11) instead of range(10). With this, the loop will start counting from 1 to 10. You can do this for any number you want.

Just as how we used definite and indefinite loops in Scratch, the same can be done in Python. To use indefinite loops (loops that run forever), all you need to do is edit the 2nd line of code in the above program.

print("Loop starting!")

While True:

print("Loop running!")

print("Loop finished!")

You have now created an indefinite loop. This is because the end condition of the loop has not been specified as each time the message "loop running!" is printed, the program directs the code execution back to the start, and the whole process is repeated until the program itself is terminated. Save the program and run it to see the output in the shell area.

To terminate the program, simply click the red 'Stop' icon. The program will terminate without ever being able to reach the last line of the code.

Using conditionals and variables
Open up a new project by clicking the 'New' icon and in the scripts area, input the following line of code

userName = input ("What is your name? ")

Save the program and run it. The output of this program is that it displays a message asking for your name. After the end of the message, left-click the empty space, write a name, and hit ENTER. Nothing will happen in the program, but if you shift your focus to the right towards the variables window, you'll see that a variable 'userName' assigned with the value you just entered has been created.

To demonstrate how to use variables in python, we will pair the 'userName' variable with a conditional statement. In this demonstration, the program will ask us for our name, and based on our answer; it will give us a specific response.

if userName == "Clark Kent":

print("You are Superman!")

else:

print("You are not Superman!")

Now run the program after saving it and notice the output. In the first scenario, when the program asks us for our name, it compares it with the variable's value "Calrk Kent" to see if it matches. If our name matches the one in the variable, then the condition is said to be True; if it does not match, then the condition is said to be False. Depending on the result being True or False, the conditional statement instructs the program to execute one of the following lines of code.

Also, notice that instead of one equality "=" symbol, we used a double equality symbol "==." This is because a single equality symbol assigns a value to a variable, or in simpler terms, makes this value equal to this variable. While the double equality symbol makes a direct comparison. One is an assigning operator, while the other is a comparative operator.

Also, a text in quotation marks is referred to as a String. A number with or without quotation marks is referred to as an Integer. When you are combining two different types of information, for example, the text "How old are you?" with the reply 22, you will have to convert the integer into a string before they can be joined.

When working with numbers, you can also use the greater than '>' and lesser than '<' comparative operators. But to use the equal to operator, you'll have to use '==.' Similarly, equal to or greater than '=>' and equal to or less than '=<' can also be used.

We will now use some comparison operators in the loop example we used before.

while userName != "Clark Kent":

print("You are not Superman – try again!")

userName = input ("what is your name")

print("You are Superman!)

Upon running this program, you'll see that instead of quitting the program after telling you that you are not superman, it will keep inquiring your name until it is confirmed that you are indeed the superhero Superman.

Chapter 8

Raspberry PI Models

Model A/B

The very first line of Raspberry Pi models was known as the Model A and the Model B (as shown in the image above). Both models had the Broadcom BCM 2835 SoC within them, but had different specifications: Model A, for instance, had 256 MB of RAM, one USB port, and zero networking qualities; Model B had either a 256 MB or 512 MB of RAM depending on the date of the purchase, a 10/100 wired network port, and two USB ports. These models were distinguishable because of their smaller than usual GPIO port, which has only 26 pins where is the larger, more advanced one has 40 pins. Both models also possess a full-size SD card storage instead of the compact microSD cards that the newer models come with. Although there are no longer manufactured, both the Model A and B are still compatible with most of the software that's designed for the newer models, except they don'tuse add-on hardware based on the HAT standard.

Model A+/B+

The original models proved to be very popular, but more than swiftly replaced with a new board design called the Plus. These later model iterations came with the 40-pin GPIO header while improving some of the other features. However, they didn't deviate from the BCM 2835 SoC, which means that there was not much of a difference in performance between the Plus models and the older models.

The hardware difference between the Model A+ and Model B+ is similar to the previous Model A and Model B: the A+ model, which has a smaller footprint than the A Model, either has a 256 or 512 MB of memory depending on the launch of the product, zero network capabilities, and a single USB port; the Model B+ has a 512 MB of memory, a 10/100 wired network port, and four USB ports.

A+ and B+ are quite compatible with each software and device mentioned in this guide and have identical GPIO layouts as the newer models these days. If you have either of these models, the only reason you should upgrade is to gain additional memory, enjoyed built-in wireless capabilities, or improve performance.

Raspberry Pi 2

Whereas the Plus end previous other boards use the same BCM 2835 SoC processor, the newer Raspberry Pi 2 uses the new BCM 2836 SoC processor. Instead of one core like the original, the new processor features over four cores as well as 4 to 8 times the performance of the original – which makes everything from word processing to compiling code a much faster process. This new version also contains over 1GB (1024 MB) of RAM, doubling what was available for the previous one, which made memory-intensive applications and multitasking go much smoother and a lot more responsive.

When it comes to layout, not much has changed from the Model B+. For instance, the Raspberry Pi 2 has the same four USB ports, 40-pin GPIO header, 10/100 wired network ports as well as other ports. If you indeed have an add-on device or a case that works with the Model B+, it will work well with the Raspberry Pi 2 – only faster.

The new board comes with bigger software compatibility than the previous versions: even the proprietary operating system, Raspbian, can run operating systems such as Windows 10 IoT Core and Ubuntu that wasn't made available for the Raspberry Pi's predecessors.

Raspberry Pi 3

The last model before the fourth iteration, the Raspberry Pi 3, came with a newer processor at the time: the Broadcom BCM 2837. Being the 64-bit processor, not 32-bit, the new processor was considerably faster than the BCM 2836 found in the Raspberry Pi 2 version, which at the time was a massive upgrade from the BCM 2835 of the original and the Plus series. The Raspberry Pi 3 was also the first model to get built-in wireless support, which included a radio that connected to 2.4 GHz Wi-Fi networks and Bluetooth devices.

Like Pi 2, nothing much was changed with the layout: you would get the same four USB ports, 40-pin GPIO header, 10/100 wired network port, and several other ports that came with the last models. The only minor change comes with how the board interacts with specific add-on hardware, so if you're sure about whether a device is compatible with the Pi 3 model, then you should contact the vendor or manufacturer before buying to ensure that the software factored in that change.

One great advantage of the new Pi 3, other than the built-in wireless features and, of course, the improved performance, is its 64-bit processor. Switching over to this model given its new processor means that you will have better software compatibility performance and security over the 32-bit version of the previous models.

Raspberry Pi Zero

The Raspberry Pi Zero is by far not only the smallest board in the entire Raspberry Pi family, but it's also the cheapest of them all. Despite being the size of a couple of sticks of chewing gum that are stacked on top of each other, the Raspberry Pi Zero hardly lacks what the other models too: it has the same BCM 2835 SoC as well as 512 MB of RAM like the Raspberry Pi Model B+, and runs in a slightly faster speed for better performance.

However, Pi Zero needs the aid of certain caveats when it comes to using. For example, the mini-HDMI port and single micro-USB port require adapters before they can be connected to standard peripherals; there's no DSI port; the 3.5 mm AV jack is gone, the CSI port needs an adapter; and while it's present, the GPIO header needs pins that have to be purchased and soldered into place before it can be used.

We don't recommend the Pi Zero if you're a beginner. But if you are a more experienced user and want to bring more intelligence to embedded projects – especially when you experience troubles with cost, power draw, and size – the Pi Zero is the board you need to get your hands on.

The Raspberry Pi 4 Model B

Now, we were going to look into the latest Raspberry Pi 4 Model B, see what it's made of and how you can make it work. Although it seems like a lot is going into this tiny board, we assure you that the Raspberry Pi board is quite easy to understand - especially its components.

One of the most critical components is the *system-on-chip* (SoC), which is the centerpiece covered in a metal cap. It is called system-on-chip as there is a silicon chip underneath the metal cover if you pry it open. This chip is also known as an integrated circuit that contains most of the Raspberry Pi's operating system. Some of the most critical aspects contained within the chip are the graphics processing unit (GPU), handles the visual side of things, and the central processing unit (CPU), also known as the brain of a computer.

But without memory, the CPU would be of no use. But if you were to look to the side of the SoC, you'll find another small, black, plastic square chip (as the image shows), which is the board's random-access memory (RAM). This RAM, when in use, holds whatever you're doing and will write it to the microSD card when you save your work. To reiterate from what we said earlier, the RAM is volatile, which means when the Pi board is powered off, you lose your data. On the other hand, the microSD card is non-volatile, and if you save your data in it, you won't be able to lose it even when the power is out.

Then at the top left a corner of the board. You'll come across another silver lid which covers the radio, which is what gives the Raspberry Pi its ability to connect with other devices wirelessly. The radio behaves as two separate components: a Wi-Fi radio that wirelessly connects to other computer networks; and the Bluetooth radio that connects to peripherals like keyboards and mice or for sending or receiving data from nearby smart devices such as sensors or smartphones.

Then there's the USB controller represented by a black, plastic-covered chip that's at the bottom edge of the board just behind the middle set of USB ports. This component is responsible for running all four of the USB ports. There's the even smaller network controller chip that handles the board's Ethernet network ports. And then finally the smallest black chip that's a little over the USB Type-C power connector that's located to the board's upper left side, known as the power management integrated circuit (PMIC). This chip is responsible for turning the micro USB port power into the power that the Raspberry Pi requires to run.

Conclusion

Thank you for reading this book. The next step is to use the information that you have learned in this book and get to coding with Raspberry Pi. You are going to be able to create a lot of projects that are going to improve your life so that it is more comfortable. The Raspberry Pi is indeed a technological marvel, and it will always be surprised as to what this tiny machine is capable of. Not only does this little monster pack a punch in terms of power and capability, but the Raspberry Pi is also in a league of its own with regards to its adaptability to an entire array of possible applications.

Just as how the Raspberry Pi's usefulness knows no limits and has no defined boundary, we could only learn so much in this beginner's level book. There's still an entire island's worth of knowledge to still explore regarding the Pi and its capability and how we can use it to the best of its abilities. However, this book has addressed all of the essential concepts to their basic form so that the reader will be able to tackle any problem he comes across if he wants to use the Raspberry Pi as a pocket computer or as a project piece.

Be humble in the way that you approach everything. Don't be afraid to admit that you're wrong or that you aren't as capable as what you want to think and ask for help on one of the communities. The Raspberry Pi is altogether one of the coolest pieces of technology out there right now, and it can do so much. Still, it can also be frustrating to the programmer because it can do exactly as much as the programmer can make it do.

The Raspberry Pi is indeed a wonderful device. It's small and handy so that you can carry it with you anywhere. It is very affordable and widely accessible, so you can easily purchase a dozen without breaking your budget. You can never have too many Raspberry Pi devices for your projects.

If you want to hone your skills, unleash your creative side, and create things that are useful and unique, you should keep working and practicing. Remember that you can get tips and advice, as well as share your ideas with other Raspberry Pi users. You may even form friendships from the online community.

The affordability and accessibility of the Raspberry Pi can help you work on multiple projects. If you made a mistake, you could try again. You can even patent and sell your work. From simple devices, you can come up with tools that the whole world can benefit from. The opportunities are limitless, and you can reach for your dreams with the help of the Raspberry Pi.

Rather than pass the time watching TV, checking your social media, or mindlessly surfing the Internet, you can be productive and use the Raspberry Pi to experiment with projects.

The Raspberry Pi is truly one of the greatest inventions today. With such a tiny device, great things can be achieved.

Top-notch programmers don't give up along the way. Go ahead and practice to conceptualize all the ideas you have learned in this book. Remember, the rule of thumb in learning - Raspberry Pi included - is practice; and undoubtedly: Good practice makes perfect.

I wish you the very best of luck!

CPSIA information can be obtained
at www.ICGtesting.com
Printed in the USA
BVHW040759250222
630007BV00017B/812

9 781990 151361